Attaining the Way

ATTAINING THE WAY

A Guide to the Practice
of Chan Buddhism

CHAN MASTER
Sheng Yen

SHAMBHALA
Boston & London
2006

SHAMBHALA PUBLICATIONS, INC.
HORTICULTURRAL HALL
300 MASSACHUSETTS AVENUE
BOSTON, MASSACHUSETTS 02115
www.shambhala.com

9 8 7 6 5 4 3 2 1

First Edition

Printed in the United States of America

Designed by Lora Zorian

∞ This edition is printed on acid-free paper that meets
the American National Standards Institute z39.48 Standard.
Distributed in the United States by Random House, Inc.,
and in Canada by Random House of Canada Ltd

LIBRARY OF CONGRESS CATALOGING-IN-PUBLICATION DATA

Attaining the way: a guide to the practice of
Chan Buddhism/Sheng Yen.
p. cm.
ISBN-13: 978-1-59030-372-6 (pbk.: alk. paper)
ISBN-10: 1-59030-372-5
1. Spiritual life—Zen Buddhism. I. Shengyan, 1930–
BQ9288.A88 2007
294.3'927—dc22
2006014679

Contents

Contents

PART 3:
THE ESSENTIALS OF CHAN PRACTICE
BY MASTER XUYUN (EMPTY CLOUD)

PART 4:
ATTAINING THE WAY FROM RETREAT TALKS
BY MASTER SHENG YEN

Contents

Translator's Preface

Notes on Terminology

There are several key terms and concepts relating to the methods of practice that the four masters whose teachings are presented here mention without much explanation. The reason for this omission is that their talks were either extemporaneous, given during intensive practice retreats where the practitioners were already familiar with such ideas, or written for seasoned practitioners. Also, many modern readers may not be familiar with these masters. For the sake of understanding the contexts of these teachings and appreciating why they were given, Master Sheng Yen asked me to write this short essay on his behalf.

The primary methods of meditation mentioned in this volume are *gong'an* (literally, "public case") (Jap., *koan*), *huatou* (Jap., *wato*), and *mozhao* (Jap., *mokusho*). This last method is translated here as "silent illumination," and it is the origin of the Japanese Zen method of *shikantaza*, or "just sitting." This method is often misunderstood by practitioners of the past and present as a form of quietism, but since Master Sheng Yen clears up this misunderstanding in this volume, I will not expand on it here. Gong'an and huatou, however, need some explanation.

The term *gong'an* literally means "public case," as in a court case, but in the Chan context it refers to an encounter between a Chan master and a student that often results in some insight or awakening. Beginning in the early Song dynasty (960–1279), Chan masters began to collect these stories into anthologies and drew from them methods for training and testing practitioners. It is said that there were as many as seventeen hundred gong'ans collected during the Song. Some of the famous collections are the *Gateless Gate,* the *Blue Cliff Record,* and the *Book of Serenity.*

The term *huatou* literally means "source of spoken words before they are uttered," or "before the spoken word." This is an indirect way to point out that which is beyond language and concepts. This "source" is variously referred to in Buddhism as buddha-nature, self-nature, no-self, no-mind, and intrinsic wisdom. All are alternative names for the nature of "emptiness" in the Mahayana teachings. But these are only semantic explanations of the gong'an and the huatou.

In actual practice one does not engage in thinking or reflecting on any of these labels or ideas. In practice a gong'an is not some interesting story to be figured out through reasoning but is internalized as a fundamental and existential dilemma. Likewise, a huatou is used as a "critical phrase" to generate an intense questioning of who we are before the onset of words and language, and of the meaning of ultimate truth.

This is a famous gong'an in the *Gateless Gate* collection:

> One day a monk asked Master Zhaozhou [778–897; Jap., Joshu], "Does a dog have buddha-nature or not?"
> Zhaozhou replied, "No!" [Chin., *wu;* Jap., *mu*].

Clearly, Buddhist scriptures teach that all of us, including other sentient beings such as dogs, have buddha-nature—the potential to become a buddha. So why did Zhaozhou answer "No"?

Using this case as a gong'an means internalizing it by reflecting on and questioning single-mindedly the entire story. Using this same case as a huatou, or "critical phrase," on the other hand, means just concentrating on the question "What is *wu*?" and relating to it as one's own dilemma.

Chan master Dahui Zonggao (1089–1163), a great advocate of the huatou method, said that rather than meditating on the entire gong'an, which may lead to discursive thinking, Chan adepts should just meditate on the critical phrase or fragment from the gong'an. For this reason, Chinese practitioners typically use the huatou instead of the gong'an, or koan, method favored by Japanese Rinzai adepts.

Despite the differences between the gong'an and the huatou, the most important thing is to make these meaningless stories "come to life" in practice. Hence, Chan and Zen masters often speak of turning "dead words into live words." To do this you have to generate what is known as the doubt sensation. In other words, just becoming one with the method is insufficient. You must go beyond that and generate a "great ball of doubt," reaching the state of oneness, and then break through this doubt to the state of no-mind or no-self.

The doubt is a process of questioning, but you are not allowed to use any thinking or intellectual reasoning whatsoever. The point is not to "answer" the question but simply to reflect on the huatou or gong'an again and again until you become completely absorbed in the sense of questioning and wonderment. This sense of not knowing can come alive only by making the question your own. Hence, "Why does a dog have no buddha-nature?" is really "Why don't I have buddha-nature?" or "What is my buddha-nature?" The more earnest the questioning, the stronger this doubt sensation will be. This is the most crucial point in this method. Hence the Chan saying "Great doubt, great enlightenment; small doubt, small enlightenment; no doubt, no enlightenment."

Sometimes a practitioner gives rise to doubt spontaneously, without using the huatou method. For example, Master Dongshan (807–869), one of the cofounders of the Caodong (Jap., Soto) lineage, had a natural doubt induced by his master when he bade farewell to him. Dongshan asked his master, "After you have passed away, how can I answer those who want me to describe you?" "Just this!" his master retorted. Dongshan was dumbfounded and became silent. His master said, "You must be very careful, and take care of *this*." Puzzled by this whole incident, Dongshan left his master in that state of wonderment, traveling alone in the mountains. One day he saw his own reflection in a river and suddenly his doubt was shattered. If Dongshan had not been deeply absorbed by doubt about his master's words, he might not have realized enlightenment.

A similar case is the story of Japanese Zen master Dogen (1200–1253), who in his youth could not understand why Buddhism teaches the intrinsic enlightened nature of all sentient beings and yet buddhas and bodhisattvas still need to arouse the desire for enlightenment. This question perplexed Dogen greatly for years and drove him from his seclusion on Mount Hiei across the sea to China. Dogen's doubt became the fundamental question of his own being. Years later, practicing under the Chinese master Rujing (1163–1228), Dogen heard the master scold another monk who was dozing off in meditation, "In Zen, body and mind are cast off; why are you sleeping?" When Dogen heard these words, his original doubt was shattered and he experienced enlightenment.

From these stories we can see that Chan doubt is not something contrived but is something that drives us forward in practice; it must be connected to our own lives. In Chan this is called the fundamental question, which is very similar to what modern people refer to as the sense of questioning but not knowing who we are, as in the sense of "What am I doing here?" Ultimately, it does not matter what method we use or what kind of Buddhism we practice; the fundamental question must be there. Shakyamuni's fundamental question before he became a buddha was how to end human suffering, and that question was suddenly and completely resolved after six years of austere practice when he saw the morning star after six days and nights of meditating under the Bodhi Tree.

Huatou and gong'an are merely devices. As methods, they are problems created by Chan masters for practitioners to use in meditation. Traditionally, some Chan practitioners used a single huatou all their lives, even after breaking through the doubt and realizing enlightenment. Virtually no one in this day and age can realize thorough enlightenment all at once. For this reason, the same huatou can be used over and over again to generate the doubt sensation, which is then shattered repeatedly until all vexations, self-attachment, and unwholesome habits are relinquished in the full manifestation of wisdom and genuine compassion.

These methods are not suitable for everyone; it is extremely important that they be used only when the student is ready and under the close guidance of a Chan or Zen master in a retreat setting. Otherwise they can lead to the kinds of problems detailed in the teachings of the four masters in this volume.

Master Boshan

The first master in this volume, Wuyi Yuanlai (1575–ca. 1630), was one of the most revered masters in the Caodong lineage during the Ming dynasty (1368–1644). He left the household life at age sixteen after hearing lectures on the *Lotus Sutra*. After becoming a monk, he practiced the Tiantai method of stillness and contemplation (*shamatha-vipashyana*) for five years before studying under the eminent Chan master Wuming Huixing (1548–1618). Through the practice of gong'an and huatou, Yuanlai had numerous insights, which by today's laxer standards would be considered experiences of "enlightenment." However, Huixing did not affirm any of Yuanlai's realizations. Again and again, Huixing scolded Yuanlai and turned him away, thus generating more "doubt" in him. One day, while watching someone climbing a tree, Yuanlai's doubt was completely shattered; he experienced thorough enlightenment, and life and death no longer had a hold on him. It was only then that Master Huixing affirmed Yuanlai's understanding. At the time, Yuanlai was only twenty-seven. Later Yuanlai studied the precepts under Master Yunqi Zhuhong (1535–1615) and traveled broadly. He finally settled down on Mount Bo (Boshan) to teach for the rest of his life. In the Chan custom of referring to eminent masters by their place of settlement, he then became known as Master Boshan.

The two tracts of Boshan's translated here are excerpts from his record of discourses delivered at Mount Bo. The record bears a preface that dates to 1611. The context in which these teachings were given appears to be intense retreats. The original title of the first tract is "Exhortations for Beginning Practitioners" and the second, "Exhortations on the Inability to Arouse the Doubt Sensation." Together they are titled in this volume as "Exhortations on Investigating Chan." These two tracts were chosen because they point out all the common mistakes and erroneous views that practitioners encounter even today; they also reveal what it takes to seriously practice the gong'an and huatou.

Though Boshan belonged to the Caodong school, he freely used the gong'an and huatou methods, which are usually associated nowadays with the Linji (Jap., Rinzai) school. However, in Chinese Chan the methods of practice were always flexible, not surprisingly, since the methods are only expedient means, devices used to awaken the student's wisdom. But there are other social and historical reasons behind Boshan's style of teaching.

The late Ming was a period when gong'an collections were

widely circulated. The widespread use of printed books helped to infiltrate all levels of the society, elevating the level of literacy among even the common people who were familiar with Chan sayings. The gong'an collections and Chan discourse records were easily accessible, but this accessibility also caused Chan teachings to be secularized and misunderstood. For example, the extent of influence of Chan can be seen in the writings of the elite literati, who not only read and studied gong'an collections but also developed their own systems of meditation, touting a form of awakening experience that corresponded to their own ideas of "realizing sagehood." Many acted as if they were enlightened without ever seriously engaging in practice, leading only to lip service. There were also popular religious cult leaders who taught a vulgar form of Chan based on their mystical experiences. Sometimes Buddhist clerics, after years of practice without results, turned to these cult leaders for guidance. Many of these clerics in turn broke the Buddhist precepts and caused much criticism of Buddhism. In short, there seems to have been widespread deterioration in the correct understanding of Chan. We get a sense of the many deviant ways people practiced Chan in Boshan's teachings here. Thus, his insistence on clarifying all the ills of Chan practice should be seen in this light.

Master Jiexian

The second master presented in this volume is Yuanyun Jiexian (1610–1672), a follower of the Linji school of Chan. He was a younger contemporary of Boshan and was the Dharma heir of Master Jude Hongli of Lingyin Monastery. The teachings presented here are excerpts from Jiexian's writings on Chan training, geared toward other contemporary teachers. This work bears a preface that dates to 1661, a time when Jiexian was already mature in his career as a Chan master.

Not much is known about Jiexian's personal life. However, fragments that appear in local gazettes from Jiangsu and Xiangxi provinces, in Lingyin monastic records and inscriptions, and in miscellaneous passages in Chan anthologies can be used to reconstruct some details of his life. Jiexian's father was a literatus who had great interest in Chan, and so at an early age Jiexian not only received a great education but also became familiar with Buddhist teachings. By age twenty-nine he had already received the lay bodhisattva precepts and worked as a local teacher. At the demise of the Ming dynasty (1644) he burned all of his poetry at a Confucian temple, terminated his literary involvements, and became a Buddhist monk. At the age of thirty-five he received the full monastic precepts and began to study them intensely. Soon he started his Chan training with Master Hongli. It was at a three-month winter retreat that Jiexian experienced his awakening and received recognition from Hongli.

Jiexian continued his practice and traveled to many places, refining his understanding and experience. In 1651 he settled down at Yunju Monastery to teach, focusing on training disciples and reviving the study of Buddhist precepts, which he saw as the means to strengthening Chan practice. During this time he also rebuilt several training monasteries. When Hongli died, Jiexian became the residing master at Lingyin Monastery.

The work included here taken from the records of Master Yuanyun Jiexian was written when he was teaching at Yunju Monastery. From this tract we can see that he was someone skilled not only in guiding and tempering students but also in the Buddhist doctrine. This work is extremely precious in that although past Chan masters received students of varying spiritual capacity, none of them, to the best of my knowledge, has written down a "manual of strategies" for guiding Chan practitioners. Most of what we know of other masters' teaching styles can only be culled from bits and pieces of their discourse records.

Modeling his work on the famous tactics in *The Art of War* by Sun Zi (Sun Wu, Sun Tzu; sixth century B.C.E.), Jiexian's "Discourse on Chan Training" is a composite of ancient wisdoms in the Linji lineage that had passed down to his time. He drew freely from earlier masters' teachings and created a system of principles for disciplining Chan adepts. In this work Jiexian details how to distinguish the spiritual capacities of students, how to test their understanding, when to give Dharma talks, how to structure an intense retreat, and how to utilize the principles of the Chan teaching, and points out the necessity of continuing to practice after enlightenment. This work not only reveals the high standards of the ancient worthies but also offers useful strategies as references for Chan and Zen teachers today. His words are extremely inspiring and humbling, reminding us not to be satisfied with small accomplishments.

Master Xuyun

The third master in this volume is Yanche Deqing (1839–1959), better known by his self-styled name, Xuyun (Empty Cloud). The most illustrious Chan master in recent times, Xuyun was known for many things, such as his meditative absorptions and ascetic practices, which included extended fasting, never lying down to sleep, burning one of his fingers (out of filial piety for his deceased mother) as an offering to the Buddha, and prostrating every three steps for thousands of miles during his pilgrimage to holy sites.

Xuyun's enlightenment occurred at age fifty-six, during a three-month retreat, when an attendant accidentally spilled hot water on Xuyun's hand, thus causing Xuyun to drop his teacup. Xuyun's enlightenment ensued from the sound of the teacup shattering on the floor. Although his enlightenment occurred relatively late in life, he lived for another sixty-four years, to a ripe age of 120! During these years he focused on holding intensive Chan retreats for both laypeople and monastics and on rebuilding ruined temples throughout China. (More biographical information can be found in the book *Empty Cloud: The Autobiography of the Chinese Zen Master Hsu Yun,* translated by Charles Luk [Lu K'uan Yu].)

The tract translated here, "The Essentials of Chan Practice," is geared toward serious beginners. One distinct feature in this teaching is Xuyun's advocacy of reciting Buddha's name as a Chan method, which some scholars and Zen practitioners today believe to be a "degeneration" of the "pure" form of Chan of the Tang dynasty (618–907). This, of course, is ludicrous because there never was a "pure form" of Chan. The methods of Chan have always been fluid, adapting to changing times and appropriating other Buddhist methods when suitable for practitioners. In fact, some of the founding fathers of Chan had already used this method in guiding students as early as the sixth century.

In Chinese Buddhist history, reciting Buddha's name as a method became particularly popular in the Ming period. Hence, many masters used this method to teach Chan but gave it a new twist. Instead of reciting Amitabha Buddha's name in order to be reborn to the Pure Land, they encouraged those who had reached a state of oneness by asking, "Who is reciting the Buddha's name?" In other words, reciting the Buddha's name was turned into a huatou. Xuyun's usage of this method should be seen in this context.

In his teachings, Xuyun not only lays out the purpose, methods, and attitudes in practice but also stresses the theoretical background and similarities between Buddhist contemplation techniques and the huatou.

At the end of Xuyun's discourse we include a never previously published translation of a dialogue between Xuyun and his disciple Lingyuan Hongmiao (1902–1988) on the relationship of mind, wandering thoughts, and meditative absorption. This dialogue took place on a seven-day winter retreat in 1947. It not only gives us a glimpse into how retreat interviews work but also reveals indirectly the nature of mind and how Chan adepts cultivate meditative absorption after enlightenment, which is radically different from ordinary meditative states.

Master Sheng Yen

The last master included in this volume is Huikong Shangyan (better known as Master Sheng Yen; 1930–), who is the Dharma heir of Master Lingyuan (mentioned above). Master Sheng Yen is a third-generation heir of Xuyun who became a novice monk at age thirteen in China because his farming family was too poor to raise him. He remembers being slow-witted as a young boy because of malnourishment. However, this all changed when he entered the monastery. The abbot, seeing the young monk's slowness in developing, told him to prostrate to Guanyin (Avalokiteshvara) Bodhisattva every day. Eager to make progress, Sheng Yen woke up before everyone else and prostrated five hundred times each morning, and the same after everyone else went to sleep. One morning after prostrations he experienced a sudden outpouring of sweat that left his mind extremely clear. After that he was able to memorize sutras with ease.

Sheng Yen later met his Dharma master in the depth of a spiritual crisis. In Shanghai, in order to escape the Communist takeover, he joined the Youth National Army at age eighteen to escape to Taiwan. He was falsely promised to be released after a short period of service, but his time in the army lasted ten years. During this time everyone still called him a monk because he continued his meditation and scriptural study. Because he had no teacher to guide him, his frustrations from being stuck in the army and his reading of various contradictions in the Buddhist scriptures developed into a natural "doubt sensation," to the point where he was able to obtain a temporary leave from service. As soon as this opportunity came up, he visited monasteries. His doubt was suddenly shattered one night in 1958 when pouring out his endless questions to Master Lingyuan, who finally exclaimed: "Put [it] down!" Upon hearing this, Sheng Yen put down all of his doubts about his body, mind, and world. He was then twenty-eight years old. A year later, with the help of friends, Sheng Yen was released from service and returned to the life of a monk under the Caodong master Dongchu (1907–1977). Two years later he entered a six-year solitary retreat in the mountains to deepen his practice.

Realizing the deplorable state of Chinese Buddhism and society as a whole, Sheng Yen vowed to raise the educational level of clerics and spread the teaching of Buddhism in ways that modern people could understand. Thus he went on to Japan to Rissho University to become the first Chinese Buddhist cleric to receive a doctorate (Litt.D.) in Buddhist literature. In 1976 Sheng Yen came to the United States to teach Chan. He later returned to Taiwan to start a Buddhist university to fulfill his vow of developing Buddhist education.

The teachings presented here bear witness to a further development in Chan teachings, one geared toward modern people. Sheng Yen's retreat talks are a unique blend of practical Buddhadharma and methods of Chan. His teachings on relaxing the body and mind in all situations and incorporating Chan in all affairs of life reflect his mottos, "Where one saves power is where one gains power" and "The business of daily life is inseparable from Chan practice."

In the beginning of his teaching career, Sheng Yen focused on the aggressive approach of huatou practice but soon found that there were some negative side effects for modern people. He felt that people were too lacking in a stable sense of self and a correct understanding of Buddhadharma to be using this very intense method. So in retreats he began to give more Dharma talks in order to integrate Chan methods with basic concepts of precepts, concentration, emptiness, and compassion. He felt that instilling a correct view was essential to Chan practice. During his retreats he also invented some methods that would incorporate these views in a practical way, such as slow prostration meditations on gratitude, and direct contemplations of forms and sounds in nature to strengthen a nonconceptual awareness. To build up people's ability to practice, he also revived the gentler practice of *mozhao,* or silent illumination, to stabilize the practitioner's awareness in all situations of life.

In this book Master Sheng Yen's remarks have been selected from four seven-day Chan retreats: one at Nongchan Temple in Taiwan (1991) and three at the Chan Meditation Center in New York (1992). The remarks were compiled, edited, and grouped by roughly defined categories rather than chronologically. Needless to say, the categories are not hard-and-fast but overlap seamlessly.

Master Sheng Yen has received Dharma transmission from Master Lingyuan in the Linji line as well as from Master Dongchu in the Caodong line.

The teachings collected in *Attaining the Way* are the result of years of struggle and spiritual maturation by these four Chan masters. Responding to their times, they creatively transmitted the Chan wisdom to us in hopes that we would continue the teachings. It is in this spirit that these teachings are being presented here.

GUOGU (JIMMY YU)
Princeton, New Jersey
November, 2005

Conventions Used in This Book

Translation and Textual Conventions

- The Chinese do not make a sharp distinction between the concepts of "mind" and "heart." The qualities of the Western notion of both mind and heart are conveyed in the Chinese word *xin* (pronounced *shin*), which we will render as "mind" unless it is obvious that the context calls for a more emotive rendering as "heart." *Xin* also connotes more than the ordinary mind. In Chan it sometimes refers to the ultimate state of enlightenment, free from delusion. In this case, *Mind* will be capitalized; otherwise, *mind* in lowercase will be used for ordinary mental states.
- All references to the Buddhist path, or *dao,* will be rendered as "the Way."
- The word *buddha* is capitalized when it refers to a specific buddha, such as Shakyamuni Buddha; otherwise it is left in lowercase. The same is true for the word *bodhisattva*. *Buddhadharma* is capitalized because it refers to the teachings of the historical Buddha, Shakyamuni.
- *Dharma* is capitalized when the context refers to the teachings of the Buddha. Lowercase *dharma* refers to phenomena, including objects of the mind.

- All words from the Sanskrit are rendered in the romanized version of the Chinese rather than their original Sanskrit, such as "Guanyin Bodhisattva" rather than "Avalokiteshvara," unless the word is already in wide use.
- Diacritical marks are not used, as this volume is geared to a general audience. For example, *sūtra* is rendered as "sutra."
- In the translations, parenthetical comments in the main body of the text provide explanatory information for the reader; text in square brackets supplies interpolations by the translators to make the texts read better.
- Some references from the Buddhist canon made by the four masters have been cross-referenced to the modern *Taisho shinshu daizokyo,* which is abbreviated in the endnotes as *T.,* followed by the catalog number, volume number, page number, and register column(s): a, b, or c. For example, Boshan cites a poem by Master Huangbo Xiyun in his talk. The note citation reads, "See *T.* no. 2012, 48: 387b." Cross-references to the *Xuzang Jing,* the *Extended Buddhist Canon,* are abbreviated in the endnotes as *X.,* followed by the catalog number, volume number, page number, and register column(s): a, b, or c. The decision to include this technical convention was made for the benefit of those who would like to locate the original Chinese in the Buddhist canon.
- In the translations in the main body of the text, square brackets are interpolations by the translators to make the texts read better.

A Word on Pronunciation

Chinese names have been transliterated in roman letters in this volume using the standard Pinyin system. To get a rough idea of the pronunciation of some of the common letters, please see the simple guide that follows:

c	pronounced like the English *ts*
q	pronounced like the English *ch*
x	pronounced like the English *hs*
zh	pronounced like the English *j*

The Pinyin system of transliteration does not separate conjoined characters with a hyphen. However, when conjoining a word could cause confusion in its pronunciation, an apostrophe has been used: for example, gong'an. This is to avoid pronouncing the word wrongly as *gon gan.*

Acknowledgments

I would like to acknowledge the following individuals who have contributed their skills and efforts to making this book possible: Guogu (Jimmy Yu), who translated the teachings by Boshan and Xuyan, as well as supplementing the translations of the Jiexian and Sheng Yen sections; J. C. Cleary, who translated the article by Jiexian as well as my own portion of this book, which is based on talks from four Chan retreats: one at Nongchan Temple in Taiwan (1991), and three at the Chang Medication Center in New York City (1992); Lin Ch'i-hsien and Kuo Hui-hsin, who edited the Chinese transcript of the Nongchan Temple retreat, which was then translated into English by Mr. Cleary; Ming Yee Wang, who provided concurrent English translations of the New York retreats, which were then transcribed and edited; Ernest Heau, who acted as general editor; Mike Morical, who reviewed and proofread the manuscript; Iris Wang, who provided essential support throughout the publication phases of this book.

We are greateful to Shambhala Publications for their faith and commitment to this endeavor, particularly to David O'Neal, Katie Keach, and DeAnna Satre for their dedicated and skillful editing.

Finally, without the help of the anonymous bodhisattvas who

contributed their time and effort, and without the earnest attention of the practitioners past and present who received these teachings, this volume would not be possible. I am grateful to them all and dedicate this book to them.

I take great joy in sharing these teachings with you, and may peace prevail in the world.

MASTER SHENG YEN

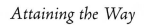

Attaining the Way

Introduction: Resolving the
Great Matter of Birth and Death

FOR NEARLY THIRTY YEARS, causes and conditions have allowed me to use my experiences in Chan to help others in their own practice. During this time I have led close to three hundred intensive Chan retreats—lasting from seven to forty-nine days—in the United States, Europe, and Asia. While I have edited and written many works on Buddhism and Chan in Chinese and English, there is a still a need for translations of original works. This volume is part of the continuing effort to meet this need.

Attaining the Way is an introduction to the teachings of four masters on Chan practice—two from the Ming dynasty and two from modern times. They are masters Wuyi Yuanlai, also known as Boshan; Yuanyun Jiexian; Yanche Deqing, better known as Xuyun; and myself, Huikong Shangyan, also known as Sheng Yen. From these teachings one may discern the masters' individual approaches to addressing the common issues that arise in Chan practice. They not only deal with the challenges of using the methods but also point out the correct attitudes, concepts, and mental states that a practitioner may encounter on the Path. While using distinct approaches to teach and temper students with different dispositions, their principle remains the same: that genuine awakening depends not only on proper understanding of Buddhadharma, correct use of the methods, and earnest practice but also on the guidance of skillful masters.

While Chan is not the only way to cultivate Buddhadharma, it is the essence or common ground of all practices. What I mean is that Chan not only is established on ethical living and stability of mind but also takes as its goal the blossoming of *bodhi*—the full realization of wisdom and compassion. From the time of Shakyamuni Buddha, all bodhisattvas, Chan masters, and sincere practitioners have trod this path. Because there is no single fixed method called "Chan," various methods have been embraced by Chan, including reciting a buddha's name, mantra recitation, prostrations, and studying scriptures. Chan is neither limited to sitting nor separate from daily life. If any of the methods is used to the point where the mind is settled and focused, then with the guidance of a master, methods like huatou or silent illumination can be used to generate wisdom. Once genuine wisdom is experienced—the letting go of body, mind, and the world—confidence will become firm, character will be improved, and compassion will be free from conditions.

This volume is not sectarian, in that it does not align with the Linji (Jap., Rinzai) or the Caodong (Jap., Soto) branches of Chan (Jap., Zen) in method or view. The teachings are presented chronologically, while their selection is based on what I perceive as useful, clear, and appropriate for Western practitioners. I encourage Chan and Zen teachers to use these texts as resources for preparing and guiding students in "attaining the way" of the buddhas and bodhisattvas. In this ocean of wisdom, all the "pearls" of the Dharma already exist, waiting for practitioners to harvest and string them together.

The hope for this volume is that it will show that Chan is a supreme way of resolving "the great matter of birth and death," that is to say, attaining enlightenment. Among the ancient masters and adepts, Chan was known as the Dharma gate of "letting go of one's life" and "putting to death one's delusion." When one can die the great death of delusion, then one can live the great life of awakening. This is the meaning of resolving the great matter of life and death. This book is for teachers, practitioners, scholars, and those who wish to learn more about how one may approach the practice of Chan and Zen. May this book help you to realize your innate wisdom and act toward others with limitless compassion.

MASTER SHENG YEN
Pine Bush, New York
2005

PART ONE

EXHORTATIONS ON INVESTIGATING CHAN

by Master Boshan

Excerpts translated by Guogu

What Beginning Chan Practitioners Should Know

AT THE VERY OUTSET OF PRACTICE, arouse the aspiration to break through the mind of birth and death.[1] With determined resolve, see through the universe, body, and mind, and realize that everything is [the coming together of] provisional conditions— without a substantial self. If you cannot discover the Original Great Principle[2] that is within you, the mind of birth and death will never be shattered. When the mind of birth and death is not shattered, the slaying ghost of impermanence will continue without end in your each and every thought, [haunting you]. How will you ever stop it? Just take this single thought of shattering the mind of birth and death like a tile that knocks [down] a gate. [You should be like someone] sitting in the midst of a raging fire, wanting to escape. Do not step haphazardly; do not stand still. Give rise to no other thoughts, and don't count on the help of others. At this point, throw away your concerns about the raging fire, your very life, your anticipation of others' help; with no other thoughts and refusing to halt, just directly dash forward. If you can break out [of the raging fire], then you're a person of [great] abilities!

In the course of practice, the most crucial thing is to arouse the "doubt sensation." What is this doubt? Not knowing where you came from prior to your birth, you have no choice but to wonder where you are from. Oblivious to where you will go after you die, how can you not question where you will end up? Your inability to shatter this barrier of birth and death will suddenly arouse the doubt—like a curled knot on our eyelashes, which you are unable to untangle or get rid of. One day you will suddenly shatter this mass of doubt and realize that the term *birth and death* is useless garbage! The ancient worthies said: "Great doubt, great enlightenment; small doubt, small enlightenment; no doubt, no enlightenment."

In the course of practice, the most fearful thing is to settle into a state of stagnation and attach to quiescence, becoming dry and lifeless, unknowing and ignorant, and detesting activity while taking pleasure in quietude. Since practitioners have always lived amid noisy, busy situations, experiencing quiescence is like eating candy and honey! This is also like an exhausted person enjoying a long sleep! How will they know that they're already stagnating in quiescence? (Section omitted) In the midst of stillness, we must discover this precious thing hidden under the lining of the garment.[3] You can only resolve the Great Matter [of birth and death] in the midst of stillness while not knowing that you are in stillness. But if you seek to resolve this Great Matter in stillness, then you'll never attain it! If you don't seek, then you are sure to get it.

In the course of practice, when you look up you do not see the sky; when you look down you do not see the ground. You do not see mountains when looking at mountains, or water when looking at water. Not knowing you are walking when walking, not knowing you are sitting when sitting. In the middle of thousands and millions of people, not a single person is perceived. Throughout your whole being—inside and out—there is only the mass of doubt sensation. Even when the world is completely chaotic, vow not to rest in your mind until you shatter this mass of doubt. This is the most important thing in practicing.

In the course of practice, do not fear that in death you will not live; instead, fear living without [having experienced the great] death! If you can fasten yourself to the doubt, there will be no need to leave behind motion and stillness—they will depart by themselves. Nor will there be a need to purify the deluded mind—the deluded mind will be purified by itself. At that time, the gates of the six roots[4] will naturally be expansively open, like empty space. Touch "it," and you'll arrive; call "it," it will respond.[5] Why worry about not living?

When practicing well, [the doubt] will feel like a thousand pounds on your shoulders and being unable to put it down. Like searching for something extremely important that you've lost—vow not to rest until you find it. During this process, do not give rise to any attachment, clinging, or schemes. Attachment will become illness, clinging will turn into a demon, scheming will only place you outside [the Way]. If you can practice single-heartedly—with one intent—like searching for an important thing you have lost, then you will not encounter the above three situations. Know this: When the mind arises, thoughts will stir up. This is departing from the principle of Dharma.

When bringing forth the huatou, be alert and clear, like a cat catching a mouse. There's an old saying, "Don't rest until the [cunning] ferret is killed."[6] Or else, you will sit there dwelling in the cave of ghosts, spending your life in dullness and confusion—what will be the use of that?

When a cat is trying to catch a mouse, its eyes are wide open and its four limbs are firmly on the ground. It will not rest until the mouse is in its mouth. Even if there are roosters or dogs at its side, the cat will not be distracted. It should be the same for those who investigate Chan. Have the determination to actualize this principle. When confronting the eight winds,[7] do not be distracted. However, as soon as other thoughts arise, not only will you be unable to catch the mouse but the cat will be gone too.

When practicing, do not guess or measure the gong'ans of the ancient worthies and make deluded interpretations. Though you may indulge yourself in these gong'ans and think you understand them clearly, they really have no connection with you. In reality you do not understand a single phrase or word from the ancient worthies. The gong'an is like a great raging fire, you can't get near it or touch it; not to mention trying to sit and lay in the midst of it! Furthermore, it is useless to ponder or theorize whether this gong'an is more or less profound than that one. Very few people can go on like this without harming their bodies or losing their lives!

If you can have faith, then you are a vessel [of the Dharma]; if you cannot have faith, then you are not a vessel [of the Dharma]. Practitioners who wish to enter the principle of this Great Vehicle [of the Mahayana] accomplish it through faith. This word *faith* can be shallow or profound, specious or true. You must be clear about the differences! When those who have shallow faith enter the Dharma gate, you cannot really say they lack faith, but their faith is in the Dharma gate and not in their own minds. Even those who have profound faith, such as bodhisattvas of the Great Vehicle, do not have complete faith. For example, you cannot say that these bodhisattvas don't believe that mind is buddha. But if you ask them, "Are you a buddha?" they will not be able to affirm it with conviction or take on the title. When you consider your own mind as the buddha, that is genuine faith. If you seek the Dharma outside of your mind, that is specious faith. You must personally verify this and put it into practice until you have no more qualms about it. This is genuine faith. But if you have the slightest skepticism about this, then even though you say that "the mind is buddha" but have not personally come to know your own mind, then this is still heretical faith.

Do not be stained by or attached to worldly dharmas in the course of practice. Even Buddhadharma should not be attached to, much less worldly dharmas! If the doubt sensation truly manifests, you will not feel cold when stepping on ice or hot when walking on fire. Even if you were to walk through a dense, thorny forest, you would not feel obstructed. When you have reached this point, then you can freely come and go in the midst of worldly affairs. Otherwise you will be turned by situations. In this state, even though you wish to reach the point where your practice is pervasive and seamless, you cannot dream of it. Not even in the year of the donkey![8]

Chan master Huangbo Xiyun (d. ca. 850) once said: "Relinquishing the dust [of vexations] is no ordinary affair; you must practice rigorously, like fastening a tight knot on a rope. If you have not endured through the bone-chilling winter, how can you expect to smell the scent of plum blossoms?"[9] These words are most intimate to us. If at all times you can admonish yourself with these words, you will naturally have practiced well.

In the course of practice, it is crucial to be "earnest."[10] Being earnest is most powerful. If you are not earnest, you will fall into laxity. Because of this laxity, you will be indulgent and lazy. At that point, anything can happen. If you can really apply your mind and be earnest, from where can laxity arise? (Section omitted) Being earnest can free you from mistakes and in an instant you can transcend the three natures of good, evil, and indifference.[11]

In the course of practice, the worst thing is to start thinking and composing verses, poems, and various prose works.

In the course of practice, do not anticipate enlightenment. (Section omitted) Only under severe crushing pressure will enlightenment happen. (Section omitted) When the causes and the conditions are ripe, you can work on the huatou with certainty and crushing force. Then enlightenment may happen. Enlightenment will not happen when you anticipate it. At the time [of enlightenment], it will be like dispersing the clouds and seeing the sky, expansive and open, with nothing to lean on. The heaven will whirl and the earth will spin—a sweeping state of reversal.

Your practice must be taut,[12] impenetrable, and integrated and pervasive.[13]

What is taut practice? Our human life exists in the in and out of our breath. Without resolving this Great Matter [of birth and death], when the next breath does not come you will be completely lost as to your destiny. Since you don't know where you will go [after you die], you have no choice but to be taut in your practice.

What is impenetrable practice? It is like the [nonexistent] gap between the hair of the brows and space. Needles cannot penetrate it and water cannot wet it. [Your practice] should not have any gaps. If there is even the tiniest gap, that is where demonic situations can gain entry.

What is integrated and pervasive practice? When the world expands ten feet, the ancient mirror expands ten feet. [But] when the ancient mirror expands ten feet, the firing furnace also expands ten feet. You shouldn't attach to or abide in any place. Do not seize the snake's head nor snatch at both ends of it. Just be boundless and limitless. An ancient worthy said, "The Way is perfect like great space/Without lack, without excess."[14] When you have really attained the stage where your practice is integrated and pervasive, then internally you will not perceive a body and a mind. Externally, there will be no [such thing as the] world. This is the beginning of gaining an entry into genuine practice.

When practicing, it is crucial not to arouse the least bit of extraneous thought. Whether walking, staying, sitting, or lying, simply bring forth the fundamental question of the huatou to arouse the doubt sensation and generate a great resolve to find out the answer. If there is the least bit of extraneous thought, it is what the ancient [ones] refer to as "fatal poison entering the heart." Not only will this harm your physical life; it will also harm your wisdom life. Adherents should be careful!

The so-called extraneous thoughts are thoughts that relate to worldly phenomena. Other than the thorough investigation of Mind, all other good things within the Buddhadharma are considered extraneous thoughts. Not only all the [good] things within the Buddhadharma but also whatever can be grasped, shunned, attached to, or transformed outside the mind essence is considered extraneous thoughts.

In the course of practice, most people complain that they cannot apply their efforts well. Precisely because they cannot "apply themselves," they should apply themselves even more! It is like a person who is lost; it makes great sense for him to find his way. He cannot say, "Well, since I am lost, I will quit." (Section omitted) An ancient worthy once said, "The gate of liberation is gateless; one enters the Way without intentions."[15] The most important thing is to personally enter it.

The most fearful thing in practice is a witty or clever mind.[16] The witty mind is like food that annuls medicine. If you give rise to the least bit of wit, then even when genuine medicine appears in front of you, it cannot cure you. If you are a true person of Chan, your eyes should be blind and your ears should be deaf. When thoughts arise, they should be like they're smashed up against a silver mountain or an iron wall. When you can be like this, you will conform to genuine practice.

In the course of practice, do not fear mistakes; rather, fear not realizing that you are wrong. Even though you make mistakes, if you turn your thoughts around and admit them, then this is having what it takes to become a buddha or a patriarch; this is the essential way out of birth and death; this is the useful weapon to rip through Mara's grip.[17] Shakyamuni Buddha attained all levels of practice of the heterodox path. However, he did not dwell in those old ruts. By knowing and relinquishing that which is wrong, he directly ascended from the ordinary to the holiest stage.

In the course of practice, you should not avoid noisy situations and crave quiescent states. This is like closing one's eyes so as not to see a single thing, like sitting in the "dark cave of ghosts" wasting away time. What kind of attainment can you achieve by sitting beneath the dark mountain immersed in stale water? You have to learn to apply yourself in different circumstances. This is where you really gain power! Just use a huatou as if [something were] stuck between your eyebrows and eyelashes; whether walking, sitting, dressing, eating, or receiving guests, just clarify where this huatou is going. One morning when you wash your face and touch your nose, you will realize how close you are! This is where practice saves power.

In the course of practice, it is most dire to mistake phenomena arising out of subconsciousness as buddha activities.[18] When such phenomena arise, you may raise your eyebrows, wink, shake your head, and turn your face and say that you have attained great spiritual powers. If you take the phenomena arising from your subconscious as something extraordinary, then you are not even worthy of being a slave to heterodox practitioners! When practicing, it is crucial that the workings of the deluded mind be extinguished. Do not construct different ideas in your head, and never try to theorize those occasions of encounter dialogues.[19] (Section omitted) When you penetrate the Great Principle thoroughly, all the various *samadhis* will issue forth naturally from your mind. But if you try to conceive or construct some notion of this, you will be as far apart as heaven and earth.

In the course of practice, just wholeheartedly work on one gong'an. Never try to analyze or interpret all the gong'ans. Although you may be able to interpret them, they will remain mere interpretations, not enlightenment. The *Lotus Sutra* says: "The Dharma cannot be attained by means of thinking and discrimination."[20] The *Sutra of Complete Enlightenment* says: "If one tries to measure the state of Tathagata's complete enlightenment by means of the thinking mind, then it will be like using the light of the lightning bug to heat up Mount Sumeru. It will never be accomplished."[21] Chan master Dongshan Liangjie (807–869) once said, "If one plans to learn this profound Dharma by means of the conscious mind, it will be like a person walking west trying to go east."[22] In sum, anyone who tries to fathom the meaning [of a gong'an] must feel ashamed and know humility.

When bringing forth the huatou, without giving rise to a second thought, just know that this doubt sensation hasn't been shattered. (Section omitted) The Way is inseparable from everything else. If it is something separate, then it cannot be called the Way. Likewise, practice cannot be off and on. If your practice can be interrupted, then it is not genuine practice. True practitioners investigate as if their eyebrows and heads were on fire. How can they give rise to trivial thoughts? An ancient worthy said, "Like a man confronting a thousand enemies, at that moment, face-to-face, how can he blink his eyes?"[23] Observing this phrase in the course of practice is crucial, which is something that must be known.

When practicing, if you have not thoroughly "broken through" [to enlightenment], you must mind your own business—do not try to instruct others. If a person has never been to the capital yet talks of various affairs there, then this is deceiving not only others but also himself.

If in your practice you attain the state of "light and ease," or some kind of insight, do not take this to be enlightenment.

Once I, Boshan, was investigating a line by the Boat Monk, "without a trace."[24] Later I read a dialogue between Chan master Zhaozhou (778–897) and another monk in the *Transmission of the Lamp* that said: "One must meet someone [face-to-face] from three thousand miles!"[25] Without any intentions, this "sack" was sloughed off.[26] Like putting down a thousand pounds of burden. I thought I had attained great enlightenment. But later, when I met Chan master Baofang,[27] it was like trying to fit a square peg into a round hole! I felt ashamed. If after some insight you do not meet a great spiritual teacher, then even though you have attained a state of ease of bliss, this will not resolve [this Great Matter of birth and death].

Master Baofang encouraged me with a verse: "Using emptiness to crush emptiness is the greatest merit. Using existence to pursue existence, the merit will be small. How can the slandering of Mahakashyapa be considered reasonable? When things are easily attained, this is where you lose that thing."[28] This is the stage where one has to take another step beyond the one-hundred-foot pole. We patch-robed monks cannot be careless. I often advise practitioners, saying, "I only received two words of instruction from Baofang: 'Not yet!' But the usefulness of these two words never seems to exhaust itself."

In the course of practice, you should not try to rationalize things. Just persistently and stubbornly work on your investigation until you arouse the doubt sensation. If you rationalize about your practice, then your practice will be dry and stale. Not only are you unable to break through this Great matter [of birth and death] thoroughly, you cannot even give rise to the doubt sensation.

In the course of practice, do not engage in idleness. You must have a strong determination to understand this principle. If you are idle, then you will spend your life as an idler. This Great Thing hidden under the seam of your cloth will never be discovered.[29] It is like a person searching for something that has been lost. If you can find it, then your task will be fulfilled. If you cannot, then you may come to a halt, in a state of idleness. If you cannot arouse the intention to search for it, then even if the lost article appears in front of you, you will not be aware of it. This is because you are not searching for it.

In the course of practice, you should pay no attention to those so-called experiences that are like sparks from struck flint. What is the point of being caught up with those fleeting experiences of lights and images at [your sensory] entrances—sometimes appearing, sometimes not? You must personally experience and verify [enlightenment]. If you can truly fulfill and achieve this, it will be like seeing your own parents in broad daylight[—there's no mistake about it]. No worldly pleasure can surpass it.

In the course of practice, never ask someone else to reveal the truth to you. If they tell you, the answer will still be theirs. It will have nothing to do with you. Like a person asking for directions to the city of Chang'an,[30] who should only expect to be told where to find the road leading there, not about the affairs in Chang'an. Even if the affairs there are clearly explained to him, it will only be what the other person saw, not what the person asking for directions might see. The same is true when you don't work hard but instead beg the answer from others.

When practicing, you should not "recite" the gong'an. What is the use of mere recitation? (Section omitted.)

I do not teach people to recite the huatou but just continuously try to bring forth the huatou [to their attention]. If you are observing the word *wu*,[31] then from the word *wu* the doubt must arise. If you're observing "the cypress tree,"[32] then it is from these words *the cypress tree* that the doubt must arise. If you are observing the huatou "Where does the one return to?"[33] then naturally, this is where the doubt sensation will arise. If you can arouse the doubt sensation, then the ten directions all become this mass of doubt.[34] You will not know the existence of the body and mind that your parents gave you, through and through; your whole being is just a mass of doubt. Unaware of the existence of the ten directions, no inside or outside, everything is fused into one great mass. It will [then] only be a matter of time before the metal band around the barrel explodes!

When practicing, never lose the correct thought. If you lose this thought of investigation, then you have strayed off into extremes, forgetting to return [to the method]. Like a person sitting in quietude, preferring only stillness and clarity, thinking that the essence of Buddhism is just this purity. This is called losing the correct thought and falling into the state of utter clarity. Or, if you take the abilities to articulate, converse, maneuver, or be still as Buddha's activities, then this is losing the correct thought and taking the mere conscious mind as the workings of Buddha's activities. Moreover, if you try to repress or prevent deluded thoughts from arising, thinking that the Buddha's activity is the nonarising of wandering thoughts, then this is also called losing the correct thought. Using wandering thoughts to press down wandering thoughts is like a stone pressing down on the grass. (Section omitted)

In addition, if you contemplate the body and mind as empty space, without giving rise to thoughts, like a wall, then this too is losing the correct thought. Chan master Xuansha (835–908) once said, "If you intend to freeze the mind and collect your thoughts, taking in all the affairs and returning them to nothingness, then you will fall into the dead emptiness taught by the heterodox path and live out your days like a dead person whose soul refuses to disperse!" At any rate, all of these cases are considered losing the correct thought.

The Doubt Sensation and the Arising and Perishing Mind

You are unable to give rise to the doubt sensation precisely because of your discriminating consciousness. With the turning of a thought, if you can acknowledge your mistakes and put down your body, then when you see a virtuous teacher you will gain entrance [of the Way].

Some people cannot generate the doubt sensation in their practice, so they try to control the wandering mind or stop it from arising. If they practice like this, they may reach a point where the wandering mind does not arise. When they reach this point where nothing arises, they will experience the state of stillness, clarity, and purity, without the slightest taint. However, if you consider this as your practice, then you will never shatter the root of the discriminating consciousness. Even if you meet a person who points out "the spot where it hurts" to you (that is, points out your mistake), your response will be like a person trying to press down the gourd floating on top of the water. Yours is the mind of arising and perishing, not Chan.

All of this is because in the beginning you refuse to investigate the huatou to arouse the doubt sensation. Even though you are able to force the body and mind not to stir, you are like a stone pressing down on grass. After you die, this discriminating consciousness will lead you to annihilation; for sure you will be [reborn] into the realm of nothingness of the heterodox path. And if you do not go to the [realm of] annihilation, then when meeting conditions, your discriminating consciousness will stir up again. Interpreting the state of utter stillness and clarity as holy, you will probably think you have entered the door of great enlightenment! If you follow this line of thinking, you will for sure become insane. If you attach to it, you become the demon. Amid the worldly phenomena you will be an ignorant, deluded lunatic creating evil karma and causing people's faith to regress. This is obstructing the Way of *bodhi*.[35]

When you cannot arouse the doubt sensation, you might resort to neglecting your body, your mind, and the world to a state of "voidness," not giving any care to them, without any retention. Not perceiving a body, mind, or world, no inside or outside, everything is just this emptiness; believing this to be Chan, taking this kind of voidness as buddha, walking is voidness, sitting is voidness, this is voidness, that is voidness; and if in the midst of walking, standing, sitting, and lying, you feel as if they are all done in voidness, then this is also the mind of arising and perishing, not Chan.

Detaching yourself from this state, you end up in the dark state of unknowing. Attached to it, you become a demon, saying that you have already entered the door of great enlightenment.

If you are really a Chan adept who can arouse the doubt sensation, then your huatou will be like a long sword extending to the heavens. Anything that comes in contact with it will lose its life!

If you cannot arouse the doubt sensation, then even though you have seen through body and mind as [the coming together of] false conditions, still there is a thing that is coming and going, moving and settling. It may be shapeless and formless, at the gates of the six sense faculties emitting light and shaking the ground. When diffused, it can pervade and fill up as many realms as there are sands in the Ganges River. When withdrawn, not a single particle of fine dust can be found. You may convince yourself in this very state—refusing to arouse the doubt and make further investigations—that you are a free man who has resolved this Great Matter [of birth and death]. This is the mind of arising and perishing, not Chan!

Little do you know that without shattering this mind of birth and death, you have already become content and indulgent, regarding [what you have achieved] as rapturous. This is just sporting with the discriminating consciousness. When the light of your eyes drops to the floor,[36] you will not be your own master. Then you will simply be dragged by your consciousness [to your next birth], following your karma and receiving retributions.

From this we can see that practicing Chan depends completely on meeting a good master. If you try to go about your own way, you will never make progress.

If you cannot arouse the doubt sensation, you might start to have aversion toward certain situations that you face, enjoying yourself only in meditating in desolate or quiet places. Feeling engrossed, you might think that you are progressing. If you feel repelled when meeting active situations, then this is the arising and perishing mind, not Chan.

After a long time of meditating like this, you may come to accord with the realm of serenity and quietude, becoming gloomy and unknowing, cutting off all interactions and responses. You may even achieve *samadhi*, fixating your mind without motion. But what would be the difference between this and the path of those following the Small Vehicle?[37]

When confronting the slightest adverse situation, you don't feel at ease; when hearing sounds and seeing forms, fear rises in you. Because of this fear, you will give demonic forces a chance to enter. When demons possess you, your actions will be evil and your whole life's practice will be wasted. All of this is because in the beginning you misused your mind, not arousing the doubt sensation, unwilling to see a teacher or trust others, only going about your own way, dwelling in your own quietude. Even if you meet a virtuous friend, you refuse to realize your mistakes. Although a thousand buddhas may appear in this world, they will be unable to help you!

PART TWO

DISCOURSE ON CHAN TRAINING

from the records of
Master Yuanyun Jiexian
(1610–1672)

Translated by J. C. Clearly *with* Guogu

Jiexian's Preface

WHY DO I MODEL THIS DISCOURSE on Chan training on the principles of Master Sun Wu?[1] If the nation is ruled correctly and military forces are used strategically, then the words of the court counselor [who is advising the ruler] must be accurate. For those who occupy the position of masters in Buddhism, ruling over the Chan community is like ruling over a nation. Using strategic methods to train the Chan congregation is like using military strategy. Surprise tactics and standard tactics depend on each other: this is an unchanging principle.

The Chan transmission began with a single gesture—Buddha holding up a flower. The masters of this strategy included twenty-eight [patriarchs] in India and six [Chan patriarchs] in China. Though they revealed ultimate principles, they were secretly in accord with Sun Wu. When it came to the Galloping Colt (that is, Chan master Mazu), it was like [the great Song dynasty general Hong Hao, known as] Gangbi shifting the defensive lines [to block the Jerchen advance for many years and allow the Song dynasty to survive in south China]. Mazu's successors included the Chan masters Huangbo (d. ca. 850), Muzhou (780–877),[2] Yunmen (864–949), Fenyang (947–1024), Zhiming (986–1039), Wuzu (1024–1104) of East Mountain, and Yuanwu (1063–1135). Sometimes empty, sometimes solid, sometimes killing, sometimes giving life, they used pure strategy. When it came to (Yuanwu's disciple Dahui Zonggao) Miaoxi, he specialized in holding a bamboo comb when teaching. He made extensive use of surprise tactics, winning people over on the widest scale. Each of the Five Houses of Chan[3] established its teaching and its own set of guiding principles. Their strategies were refined and rigorous and so firm no one could break through them. Their command of strategy was complete.

From the Yuan period into the middle years of the Ming dynasty, the methods of training and tempering Chan practitioners were neglected. [Misguided methods of] "cold ashes and dead tree" [meditation] trapped and killed people [who tried to employ them to practice Chan]. Fortunately, in recent times old man Yuanwu of Tiantong Temple picked up his three-foot-long Dharma sword and opened up the frontiers of the Chan school. Old man Zang (Fazang; 1573–1635) of Sanfeng Temple succeeded him, reviving the guiding principles of Chan and taking up Miaoxi's bamboo stick again. Thus the correct methods for training and tempering Chan practitioners were again put into practice. These two genuine masters burst through the enemy lines and produced a multitude of "dragons and elephants" [outstanding Chan people]. Succeeding them, my own master, Lingyin, added a further mastery of adaptive change. He used many methods to break through from outside [the shell of delusion] while the practitioner simultaneously breaks through from inside. He used all sorts of unfathomable strategies and came out with a profusion of surprise tactics. Thus the Chan masters' book of strategy became even more complete.

In years past I served as the head seat [4] [in Lingyin's congregation] and awakened to his Dharma. Now I do not shrink from the task of adding to my masters' methods. I have devised methods for Chan masters to accompany their assemblies of practitioners in their walking meditation, to strike blows [against their ignorance], to turn their minds around, to capture them and peck through their shells, and to split apart their delusions. These methods are very effective for this time. Although there will be hard fighting on the battlefield, there will be victory and many captives. Overall, this is where the use of extraordinary, complex, deadly poisonous strategy reaches its culmination.

No matter whether people's faculties are sharp or dull, if they receive training and tempering [from a genuine Chan master], they are all capable of insight and enlightenment. But these days, because most people [who play the part of Chan masters] cling to dead methods and do not let down their hands from the perilous cliff [to reach out to their practitioners], even if there are capable people [who come to practice with them], most are sadly made dull. Being mindful of this, I dare not keep these methods secret, and so I am composing a discourse on Chan training to be put into circulation in the Chan schools. Even when they find this discourse, the old masters and seasoned monks will not necessarily be able to put the methods I set forth here into practice. Not only won't they put them into practice; they will contemptuously criticize them instead. Those who are just beginning in the role of Chan masters still have bodies that are brave and strong and energy that is fierce and sharp. If they adhere to this strategy and diligently take charge of perfecting their practitioners, they will surely be able to enlighten many people and produce great Dharma generals. My hope is that the weapons and armor of the Three Mysteries[5] [of the Linji school of Chan] will be forever strong, and the banner of the Five Stations[6] [of the Caodong school of Chan] will never falter.

[As Confucius said of himself, regarding the *Spring and Autumn Annals,* this work will be how other people can] both know me and find fault with me, and there is nothing to regret in this. So I hope this work may be thought of [as a classic on the strategy of Chan training], as the [work of] Sun Wu is [*on the Art of War*].

Early spring, fifteenth day of the first lunar month, 1661.
Composed by the mountain cleric Yuanyun Jiexian of Eastern Wu,
who lives on Mount Hui in the Yunju Temple complex.

Making Firm Vows and Enduring Suffering

A CHAN MASTER OCCUPIES the true position of the buddhas and patriarchs, so he must continue the family heritage of the buddhas and patriarchs. He functions as a master and exemplar to humans and gods, and so he must open the eye of wisdom for humans and gods. What is the eye of wisdom of humans and gods? It is buddha-nature. What is the family heritage of the buddhas and patriarchs? It is finding people [capable of sustaining the enlightened lineage]. If you act as a Chan master but you cannot cause sentient beings to awaken to their buddha-nature, this is called stealing the name of Chan master. If you occupy the true position [of the buddhas and patriarchs] but you cannot develop and expand human potential on behalf of the buddhas and patriarchs, this is called usurping the position. To enable sentient beings to awaken to their buddha-nature, you must take great pains with your mind. You cannot make them awaken to their buddha-nature unless you have figured out how their minds work and trimmed away their false consciousness and brought all the machinations of their conditioned minds to an end. To develop and expand human potential for the buddhas and patriarchs, you must work hard with your body. You cannot find suitable people for the Dharma gate unless you make them work diligently and courageously and fully mobilize their energies and undergo a rigorous course of tempering and training.

Therefore, to become a Chan master, you must first undertake a great vow and establish a great resolve. Only then can you manifest the great potential and exercise the great function [of a real Chan master]. What is this vow? First, to become a Chan master, you must make a vow to the dragons[7] and gods and call upon the buddhas and patriarchs. You must vow that if you can enable sentient beings to awaken to their buddha-nature, you will exert yourself to the utmost and sacrifice yourself in the attempt, and you will not shrink back from this mission even if it means wearing out your physical strength and your spiritual energy, even if it is as difficult as boring through a mountain to open up a road. You must vow that if you can develop and expand human talent for the Dharma gate, you will endure the hardships and not be afraid to continue even if it means working day and night without sleep or food, "gnawing on snow and swallowing felt" [to assuage your thirst and hunger]. (Section omitted)

For the Chan masters, their path is to serve as a bridge across the realms of desire, form, and formlessness and to rescue the four classes of sentient beings. They must add to the age-old life of wisdom of the buddhas and patriarchs and open the eye of enlightenment for the world's sentient beings. What a heavy responsibility this is! In terms of the amount of loving care and painstaking effort involved, (section omitted) they must live aloof [from worldly concerns] and act with uncontrived wisdom. If a so-called Chan master interrupts the Chan stream, if he covets honor and privilege, if he lives at ease and does what he pleases, if he views the Chan monastery as a place to rest and the Chan community as something poles apart from him, if he views the monastic regulations as a dead letter, then is he not turning his back on the buddhas and patriarchs above him? Should he not look up with shame to the dragons and gods? Is he not betraying his masters? He becomes a criminal in the Dharma gate!

Bodhisattvas who teach the Middle Way will tirelessly endure great hardships and sufferings for countless ages for the sake of a single sentient being. These days the Chan communities number tens or hundreds or even thousands, so it is not just one potential vessel of the Dharma with whom the Chan master is faced.

It is also said that a bodhisattva vows, if necessary for the sake of sentient beings, to relinquish his head and his eyes and his marrow and his brain, his blood and his flesh and his hands and his feet,[8] until [over many lifetimes through the ages] these would cover the earth and pile up as high as Mount Sumeru.[9] He swears never to retreat from his great aspiration because of the pain and suffering. If we compare the effort and pain and privation of training a Chan community to a bodhisattva's sacrificing his head and eyes and flesh and blood, even if we multiply it ten or a hundred or a thousand times, it still cannot measure up to a millionth part of the bodhisattva's sacrifice. Having entered this gate, the path of a Chan master, you must act worthily as an enlightened man of knowledge, a spiritual good friend. Once you are a Chan master, you cannot but take upon yourself the responsibilities of the buddhas and patriarchs. If you occupy the position, you must carry out the tasks [that go with that position]. If you take on the name, then you must fulfill the reality of the name.

For the Chan communities, a genuine Chan master is the great means upon which they rely in order to become enlightened. Tempering and training is in truth the great key that all the patriarchs have used to obtain people [capable of perpetuating the Buddhist Dharma]. If the Chan master does not make a diligent effort to temper and train his practitioners, then he will certainly not be able to open the eye of wisdom for sentient beings and allow them to enter [the Way]. If the Chan master does not take the bodhisattva vows, then he will certainly not be willing to endure hardships.

Therefore, before setting forth the methods of tempering and training practitioners, I ask you to make a firm vow. When this vow is made, then the great basis will be correct. That is why this section is called "Making Firm Vows and Enduring Suffering."

Distinguishing Practitioners' Capacity and Giving Huatous Accordingly

If you want to train Chan practitioners, you must teach them genuine investigation of Chan. If you want to apply the hammer and tongs, first you must distinguish which practitioners are potential vessels of the Dharma. Master Linji said, "Here I distinguish three categories [low, middle, and high] of inherent capacity for the Dharma among my practitioners. Depending on the capacity of the practitioner, sometimes I take away the person, sometimes I take away the phenomena, sometimes I take away both, and sometimes I take away neither."[10] This is the main essence of distinguishing and testing potential vessels of the Dharma.

During the Tang dynasty [when Linji lived], the influence of Chan was strong, and there were people of uncommon potential for the Dharma. When the Chan masters of those days received people, they always manifested the great function of the whole potential and abruptly cut off the root of life.[11] They used living devices only and had no dead methods. From the Song dynasty onward, people used [the method of] huatou to investigate Chan, and dead methods were established.

Coming to the Dharma Ending Age,[12] people's basic capacity grew more and more inferior, and their intellectual cleverness became more and more deeply rooted. Craziness and confusion became more and more prevalent, and meditative concentration and wisdom became more and more shallow. Those in charge of the teaching wanted to enable people in the Chan communities to open up to the enlightened nature inherent in them and to break through the "imprisonment barrier,"[13] so they had no alternative but to employ dead methods. The trend of the times made it so.

If they are not skillfully used, even living methods all become dead methods. If one can use them skillfully, even in the midst of dead methods, one can find living methods. What are living methods? This means discerning a practitioner's potential to be a vessel of the Dharma.

When members of the Chan community enter the [monastery] gate, the master measures them on sight and decides whether their capacity is high or low. Then the master tests them with Chan stories, which are like probing poles and grass shades [that enable a fisherman to peer beneath the surface of the water], and probes as to whether their investigation of Chan has been shallow or deep. The master plays the roles of both host and guest and carries on a dialogue with the practitioner to test whether the practitioner can mesh with the master in one continuous strand. By such means the master sees whether the practitioner knows of the existence [of the one great matter of enlightenment], and the practitioner's capacity as a person is revealed.

Sometime practitioners with very high potential to be vessels of the Dharma come, and the master receives them with a lion's teeth and claws and with the awesome ferocity of an elephant king. The master puts out golden traps and hurls such practitioners into thickets of thorns to see whether they can penetrate through the barrier. Control rests with the master.

After determining [the practitioner's] capacity as a person, the master lets him enter the Chan Hall. Once a practitioner has entered the Chan Hall, he is sure to enter the master's private room [for face-to-face instruction]. There the master will teach him a huatou, according to whether his potential is high, medium, or low. When a practitioner has previously traveled to other masters and already has a huatou [he has been working on], the master may trim away [the practitioner's previous interpretations], or he may change the huatou, or he may set the practitioner straight. Although there is no single pattern in this work, once the huatou is correct, the calibrations on the scale have been set.

Question: Some Chan masters did not use huatous. For example Linji taught people with blows, and Deshan [Xuanjian] (c. 782–865) taught people with shouts. What about this?

Answer: Such extraordinary tactics were indeed used, but they depended on practitioners of very high capacity and cannot be used in all cases.

Question: What about those masters who invariably used only one huatou, no matter whether the practitioner's potential was sharp or dull and no matter how many practitioners were in their Chan congregations?

Answer: There were indeed cases where all practitioners were treated the same, but this was when the practitioners' capacities were all lumped together indiscriminately. Then, even though they studied the huatou, most of them did not benefit.

Question: What is the reason for all of this?

Answer: The classic Chan masters who did not use huatous were truly very direct and alive and totally unencumbered. This was possible for the ancients but not for us today. Why? The basic capacity of the people of olden times was very high, and their meditative concentration and wisdom were powerful. Once they were alerted by the blows and shouts of the great craftsmen of the Chan school, once they experienced certainty, they retained this certainty forever and there was no more confusion. Once they penetrated through, they penetrated through forever and there was no more wavering. That's why the Chan masters of old could use these methods.

These days, people's intellectual cleverness is extremely deep-rooted, and their crazy confusion is extremely complicated. The only alternative is to use huatous to hem in [all of this cleverness and confusion] and lock it up tight, to pierce it to the depths so that sentiments dry up and intellect is exhausted and there is a sudden transformation of being. If Chan masters today were to think that Chan means only using the classical direct teaching maneuvers that were like sparks struck from stone and flashes of lightning, then even though some [practitioners] might get something from it, in most cases the practitioner's realization would belong to the category of reflections of the light. None of these practitioners would have seen through the verbal devices to the bloodline of the Chan masters. They might call this enlightenment, but later on they would relapse into unspeakable delusion. That is why we cannot use [such classical methods] today. It's not that we can never use them; it's that we cannot use them as a general rule. Old Huanglong (1002–1069) said to Huitang: "If you do not contemplate a huatou and investigate it a hundred times, until you see it on your own and accept it for yourself, then I will have buried you." How true is this!

For a Chan master to use only a single huatou [and prescribe it for all practitioners] seems evenhanded and simple and direct—it seems to avoid falling into picking and choosing. However, within a Chan congregation, the practitioners vary in the sharpness of their innate capacity. Their temperaments vary in their degree of purity. Their faith in the Path varies from deep to shallow. The time they have spent studying varies from long to short. When selling caps, one must fit the cap to the customer's head. When putting in a plug, one must look at the size of the hole. This is the natural course. If the master directs a practitioner who should be counting his breaths to [do the meditation that involves] contemplating the skeleton,[14] or directs a practitioner who should be contemplating his skeleton to count his breaths, the practitioner would not be able to experience the fruit of enlightenment, even if Buddha were still in the world, much less these days, in the Dharma Ending Age! Masters who understand the Great Dharma clearly examine the temperament and mettle of each practitioner before laying on the hammer and tongs. They know how to make the necessary adjustments before they bore in with the augur. That way practitioners of high, medium, and low capacities all benefit [from being taught with the appropriate methods]. If the master does not inquire how sharp [the practitioner's innate capacity is], how pure his temperament is, how deep his faith [in the Way] is, and how long he has been studying, and just uses one huatou to box the practitioners in, it is as futile as drawing a line on the ground to make a fence or nailing the oars down to the oarlock to propel a boat. [Someone who teaches by rigid formulas] makes the high ones bend down, but they cannot go low enough. He makes the lowly ones stand on tiptoe, but they still cannot reach high enough. This is what is called making a living method into a dead method. Miaoxi said: "Those who act as Chan masters without clearly understanding the Great Dharma just teach people with what they themselves have realized. They are sure to blind people's eyes."[15] Isn't this what he was talking about?

So, when a Chan master directs a practitioner to a huatou, what method should he use? It is still just a matter of deciding which of the three levels of capacity the practitioner possesses.

For practitioners at the elementary level, a huatou is very abstruse and hard to understand and is sure to put them off. In this case the master must direct them to chew on it a little in order to reveal the root.

For practitioners whose mettle is bold and acute, a huatou is something casual and relaxed, and it is easy for them to spin out more and more interpretations of it. In this case, the master must direct them to stand like a mile-high wall, in order to cut off their clinging to entanglements. For example, consider the following huatous:

> "The myriad things return to one. What does one return to?"
>
> "What was your original face before your parents were born?"
>
> "Where will you be after you have died and your body has been cremated?"

(Section omitted) Though huatous like these can be used with both the wise and the ignorant, they are particularly convenient for practitioners at the elementary level. (Section omitted) "Nanquan's not mind, not buddha, not anything"; "Dahui's bamboo comb";

"Whether you can speak or not, I'll still give you thirty blows"; "This way or otherwise—neither is right"; and others. Though huatous like these can be used with both the high and the low, they are particularly convenient for practitioners whose mettle is bold and acute.

For those who are even more conceited and whose subjective views are even more strongly held, the master's teeth and claws must be even more poisonous and astringent. Sometimes the master has to simulate joy or anger in order to cut away the proud practitioner's root of life. Sometimes the master has exhaustively pursued intricate inquiries in order to eliminate the secrets the practitioner holds within himself. Linji's "complete revelation or revealing only half of a body" and "revealing the lion's vehicle or riding the elephant kings," are devices he set for practitioners.[16] From this we see how a Chan master operates. It cannot be called simply transmitting something.

There are many different kinds of huatou, but the important point is this: Above, they must cut through the imprisonment barrier of "wondrous existence."[17] If the imprisonment barrier is there, then when practitioners use their minds, they must plug up the four gates and extinguish the six passages.[18] Below, they must cut through inquiry and questioning. The doubt sensation that the practitioner generates must be genuine. When the doubt sensation is genuine, the extent of enlightenment will be thorough. Wuzu of East Mountain established as a metaphor [for the Chan master giving his disciples a meditation huatou]: the father who is a thief locking the strongbox and having his son break through it. Isn't this [what is meant by the description of the essence of Chan as] the secret that is not transmitted [from father to son]?

There are practitioners whose potential capacity is such that they should investigate the answers [contained in gong'ans] like these:

Q: "What is buddha?" A: "Three pounds of hemp."

Q: "What is buddha?" A: "A dry piece of dung."

"The myriad things return to one. Where does the one
return to?"

"When I was in Jingzhou, I made a cloth shirt that weighed
seven pounds."

Q: "What is the meaning of Bodhidharma coming from the
West [to transmit Chan to China]?" A: "The cypress
tree in the garden."

Q: "Does a dog have buddha-nature or not?" A: "Wu."[19]

There are other practitioners whose potential capacity is such
that they should investigate the functioning of circumstantial device [of the Chan masters],[20] such as the way Deshan struck anyone
who approached his room,[21] Linji's shouts at those who entered his
quarters,[22] Muzhou's reception of Yunmen,[23] Fenyang's treatment
of Zhiming.[24] Frequently we can open the door to great enlightenment and see how the masters functioned. There were no dead
methods with them.

Sometimes these days [unqualified masters] do not know the
mechanism here. They just indiscriminately teach people to investigate sayings like "What is the meaning of the coming from the
West?" or "What is the original face?" or "What is the practitioner's
self?" This way there is no imprisonment barrier above, and they are
just addressing their plea to the empty sky. If the master does not
cut to the crucial point, then the practitioner will generate doubt
that has no power. Bobbing up and down in stagnant water, the
practitioner will grow old without awakening. Isn't it a pity to suffer from this malady?

The worst way that an unqualified master leads people into
error is to direct someone who has first entered the Chan gate, and

who has not yet awakened to the fundamental basis, to investigate such cases as Nanquan's killing of a cat, Baizhang's wild fox,[25] Tanxia burning the buddha-image,[26] or the story of the *naga* (dragon) maiden emerging from *samadhi*.[27] Using such cases on undeveloped practitioners is like trying to put a square peg in a round hole. It is simply a waste of time, and distancing practitioners [from what they ought to be doing] like the distance between heaven and earth. Shouldn't these supposed Chan masters be called phonies? (Section omitted)

Testing Practitioners and Cutting Away Illusions in the Master's Chamber

Once the master has shown the practitioner a huatou, he must direct the practitioner as to how to investigate it.

There are two methods of investigating a huatou: one is mild and one is intense. For those who investigate by the mild method, it is difficult to generate insight. They may have theoretical understanding, but when they go forth among people, they are sure to be weak. For those who investigate by the intense method, it is easy to generate insight, and once they enter the blast furnace of this method, when they appear among people, they are sure to be strong.[28] What is the reason for this?

If you use the mild method to investigate, then you will be casual and relaxed. All you will be able to do is suppress your superficial emotions and filter your coarse consciousness. After a long time, when you have become expert at this, you will come to rest in utter purity and stop there. You will be hopeless when facing critical situations. That's why I say that [when using the mild method], developing insight is difficult. Those [who investigate the huatou to the point where] a "kernel can pop within those cold ashes" may be totally without flaws, but they are still like "dead men on the ground level."²⁹ As soon as they encounter poisonous maneuvers or a courtyard full of thorny brambles, they go to pieces. How could they possibly undertake the Great Matter [of birth and death] and bear the Great Responsibility of leading a congregation so they do not go astray? That's why I say that when they go among people they are sure to be weak.

There is no alternative but to intensely investigate [the huatou] if you want people to cut off [the root of birth and death], to expose their complexities, to transform their existence amid the raging flames, to give their lives at the precipice, to be able to endure beatings and still remain at peace and unperturbed.

Although the intense method is superior, it may be hard to persevere in it. Desiring to succeed in practice within a set time period, you must undertake a seven-day intensive retreat. To set a period of seven days will not just multiply the energies of the strong and bold ones; even the weaklings will became deadly determined once they seek to enter the sanctuary and are willing to sacrifice their bodies and their lives. Therefore, seven-day retreats are a must.

If the Chan master wants his practitioners to undertake a seven-day retreat, the first thing to do is have them enter his room for face-to-face instruction. Entering the master's room is not an empty ceremony. Since the Chan master's task is to temper and train his practitioners, his mental cultivation must be painstaking, his intent must be profound, the methods he establishes must be rigorous, and his efforts must be careful and thorough. When he goes to the Chan Hall, he must first know the names and faces of everyone in the congregation and the huatou that each one of them has made his basic investigation. Only then can he set to work to train and temper them. If the master does not know the people he is dealing with, then even if they gather together for ninety days, they will be like passing strangers. (Section omitted) If the master knows the people but does not know their fundamental question,³⁰ then when the Chan master comes down to the Chan Hall and wants to engage the practitioners and press them to advance, he will have no way to do so. (Section omitted)

If a Chan master wants to know these things, the method is to have practitioners enter his private room and to probe and test them and cut away their illusions. In general people vary in their basic capacities, and there are many different kinds of investigation and learning. Some may understand huatous intellectually but lack the will to come to grips with them and investigate them. Some cannot develop a decisive will in their investigation or are hesitant to go all out. Some have the will but cannot generate the doubt sensation. Some get caught up in wandering thoughts as soon as a huatou is brought forth. Some investigate for years without knowing how to do genuine meditation work, and so accomplish nothing. Some draw theoretical principles from the scriptures and seek to align these with the huatou. Some just make use of concentrating on the huatou to dispel wandering thoughts. Some hide away inside the armor of "nondoing" and [lay to rest] their sense faculties. Some stubbornly follow their subjectivity and take it as their own master. Some recognize seamless silent annihilation as complete realization. If there is no genuine Chan master to set [the people who fall into these errors] straight, and they have no real inner doubts, all sorts of sicknesses will develop. In all of these cases, when [the practitioners who harbor these illusions] enter the master's room, the master must search out and expose these illusions one by one and utterly sweep away each and every one of them. The master must dissolve the sticking points and remove the bonds for the practitioner, banish his fixations and wipe away his confusion. The master cuts the entanglements that the practitioner brings along with him and cures the mortal illness that has entered deep within him. If the master directs the practitioner toward genuine investigation, then the road he follows is sure to be correct. (Section omitted)

Coming Down to the Hall and Giving Guidance

Let us assume that the practitioners have already entered the master's chamber to be tested and to have their illusions cut away, and this has been done carefully and correctly, so that none of them is on the wrong road any longer. Even so, for practitioners to investigate the huatou is like rowing a boat against the current. (Section omitted) For this reason, it is extremely crucial for the master to give guidance in the Chan Hall. It will not do to give this guidance only once every three or five days. It is necessary for the master to go the Chan Hall three times a day and diligently give guidance. The method of giving guidance must match what is appropriate for the practitioners' capacities and situations. The master observes whether they are diligent or lazy and sets a middle course for them between being too lax and being too tense. Although it is impossible to set any rigid rules, we may briefly discuss the starting points [from which the Chan master can guide his practitioners in their meditation work]. Broadly speaking, there are four. These are, first, to establish their will firmly; second, to show them the method of practice; third, to warn them against laziness; and fourth, to protect them against delusional sicknesses. The most urgent task of all is to cut off the entangling vines [of endless inconclusive rationalizations] in explaining the principles of the Buddhist teaching.

What does it mean to establish their will firmly? (Section omitted) If the master wants to set up the precondition for the practitioners to investigate, first the master has to instill in them a will that is as strong as iron, and to make them take a vow that is as imperishable as a diamond. This is the preliminary guidance he gives them. He has them vow that they would rather have their bones broken and their sinews dry up than stop their studies before they have a lucid understanding of the Great Matter. That they would rather lose their bodies and relinquish their lives than stop before they have penetrated through the barriers. When the practitioners are equipped with this strong and solid vow to be liberated from birth and death, then when they generate the doubt sensation, it is sure to be genuine. When the doubt sensation is genuine, then the investigation is powerful, and there is sure to be ultimate thorough enlightenment.

What does it mean to show the practitioners the method to investigate huatou properly? The ancient saying goes: "Great doubt, great awakening; small doubt, small awakening; no doubt, no awakening." Thus, if doubt is total, then enlightenment will be total. In our times there are those who teach people to hold rigidly to the huatou without arousing the doubt sensation. This is a great sickness in investigating Chan. Though studying Chan does not permit confused, random thinking, neither does it permit rigidly holding to the huatou. If you just guard the huatou, then you have tethered yourself to a withered pole, you have sunk into stale water, and you are honing the wrong edge of the knife. If you do not generate genuine doubt, so that the wheels of your mental processes are turning inside, then you will not attain enlightenment even if you keep on sitting until the [nonexistent] year of the donkey. When practitioners take delight in traveling this road, they sink down into emptiness and get stuck on quiescence, and after a long time they consider this nest to be blissful. They don't even believe enlightenment exists. When masters take delight in teaching this method, they are taking "dead wood Chan" as the ultimate. When they hear of other masters developing insight in people through a certain device, they are sure to slander them. Who among them knows that things are entirely otherwise? When someone is greatly concerned over birth and death, this gives rise to doubt, and doubt gives rise to enlightenment. Thus, when the Chan community is sitting quietly, the Chan master directs them to put aside the myriad entanglements so that not the slightest thing remains on their minds, and to take the huatou and cut off the pass above, and to investigate the huatou exhaustively until there is nowhere for them to go. Then they must gather together their minds and plunge down on the huatou and press against it with all their might. When their strength is exhausted from pressing against the huatou, then they start again from the beginning. After a long time, the emotional consciousness comes to an end and subjective opinions and perceptions are forgotten, and awakening to the Way will be easy. This is a method of practice that is not easy.

What does it mean for the Chan master to warn his practitioners against laziness? Those who investigate "Great Peace Chan" take it easy and act casual and relaxed. Half the time they float, half the time they sink. It is like a rock immersed in [stale] water. There is no progress or regress. They may practice taking great pains, but it is hard for them to unify their meditation work. They may succeed in unifying it, but it comes unexpectedly and they do not gain insight. This is because they have no one to spur them on and stimulate their development. For those who investigate Chan intensely, insight comes easily. But when they are studying, only those of superior capacity and sharp intellect manage to make progress without falling back. Those of medium or low capacity can be intense for a time, but their strength wanes, and as easily as they advance, they also fall back. Thus they need a Chan master to spur them on diligently. And these methods for spurring practitioners on should be intense rather than lax; they should be poisonous and stringent rather than mild and agreeable; they should cut through nails and shear through iron rather than slog through the muddy water. The master should constantly pierce the practitioners' sore points with harsh and painful words. If the practitioners have any spirit, they are sure to be aroused to anger and advance.

What does it mean to protect the practitioners against demonic sicknesses? The nature of the consciousness of beginning practitioners is bound to have myriad starting points of craziness and confusion. That is why, when showing them [how to practice] huatou, the master must cut off the pass above. Once this pass is tightly shut and the master has rigorously searched out and removed [the practitioner's deluded ideas of meditation work], the specious thoughts in the practitioner's cognitive ground will not be able to drag along their shadows. For this reason the practitioner will only awaken to the Way and will not get attached to delusions. If perchance the master does not observe the practitioner's capacity and assigns a huatou without paying attention to the barrier at the pass, then the practitioner's karmic consciousness will fly around in confusion and engage in crazy, chaotic, discursive thinking—[images of] familiar people and scenes will burst out of the practitioner's dark [subconscious]. Bizarre sights and sounds will make even more chaos in the practitioner's field of consciousness. Beginning practitioners do not have the wisdom to see through these things or the power in the Path to control them. They may become suspicious or they may become terrified; they may feel happy or they may feel sad. Suddenly the pass is opened and demonic phenomena come into play. (Section omitted) If the Chan master is diligent and scrupulous in offering guidance and deliberately protects [his practitioners against such things], then there is no worry that this will happen.

There are many ways by which meditation sicknesses are brought on, and I cannot mention them all. The easiest mistakes to make are to shut up the vital energy in the chest region and consider this to be a ferocious diligence, and to sit impassively in an indifferent state of mind to seek profound clarity. These two mistakes are very serious. In general, the essential secret to studying Chan is a matter of genuine, ardent doubt. This is not a matter of shutting in the vital energy. Ever since the Yuan dynasty there have been many evil masters who teach people to sit with their spines erect and their teeth clenched and both hands tightly closed and their eyes rolled up. Though the outer appearance [of practitioners who do this] is fierce, inside there is no genuine doubt. They think that if they stubbornly shut up their vital energy inside their chest every day, the force is sure to reach their mind. They feel pain and they spit up blood from the lungs. (Section omitted) The second meditation sickness is the Chan of impassive sitting. This too fails to bring on genuine doubt and the mind that is wholeheartedly fixed on [practice]. As soon as they sit down on the meditation platform, they put aside everything and return to a state of doing nothing. When they think of it, they recollect a few times phrases like "When the next breath does not come . . ." Then they think that the four great elements [that make up the physical body] do not exist and the myriad dharmas are all empty. They consider as the ultimate the indifferent mind and extinguish their wisdom in order to reach an unmoving clarity. If you urge them to do walking meditation, since their minds are blank, they cannot move an inch. If people sit this way for many years, it is bad for their circulation, and they easily develop dropsy and many symptoms of an excess of fire [among the elements of the body]. This is truly a grave sickness, but worldly doctors are helpless to treat it.

To avoid all of these troubles, it is up to the Chan master to spare no effort and to come to the hall every day and give the practitioners diligent guidance. The master must develop a strong will in the practitioners and show them how to undertake genuine investigation and warn them against laziness. He must wipe away their emotional consciousness and cut away their subjective opinions and perceptions. He must eliminate strayed paths and cut off the roots of [potential] sicknesses. Then there will be no way for demonic sicknesses and the myriad problems to creep in, and it will be possible to hope that the practitioners will attain genuine awakening.

Giving Practitioners Training and Tempering

As the saying goes, "If you do not enter the tiger's den, how will you catch the tiger's cubs?" If a supposed Chan master does not master the methods for training and tempering practitioners, then even when he is faced with "dragons and elephants" (practitioners of high potential), he will turn them all into spoiled vessels. He will go for decades without a single person developing insight. Even if one or a half [does get some sort of insight], it will invariably be a chance encounter, as when insects boring in wood happen to make a design, and not the result of any training and tempering offered by the master.

If the master clearly understands training and tempering, he will have a method for pushing forward even practitioners of medium and low capacities. If he encounters a large number of people, he will be able to develop insight in several of them. Miaoxi trained fifty-three people, and thirteen awakened. Yuanwu produced insight in eighteen people in one night at Jinshan. Though we often hear surprising things, such things have truly occurred in both ancient and modern times. What ground is without water beneath it? But if we don't drill for it, the water won't come to the surface. What wood, what stone, is without the capacity for fire? But if we don't use the fire-drill on the wood, if we don't strike the stone [with the steel], then the sparks won't come forth. All sentient beings have buddha-nature, just as there is water in the ground and the potential for fire in wood and stone. But even people of the highest capacity will look up at [buddhahood] and retreat, unless they find an enlightened master who clears their channels and opens them up and makes an impact on them with the use of wondrous strategies and poisonous hammer and tongs, so that the bottom of the bucket [of ignorance] drops out and they penetrate through the barrier [of self-grasping]. Therefore, a genuine Chan master cannot but emphasize training and tempering.

So in order to temper and refine the abilities of the practitioners, the Chan master must take great pains, and the monks in supervisory positions must exert great efforts. In the Chan system, the master must be present in the Chan Hall, sharing in the activities of the congregation. If he cannot do so, then he still must come to the hall three to five times every day and accompany the congregation during sitting and walking meditation. One implement for training and tempering practitioners involves the skillful use of the bamboo stick, which started with Shoushan (926–993), thrived with Dahui, and was wielded anew by Sanfeng. This instrument is used by many generations of the Chan masters of old for training patch-robed monks; it is not a new innovation.

The bamboo stick should be five feet long and one inch wide, slightly convex, with the knobs removed so it is convenient to use. As for the [Chan master's traditional] staff, it can be used to set forth teachings and to receive practitioners, but it definitely cannot be used [to deliver blows] to train and temper practitioners. If it is used, it will not be effective. As for [the implements called] *mani* jewels made of bronze or iron, they are only for calling the Chan congregation to order. If used at closer range to strike practitioners, their heads would split open: they are not things to use in training and tempering.

The bamboo stick's function is for pushing practitioners; its wondrousness lies in striking and signaling. When the Chan congregation is sitting in meditation, the bamboo stick can be held for patrolling the hall; when walking it is wielded as an instrument.

Three strikes signals the beginning of stillness, and the Chan master should then begin with instructions as I explained before. He cannot be perfunctory about this. When the stick of incense has burned halfway, a bell is sounded.

These days when Chan congregations do walking meditation, the method they use is to go slow at first, then go quicker, and progressively gather up speed and intensity. Holding the bamboo stick all the while, the Chan master follows along with the congregation as they walk in a circle. When the walking meditation becomes very intense, the master uses [methods akin to] military tactics. He appears when the practitioners least expect it and attacks when they are unprepared. He may grab a practitioner and hold him to his chest and press him to say something. Or he may give the practitioner a blow to the head, questioning him [on the meditation case that is] his fundamental investigation until he manages to say something. [In doing this, the master is] "grabbing the thief's spear to kill the thief." The master watches for the practitioner to change tactics; then he takes the stick and pokes him deeply. As thunder crashes and lightning flashes, the master does not allow the practitioner to stay imprisoned within his habitual knowledge. As practitioner and master lock horns in a complex interchange, the master again and again "steals [the hungry man's] food" and "drives off [the plowman's] ox." The master may throw down his staff and use the palm of his hand [to strike the practitioner], or engage him with daggers drawn. The master may strike indirectly and come out with surprise tactics when the situation looks peaceful. The master may reflect and act at the same time and join battle with arrows and slingshot. He may use blows and shouts together and open fire with artillery and crossbows at once.

While the practitioner's meditation work has not yet reached its culmination, the master gives the practitioner thousands of hammer blows and smelts and forges the practitioner thousands of times. As long as the "thief mind" has not yet totally died, the master releases and recaptures the practitioner hundreds of times. The master's task is to locate the lair of the shadows of emotional consciousness and the entangling vines of subjective opinions that the practitioner has accumulated over aeons and cut them off root and branch, giving the practitioner no way to escape. Gradually the practitioner arrives at the point where, hanging from a cliff, he lets go.

With one more thrust, the decisive moment arrives. Then it is not hard for the practitioner to cut off [delusion] and cause a transformation. Isn't this [what Sun Wu means by] "being forced with one's back to the river [so no retreat is possible], about to die, and yet coming back to life"? Isn't this "coming back to life in a perilous situation"? Training and tempering Chan practitioners is also like this.

For a Chan master to act like this on behalf of his congregation can indeed be called difficult. But if he follows this path, it will be easy to produce people [who are worthy vessels of the Dharma], and this indeed is called wondrous. There is nothing in the world that is difficult without being wondrous or wondrous without being difficult. (Section omitted)

Using Wise Strategy to Spur Development

For everything else in the world, favorable circumstances are advantageous. Only for the Chan school are adverse circumstances advantageous. When people take care of business, they are happy when things are good, but when Chan masters train practitioners, they are happy when things are bad. [In the context of Chan training], if things are not bad, they cannot [lead to what is] called the greatest good in the world, and if circumstances are not adverse, they cannot [lead to what is] called the most favorable situation in the world.

This can be compared with the Way of Heaven [wherein adversity brings later benefits]. (Section omitted)

If the Chan master does not use awe-inspiring methods in training and tempering his practitioners, then his congregation will become lazy, there will be no way to spur their development, and the master will certainly be unable to make them penetrate through the barrier of delusion and thoroughly awaken. In spurring on practitioners to develop, if the Chan master does not use appropriately adapted expedients, then strict rules and rigorous guidelines just become dead methods, and he will not be able to make practitioners mobilize their energies and advance. Therefore, in the [genuine, effective] training and tempering of Chan practitioners, there are a thousand [strategic and tactical] transformations, and the Chan master's functioning is completely alive.

To be skillful at enabling practitioners to develop insight, Chan masters should not make the periods of sitting and walking meditation overly long. If practitioners sit for too long, oblivion and fatigue are sure to set in and the huatou will have no power. If practitioners walk for too long, then their legs become tired, and as soon as they sit down again, they sink into oblivion. Thus, according to the normal guidelines of the Chan school, sitting meditation and walking meditation are done for the interval of time it takes one stick of incense to burn down. I assess this and adjust it accordingly. If the stick of incense is short, [the period of meditation] can last until the whole stick is burned. If the stick of incense is long, I just have [practitioners walk or sit] for the length of time it takes for half the stick to burn down. If they do sitting meditation for this length of time, then their quiet investigation is sure to be energizing. As soon as they are about to get tired, they leave their seats and do walking meditation. If they do walking meditation for the same length of time, their investigation while moving is sure to be intense. As soon as their legs are about to get tired, the session ends and they rest.

During seven-day sessions of Chan practice, when the session is well along and it is after midnight, the Chan practitioners gradually tend to become lazy. If the Chan master encourages them with sweet words and does not scold them, and greets them with a mild countenance and is not too severe, when he prods them on by beating the sounding board, they will be in a fog as before. At this point, if the master wants to arouse the practitioners' energies and call forth their courage, he must mobilize his wise strategic judgment and apply tactics that are very poisonous and astringent and display an outburst of anger. He may make the hall resound with his vituperation, or he may strike out with blows in all directions like a whirlwind. As the saying goes, "What people say in an outburst of anger are words that should not be listened to." The Chan master's words burn the practitioners' hearts like fire. He makes the cliffs crumble and the rocks shatter and throws them down in front of their faces, so that the Chan practitioners' confusion and laziness are instantly dispelled. (Section omitted) It is like resting on the brink of a deep chasm. [Ordinarily] no one could jump across it. But then an armed enemy or a ferocious tiger closes in on you from the rear and you make a mighty leap and get across.

Linji said: "Sometimes the Chan master uses joy or anger as a strategic expedient." Masters Fenyang and Zhiming were accustomed to using this method [too, spurring their practitioners on with displays of anger]. Is this method not something we have inherited legitimately [from our illustrious Chan predecessors]?

Thus, the Chan master's heart is most compassionate, but his actions are very poisonous. What he has within him is the heart of all the buddhas and bodhisattvas, but what he carries out are the [fierce and forceful] actions of the *asura* kings.[31] Only in this way can he push aside without fear the great citadel of the three realms of existence. With indefatigable zeal [to help sentient beings], without ever harming even a single insect, he helps people become averse [to the world of delusion], even if in the process he is cut to pieces or skinned alive or suffers the direst punishments. Only someone who has mastered this kind of functioning can pull out the nails and extract the pegs for people and knock off the fetters and chains. Otherwise he is only clinging to a path that may have once been good but is now dead. Since he cannot even save himself, how can he help anyone else?

Dahui said: "Of all the Chan masters that talk about meditation sicknesses, none surpasses Master Zhantang. This is because when the others help people, they do not apply the blade to the crucial point."

Yuanwu said: "When a Chan master takes action, it must be

extremely painful and extremely poisonous. Only then is what he gives not in vain."

The secret of the spirit immortals is not transmitted from father to son (from master to practitioner). From ancient times in the training and tempering of the Chan school, it has always been like this. If the Chan masters did not use these methods to spur the development of their practitioners, it would be like driving horses only by having them wear the traces, without also using the shadow of the whip. Even with the finest steeds that can run like the wind, without the whip it would still be hard to drive the carriage. How could we get them to perform as the splendid horses they are?

Still, there are those in recent times who conduct seven-day intensive retreats that continue through the nights without any break from meditation. This method seems very intense, but actually it is utterly useless. The original purpose of seven-day intensive Chan investigation sessions was to set a date for awakening to the Path, not to banish the demon of sleep. If the only purpose were to eliminate sleep, it would be enough to go to a forge [where it is noisy all night long] to refine away delusions, and it would not be necessary to come into the temple for Chan practice. For those practitioners who really seek insight, it is crucial to take a break from their studies in the middle of the night and to sleep for a bit. Only in that way will their wills be pure and clear on the next day and their spirit bold and energetic, so they can develop genuine doubt and vigorously seek liberation.

If practitioners do not comprehend how this works, rigidly insisting [on sitting for such and such number of] sticks of incense, then before they have pursued this method of investigation for three days, they will be in a fog as they do walking meditation. [In addition] they will be intoxicated with dreams as they do sitting meditation. This is an extreme form of being sunk in oblivion. This oblivion will press down on them like mountain *(taishan)*, and the so-called huatou [they are supposedly studying] will be cast away into the stream. How can they still expect that the mind flower will come to light? Not only will they fail in their Chan investigation, they will add more confused thoughts to their oblivious torpor. They will get attached to their visions and start to babble, and apparitions of ghosts and spirits will come forth from this. This is called idiot's Chan, with no understanding of expedient means. (Section omitted) Therefore, those with a deep understanding of how to train and temper practitioners are able to be enlightened masters and good spiritual friends only after they master skill in means and know wise strategy and keep far away from all errors and troubles.

Skillfully Turning Practitioners Around

Insight is one [skill]. But when it comes to penetrating through to liberation under the impact of a Chan master's dynamic devices and encountering insight amid impassive indifference, the effect is very different.

Those who pursue their investigation of Chan in a state of impassive indifference come to rest at the essence, but if they do not have the hammer and tongs of an enlightened master to turn them around, they may go ten or twenty years without developing insight. Even if insight touches their breasts in the dark, when it comes to [taking enlightened action in the world] where the swords cross points, they cannot make a move.

For those who penetrate through to liberation under the impact of a Chan master's dynamic devices, the mind of stealth is sure to die, the root of doubt is sure to be obliterated, and the road of [conceptual] interpretation is sure to be cut off. Being transformed under the impact of the master's dangerous devices, they are empowered with more than enough power to walk across the edge of a blade. This is why all the Chan masters down through the ages inevitably emphasized the impact of a master's dynamic devices when they were discussing enlightenment. From Mazu, Baizhang, Huangbo, and Linji, down through Fenyang, Zhiming, Wuzu, Yuanwu, and Dahui, all of these elders had great potential and great function. They were as unapproachable as flashing lightning and rolling thunder. They hammered and thrust and pressed their practitioners and turned their minds around. They abruptly cut off the root of life so that practitioners might completely illuminate the eye of correct enlightenment. These teachers were great dragons and elephants, cloaked in mist with clouds swirling around them. This is how the Chan school flourished at its zenith.

From the Yuan dynasty on, the methods that generations of Chan masters had used to train and temper practitioners were no longer put into practice. So-called Chan masters thought that the only valuable thing was dead sitting and impassive meditation, [sitting like] cold ashes or a dead tree or an incense burner in an ancient shrine. They considered being indifferent and impassive without moving or stirring to be empowerment. They slandered the previous Chan masters' use of dynamic devices as sectarian contrivances, and they rejected the guiding principles of the classic Five Houses of Chan as [a collection of] strange terminology and weird forms. These false masters caged up their practitioners, and so the style and influence of the Chan school suffered major deterioration.

Thus these false masters did not understand Linji's four methods of taking away the person but not the objects, taking away the objects but not the person, taking away both, and taking away neither, or his seven devices.[32] They did not comprehend the living methods of Yantou, biting those who go left and those who go right, biting those who go and those who stay. Therefore these false masters certainly could not meet practitioners' potential in dynamic workings of the moment and turn their minds around. Since they had lost the method for this, when practitioners asked them for instruction, all they could do was teach them dead huatous and direct them to sit impassively with indifferent minds. They led these practitioners into the dead-tree hall to practice wordless Chan. Miaoxi castigated this as the perversion of Silent Illumination Chan, but these false masters pass it on secretly in their rooms as the ultimate treasure. Now we have arrived at our own Ming period, and this [misguided style of] teaching is widely practiced. Because of this, the level of accomplishment of those who frequent the Chan schools is judged by how long they can sit like dead trees. Mentioning the word *enlightenment* is [as taboo] as uttering your father's name or breaking the laws of the nation. Thus the one effective method of studying Chan has been buried beneath people's feet.

Fortunately, Master Wu of Tiantong (Master Yuanwu) has opened his school with a blow of his staff and has revived the use of dynamic devices. Master Zang of Sanfeng (Master Hanyue Fazang) carries on the work of training and tempering practitioners with Linji's seven devices and has a thorough mastery of the guiding principles of the Chan school. My own master, Master Li of Lingyin (Master Jude Hongli), uses the wondrous secrets of the Five Houses [of Chan] to adapt effectively to practitioners from all over and to minister to a great variety of potentials. Because of them, the [classical Chan] methods of Linji's four selections, of shining with awareness and actively functioning, of [interchanging the positions of] guest and host, and of turning practitioners' minds around, are again seen in the contemporary world, and the light of the Chan school is again shining bright.

In general, when practitioners investigate Chan without attaining penetrating enlightenment, there are many sicknesses involved. To some the Path is impenetrable and they do not advance. For some there is a fine mist [of delusional states], and they do not cut them off. Some hold rigidly to the huatou and do not develop the doubt sensation. Some are infatuated with sitting in the cold ashes [of indifference] and end up at [what should be the starting point], the fundamental portion [of essential quiescence]. Some accept [every move they make, such as] raising their eyebrows and blinking their eyes, as the whole issue [of enlightened functioning]. Some cling to a word or half a phrase as final penetration. Some rationalize about the meditation cases and consider this mastery. Some try to figure out the guiding principles of Chan and consider this as the ultimate pursuit. Some consider obliterating everything as transcendence. Some consider not being caught up with any devices or states as independent liberation. Some consider the ancient and modern gong'ans as irrelevant elaborations. Some take the last imprisonment barrier as a forceful way to enter the Way. All of these [misguided approaches] result from people not being willing to study under a genuine Chan master, and therefore not attaining true enlightenment and not penetrating into the guiding principles of Chan. Therefore, arriving at some alternative knowledge and heterodox views, which are all wrong as soon as they are raised.

What is important and valuable about an enlightened master is that he or she gives medicine according to the practitioner's sickness and puts in a plug that fits the hole. An enlightened master is like the man from Ying who removed a speck of dirt [from someone's nose] by swinging his ax [so fast] it created a wind [that blew the dirt away]. He is like butcher Ding, who carved up oxen so deftly that he always cut through the gaps without hitting bone, so that his knife never lost its edge. Under the impact of a dynamic device or utterance, genuine Chan masters can enable practitioners to escape all at once from the chains that bind them and can make them open the enlightened mind's eye.

The Chan master's technique is a matter of skillfully using the method of turning practitioners around. There are many forms of turning practitioners around. They can be turned around in Dharma battles. They can be turned around in [sessions in the master's] private room. There is turning around with turning around, and turning around without turning around.

Turning practitioners around in Dharma battles involves the

master's pressing practitioners in the assembly to say things, then attacking their gaps from all sides. With practitioners who are able to spring back, the Chan master says more to press them further. To those who die under the impact of the master's devices, the master shows the sword that brings people to life. The master turns freely, brilliant and alive. His task is to leave the practitioner nowhere to stand: then it is not hard to cut off the root of life for him.

The master acts to turn practitioners around in [sessions in] his private room when the practitioner understands what's first but cannot understand what's later, or when the practitioner knows the head but does not know the tail. When "the arrow is about to leave the bowstring" [when the practitioner is on the verge of awakening], all that is needed is a single push from the master. When the spring is about to gush forth from the crevice, it is just a matter of the master's clearing the way. There is no harm in the Chan master's making the practitioner ask another question. The master may perhaps answer in the practitioner's place, so he awakens then and there, or add another word, so he empties through. This is the most wondrous skill of the spirit immortals and the supreme adepts.

As for turning around with turning around, [the master may have the practitioner investigate the huatou] "Who does not have buddha-nature?" Then the master says, "Who has it?" and the practitioner immediately awakens. [The master may have the practitioner investigate the huatou] "Entering the gate you meet Maitreya and leaving the gate you see Bodhidharma." Then the master says, "Whom do you meet when you enter the gate, and whom do you see when you leave the gate?" and the practitioner immediately awakens. [There are other similar devices], such as "Anyone and everyone," "Crazy people here, crazy people there," and "Yesterday right, today wrong." This is turning around with turning around.

Turning around without turning around [is exemplified in

Chan sayings such as the following]: "What is a single drop of water from the spring at Caoxi?"[33] Answer: "It's a single drop of water from the spring at Caoxi." "The Fire God comes looking for fire"; "The clouds of nothingness ascend the mountain range"; "The existence of the moon on the wavelike mind."[34] The Chan master simply brings them up again, and the practitioner facing them penetrates through. Although this method does not turn the question around, it nevertheless does turn the practitioner around.

The enlightened master uses all of these methods just as various insects use cocoons and other natural arrangements to nurture their young. Once the master puts them into action, the practitioner is sure to respond. Why? Because the genuine Chan master is able to put the guiding principles of the Chan school to use and receive people with living devices. With his grasp of the guiding principles, he can expertly select [the appropriate methods] and succeed in turning practitioners' minds around. His technique is refined and his eye is quick. He accurately discerns the "oncoming winds" [the mentalities of the practitioners] and makes heaven and earth turn as he pleases and the constellations change positions. He can enable each and every person to penetrate through the imprisonment barrier of transcendence. If a supposed Chan master only emphasizes the basic essence of Chan [that is, experience of emptiness] and does not have a thorough knowledge of the guiding principles of the Chan school, then when people come before him stuck in a pot of glue, bandying about devices and perspectives this way and that, the so-called master will have no way to turn them around. Then he will use counterfeit Chan to try to pass under false pretenses and get by, and the practitioner will not have thorough awakening.

Therefore, to train and temper a congregation of Chan practitioners depends on [a thorough mastery] of the guiding principles of Chan. This is no small matter.

Cutting Through the Barrier and Opening the Eye of Enlightenment

Turning practitioners around is indeed difficult, but when it comes to cutting through the layered barrier and opening people's eyes, only those with dragon's eyes and the ability to unfurl the great banner are able to do it. This is the most difficult thing of all. (Section omitted)

As for the secret of successfully cutting through [various layered] barriers, the work lies in pressing and pushing the practitioner; the abstruse subtlety lies in turning the practitioner around; and the power depends on giving the practitioner guidance and spurring on his development. If the master does not give the practitioner guidance, then he may travel a path that leads off in the wrong direction. If the master does not spur the practitioner's development, then the fire [of his determination] will not burn hot enough. If the master does not press and push him, the practitioner's discriminatory faculty will not be cut off. If the master does not turn the practitioner around, his thieflike sentiments will not come to an end. To expect a practitioner to have a decisive awakening without fully employing all [of Linji's four] methods is like expecting the rice to be cooked where the heat does not reach. It is like trying to peel fruit that is not ripe. Even if the master has a great reputation and the practitioner has great capacity, [if these four methods are not employed,] the master's teaching and the practitioner's potential will fail to make contact and they will let each other down.

Therefore a master who is good at training and tempering practitioners is not averse to taking minute care with his teaching, not averse to great complexity in his efforts, not averse to being completely thorough in his work, not averse to employing a complete range of techniques. If the Chan master will join his congregation in sitting meditation and offer them guidance like this today and spur their development like this tomorrow, then the road they travel is sure to be correct and the fire is sure to be intense. If the Chan master accompanies his congregation as they do walking meditation and pushes and presses them like this today and turns them around like this tomorrow, then their discriminatory faculty is sure to be cut off and their thieflike sentiments are sure to come to an end. The fire will be more and more intense and [their discriminatory faculty and thieflike sentiments] will be more and more exhausted. Then the master can employ his dragon's eye and use the sword that kills and the sword that brings life.

There are some practitioners who are in the prime of life and hale and hearty and full of energy but whose Chan investigation becomes shallower by the day. To deal with those who are alive but cannot put to death [their mind of delusion], the master must use killing methods. There are those who are called veteran practitioners who are deeply absorbed in their meditation work but for whom indifference has become a sickness, and who cannot transform their clinging [to this]. With them the master must use methods that bring them to life. If [a supposed master] uses methods that bring life when he should use methods that kill, he will pierce through and break the practitioner where he is weakest. [This mistaken use of methods shows that this so-called master's] Chan is not genuine. Often it is very easy to accept emptiness and receive echoes. If a supposed master uses methods that kill when he should use methods that bring life, the practitioner will be sunk in apathetic nihilism and the disease will become incurable. The master should not add more chains to the fetters the practitioner is wearing. If we assess supposed masters who are not enlightened, 90 percent of them use methods that kill, while only 10 percent use methods that bring life. This is because killing methods are easy to apply, while life-giving methods are hard to use.

But there are also genuine Chan masters who employ killing methods and life-giving methods equally. What sort of people are they? Generally they lift their heads wearing horns and are equipped with the solid bones of the buddhas and patriarchs and the singular mettle of dragons and elephants. As soon as these genuine masters see people coming who have the mettle of kings, they want to cast their nets broadly and catch and hold them, they want to set secret traps and use sharp weapons. The genuine master strikes [the practitioner of real potential] to the bone, to the marrow, and pushes him to the top of the hundred-foot pole. The master pierces deeply into the practitioner and gradually brings him to the point where he lets go while hanging from a cliff. When the crossbow is drawn to its full extent, it is just a matter of pulling the trigger. When meeting a robber on a road hemmed in on both sides, there is no time to blink. At such a time, the master cannot do any more to spur the practitioner's development or turn the practitioner around. He must use the sagely arrow that kills and brings life, he must strike like thunder, he must use cogent words, he must pierce into the practitioner's forehead so the bottom drops out of the practitioner's bucket [of ignorance] and the root of life is cut off then and there. This is like pushing someone off a mile-high cliff: you cannot stop. It is like rolling a round rock down a mile-long slope—you cannot hold it back. It is also like the eyes coming into keen focus when the esoteric needle is turning. Isn't this a very special moment?

When Mazu received Shuilao [with a kick], when Muzhou received Yunmen [by shutting the gate on his foot], when Dayu received Linji [by punching him in the ribs], when Yantou received Xuefeng [with a shout, and told him that enlightened insight must flow out from his own breast to cover heaven and earth], when the boatman Decheng received Jiashan [Shanhui] [by knocking him into the water], when Fenyang received Zhiming [with constant scolding], when Zhiming received Huanglong [with a show of anger], when Dahui received Jiaozhong and Xichan [by pressing them with classic meditation cases], weren't all of these great Chan masters using this method? Other similar cases can be seen in the *Records of the Transmission of the Lamp in the Jingde Era* and in the collections of Buddhist biographies.

All the Chan masters functioned like shattering bolts of thunder and lightning, like phoenixes soaring and dragons leaping. They acted with a rousing vitality that shines through ancient and modern times. Their feats cannot be fully recounted here. When did [the classic Chan masters] ever teach people that it was right just to stop and rest, to sit lifelessly in meditation, to cling to the cold stove, to take the mind and wait for awakening without arousing the doubt sensation?

Master Gaofeng (1238–1295) said: "Your practice must be like a sinking roof tile plummeting down into a pond ten thousand feet deep. If in seven days you are not enlightened, I will fall forever into uninterrupted hell." When did [the classic Chan masters] ever insist that people must meditate for a certain number of years, doing summer and winter retreats, sit through their meditation cushions, and cling to the nest of meditation work? When did they ever say that being bogged down like this is the ultimate way?

In sum, if practitioners do not encounter [genuine] training and tempering [at the hands of a true Chan master], then they will drink the bitter dregs to the end and totally waste their spiritual energy. They will exhaust a lifetime of strength wearing through the seat of their pants [in sitting meditation] but have no way to penetrate through to liberation. If masters do not know how to train and temper practitioners, then they will scan the horizon in vain while rigidly holding to lifeless routines, and they will be unable to take action to cut through [practitioners' delusions]. Even if they preside over so-called Chan centers for decades, it will all be in vain and they will not turn out anyone [capable of perpetuating the life of wisdom]. (Section omitted)

Studying the Guiding Principles of Chan

In what is called true Chan, there is the basis [which is the experience of enlightenment], and there is a system of guiding principles [the accumulated teaching devices and perspectives of generations of Chan masters]. If you work too soon at the guiding principles before you have awakened to the basis, then your excess of knowledge and understanding will block the door to enlightenment. You are sure to flow into the Chan of mere verbal advocacy without an experiential basis, and real enlightenment will be lost. If you have awakened to the basis but you reject the guiding principles, then you have taken it up in vain and are playing with shadows, and crude confusion becomes your style. You are sure to flow into "one-peg" Chan [where you cling to one way to teach Chan], and the purpose of the Chan school will be negated. Therefore, without enlightenment, true mastery of the guiding principles is not necessarily present, and after enlightenment, true mastery of the guiding principles must not be absent.

But in the contemporary world there are some who think that not understanding anything and vaguely lumping everything together is Chan. They only look at [Chan stories that focus on nonverbal teaching,] such as Buddha holding up the flower, Shanavasin raising his finger, Nagarjuna appearing as an orb of light, Gayashata holding up a mirror, Chuti holding up his finger, Mazu's kick, Xuefeng rolling out a ball, Hoshan beating a drum, Huangbo giving thirty blows with a staff, Mimo brandishing a pitchfork, and contend that this alone is the great potential and the great function of the Chan school. They say Chan is [invariably] this direct, this solitary and steep, and this singular and independent. They say that only this is direct pointing to the human mind without setting up verbal formulas, that only this is upholding the transcendent. If you say a word to them about the guiding principles of the Chan school, they denounce you for "intellectual interpretation" and for taking [provisional] teachings as absolute doctrines. They castigate you for getting wrapped up in entangling vines and getting stuck on names and attached to forms. Alas! Does anyone realize that this may seem correct but is actually a great error?! (Section omitted)

In general, in the investigation of Chan, the most crucial thing is for the master to use the methods of training and tempering practitioners explained above and make them penetrate through to the root. Once they have done so, it is also necessary to make them aware that in this [enlightenment] there is essence and there is function. The essence includes light and dark, facing away and facing toward, turning left and turning right, having a head and having a tail. The function includes killing [delusion] and giving life [to compassion], capturing and releasing, pushing down and holding up, lifting up and pressing down. In regard to confronting practitioners' potentials, there are the roles of lord and minister, father and son, child and mother, guest and host. In regard to the roles of guest and host, there is harmonious completion, there is contending for roles, there is merging in darkness, there is switching roles, there is guest and host without guest and host. If we make a detailed analysis, there is being verbal and being nonverbal, there is the verbal within the nonverbal, and the nonverbal within the verbal. There is both being in the light and being in the dark. There is both being born together and dying together. If we pursue the investigation to the ultimate point, there is the upward one move of transcendence and the [device of] the last word. This is what the ancients called "coming at last to the imprisonment barrier that does not let ordinary or holy pass through." When Linji had perceived this, in the midst of his directness he established [such experiential-analytical categories as] the three phrases, the three mysteries, and the three essentials, to make practitioners' eyes correct; and he established the four selections, the four kinds of shouts, the four sequences of awareness and functioning, the four permutations of guest and host, and distinguished the three kinds of capacities in order to fully realize practitioners' potentials and functioning. The classic Five Houses of Chan all established their own particular teaching methods: each had its own style, and each had its own arcane secrets. [There were] mystic barriers and golden locks, hundreds and thousands of devices to trap tigers and trick lions, releasing or capturing according to the potential of the moment. (Section omitted) If Chan teaching devices were not like this, then they would be inadequate for the task of cutting off people's root of life and cutting off people's intellectual knowledge; if they were not like this, then practitioners would never penetrate through the barrier of sentiments and it would be impossible to open the lock of discriminatory consciousness. Practitioners' subjective views of the Dharma would not be dissolved away and their whole being would merely be a formula-like mold. How could this be the treasury of the Correct Dharma Eye of the buddhas and patriarchs?

Some people offer this objection: "What is important in Chan is that it does not establish any verbal teachings or become involved in names and terms, that it is transcendent and independent of everything. Once guiding principles are established, then there is an excess of names and terminology, of set patterns and formulas. This adds to people's emotional and discriminative consciousness and increases their subjective views and makes them think there are absolute truths that they can seek. Intelligent practitioners are sure to spout rationalizations, and ignorant practitioners will become even more confused. How could any of this be important for true enlightenment?"

I reply that it was precisely for this reason that all the classical Chan masters established sets of guiding principles. Those who base their Chan on subjectivism claim they are free of emotional consciousness, but actually they are all mixed up with emotional consciousness. They claim they have cut off subjective opinions and perceptions, but they have nothing but subjective opinions and perceptions. They claim they have no doctrine they consider absolutely real, but they accept their own "one device, one perspective" [of the enlightenment experience as an absolute], and thus fall into considering this doctrine as an absolute truth. In the case of Linji with his seven items, and all the teachings of the Five Houses of Chan, this [approach] was the use of the wondrous secret hammer and tongs to probe and pierce practitioners, to sort them out, to cut away their illusions. Only then did their subjective opinions and perceptions melt away, their emotional consciousness break up, and their ideas of teachings as absolutely real get forgotten. Completely exhausting the myriad phenomena and not keeping a single one—this is real directness. Penetrating through all teaching methods and not getting stuck on a single one—this is real solitary steepness. Completely fathoming all teachings great and small and all guiding principles, and then rejecting them and setting them aside—this is real singular independence. How could real Chan people stick to a peg for tethering donkeys or rely on a cut rope or play a tailless monkey? (Section omitted)

Not only do those who reject the guiding principles fail to comprehend the eye of Chan for themselves, but when it comes to helping others, they are sure to blunder against the sharp point and wound themselves as soon as they make a move. When confronted with practitioners' devices and perspectives, they do not know how to occupy the head and take in the tail. At crucial junctures and difficult points, they do not know how to rearrange the elements and transform the pattern. They grasp at inanities and play slippery tricks, but they cannot test practitioners and distinguish their true situation. They hit out at practitioners and exchange blows, but they have no way to cut away their illusions. All they can do is rely on their own awareness as the ultimate paradigm, and they cannot talk about the familiar patterns of Chan teaching methods. This being the case, how can we fail to master the guiding principles of the Chan school after enlightenment? (Section omitted)

Therefore, after practitioners have already illuminated the basis, they must rely on a master and investigate further and achieve knowledge of the inner secret. They must work at penetrating the inner sanctum of the ancients. When the master sees that the practitioner has already penetrated to the basis, he must still use the wondrous, intimate-level hammer and tongs and pierce into him deeply to enable him to get through to the eye of the guiding principles of Chan. If the treasury of the Correct Dharma Eye is to be transmitted and flow on forever, the master must not let it become a process of the master's and the practitioner's accepting empty vanities from each other and receiving meaningless echoes.

Strict and Exacting Control of Conduct

The upward road of transcendence has not been transmitted by the thousand sages. It is like a great mass of fire: who can dare to look straight at it? It is like a poison-smeared drum: who can turn his ear to listen to it? Like a flash of lightning before the mind moves, realization already belongs in the category of laggard doubt. Pure comprehension at a phrase is still a deranged perception. What sort of thing is this that we can still keep on asking about conduct and discussing merit?

But the first patriarch, Bodhidharma, said: "When your conduct and understanding are in accord, you are called a patriarch."

Chan master Daoying of Yunju said: "You achieve complete understanding on that side (the side of transcendence), but you come back to this side (the side of action in the relative world) in order to practice." Yongquan said: "There are many people who understand at the perceptual level but not one in ten thousand who understands at the level of conduct."

Thus we know that all the Chan masters since ancient times never considered conduct and understanding as two separate things. There are good reasons for this. If there is conduct without understanding, then even though your practice is pure and refined, you do not get beyond stages. Even if you cultivate your conduct, this is all called ignorant merit. If there is understanding without conduct, then even if your perceptual level is outstanding, you are still carrying a log on your shoulder. Even if you have [a glimpse of] enlightenment, it amounts to crazy wisdom. One has eyes but no feet, and the other has a tail but no head. Neither is the ultimate level.

The Chan master's duty is to train and temper capable people, to sort out where they are one-sided and where they are complete, and to weigh the head and the tail.

What actually is the Path if the master wants to enable his practitioners to succeed from beginning to end?

Before the practitioner's eye for the Path has opened, the master first directs the practitioner to practice and investigate in order to temper his [or her] understanding. The master strikes to the bone, strikes to the marrow, and gives piercing thrusts [to spur understanding], but he is slow to ask about practice. [At this stage, what applies is the classic Chan] saying: "All that's important is for your eye to be correct, so I don't talk about your conduct." Once the practitioner has it clear about the Great Matter, then the master directs his behavior in order to refine his conduct. The master puts the practitioner on the bird's path and the mystic way,[35] so there is no selfishness where he stands, and his understanding at last arrives at reality. [At this stage, what applies is the classic Chan] saying: "Being able to say 'ten feet' is not as good as being able to go one inch."

This being so, if those who are in charge of the teaching do not employ the eye of the guiding principles in order to test their practitioners at the most subtle level, and instead just accept them on the basis of their partial, fragmentary understanding, then vulgar Chan will prevail. Within vulgar Chan, there are two kinds of deviant paths:

Those who think that subjectivism is Chan claim that the movements and actions of [the subjective mind], the ruling faculty within the field of the physical body, are the great potential and the great function of the buddhas and patriarchs. To them there is no such thing as going along [with the Way] and no such thing as going against [the Way]— everything is right. They think that active functioning is true nature. They are befuddled by these [misconceptions], and their habit energy sneaks into action. Thus they think the Great Way means eating anything indiscriminately and not choosing between pure and impure. If someone tries to set them straight, they say: "You fool; how can there be any duality in buddha-nature?" This is called gluing the door shut to accomplish the works of demons.

Those who think utter voidness is Chan claim that the undifferentiated silent obliteration of fundamental nothingness is where they establish their bodies and their lives. To them there are no buddhas and no patriarchs, and everything is empty. They think that this is the upward way to transcendence. They are confused by these misconceptions and specious views. Thus they do not shrink from conduct that other people ridicule and despise, they pay no attention to whether their actions cause an infraction or bring merit, and they act wantonly and without restraint. If someone rebukes them, they say: "You idiot! Do you still have this one (are you still attached to this)?" This is called the "iron hoe Chan," which cuts off [the roots of the] karma of cause and effect.

Although these two forms of perverted Chan are the practitioners' mistake, they are also the masters' fault. They arise because masters fail to use the guiding principles of the Chan school to temper their practitioners but just take reflections of the light to impart to their practitioners. Those whose basic capacity is inferior then give rise to misguided views and bring disaster to the Chan school. In general, if the master's bequest is correct, then his practitioners' conduct and understanding are sure to be straight. Then this will be passed on generation after generation, from one vessel of the Dharma to another. When the source is deep, the stream is long. If the master's bequest is not correct, then his practitioners' conduct and understanding is sure to be misguided. Then this will be blindly followed and become an entirely false style. How can a crow become a horse? If the reservoir is shallow, then the stream that flows from it is sure to be meager.

What does it mean for the master's bequest to be correct? It means that the master's eye for the Way is completely open and that he also emphasizes disciplined conduct. Even though he is the master, he shares the same standards as the congregation in all things. His personal life is pure and he puts his will to arduous tests. He rises early and goes to sleep late. He strives diligently to take the earlier virtuous ones as his guides. His conduct is as pure as ice and frost, as gold and jade. He is imbued inside with the practices of the Way, and the Chan community can take him as a model. This is what it means to be correct.

What does it mean for the master's bequest not to be correct? It means that the master's eye for the Way is bewildered and he despises disciplined conduct. He rests on his status as master and does not share in anything with the congregation. He demands delicious food and robes of silk. He rests early and rises late. He regards a leisurely existence of intoxication as the untrammeled freedom of Chan. He indulges in wild and perverse behavior and rejects the cultivation of practice. Thus the congregation has no one they can take as an example. This is what it means not to be correct. (Section omitted)

Overall, there is certainly more than one starting point for so-called Chan masters acting in perverse and deceitful ways. The greatest aberration is when so-called Chan masters do not go beyond the behavioral standards of an ordinary mediocre person. They may use their false daring to imitate the real Buddhadharma, falsely mimicking great Chan masters like Deshan and Linji by reviling the buddhas and patriarchs and scourging ghosts and spirits. While they are actually at the level of the most ordinary person, simply people in the midst of causal conditions, they arrogate to themselves the marks of someone at the stage of the fruit of enlightenment. They burn scriptural texts and images and tread upon the sage worthies, comparing this to the impeccable conduct of Danxia or Fozhao. They have nothing of the penetrating insight of Chan masters like Nanquan, Guizong, or Dasui, yet they kill and injure as they please, claiming that this is the majestic gait of a dragon or an elephant (that is, the conduct of a great enlightened being). They have nothing of the ability to teach through great expedients of Buddhist masters such as Kumarajiva, Baozhi, Budai, Jidian, Jiuxian, or Xianzi[, who ignored monastic discipline when necessary to further the teaching of the Dharma], but they wrongly consume wine and meat and thus break the precepts.

Such pretended Chan masters totally fail to realize that when the sages of old acted against conventional standards, they had the manifest characteristics of sages, and that when the buddhas and patriarchs broke through the customary norms that people cling to, they had the legitimate status of buddhas and patriarchs. (Section omitted) Those who take on the responsibility for the Dharma gate these days do not have the spiritual powers of the sages of old but just imitatively follow in their apparent footsteps. They do not have the spiritual uniqueness of the buddhas and patriarchs but just give free rein to their cravings. Aren't they just parasites and tricksters? Aren't they sending themselves down to Papiyan (king of the demons of delusion in hell)? Aren't they causing people to regress in their correct faith and ruining the Buddhadharma? (Section omitted)

Weishan said: "Though the practitioner may get a moment of sudden awakening to the inherent truth from causal circumstances, he still has the flowing consciousness of manifest karma without beginning. The Dharma will cleanse this away." Huitang said:

"When I first entered the Path [and experienced enlightenment], it was very easy to be self-satisfied. But when I stepped back in intro-spection, my contradictions were extremely numerous. So I worked hard at practice for three years, and only then did I reach the point that everything was in accord with the truth." Consider Zhaozhou, who said that for forty years he had not applied his mind in a mixed-up way; or Xianglin, who said that at forty he finally achieved unity. Yongquan said at forty that he still sometimes got bent out of shape. These were all things that happened after [these classic Chan masters experienced] enlightenment.

The virtuous ones of the past all knew that both favorable and adverse situations are [opportunities] for a great person. Thus they made diligent and painstaking efforts to discipline their conduct, and even in old age they never slackened in this. As the maxim goes, "Those who know the Dharma fear it." This being so, when a Chan master trains and tempers patch-robed monks, he cannot neglect to act as a model for those who come after him and to be an exemplar for the Chan school, with pure and rigorous conduct and under-standing.

Refining the Work of Study

The Great Way is not [manifested] in words, but without words there is no way to make the Way manifest. The Buddhadharma is not a matter of learning, but without study there is no way to illuminate the Dharma. (Section omitted) [Otherwise,] [without words and study,] when we enter the mundane world, we cannot respond to people. This would make people think that Chan people are all empty and raw and lacking in learning, dim and dull and lacking in knowledge. Without both inner and outer learning, how can we dig out the heart and marrow of the buddhas and patriarchs, how can we be persuasive to the world's outstanding people, including both monks and nuns and laypeople? (Section omitted) There are two concepts here: investigation and learning. There is a definite order in what the Chan masters set forth. Although we cannot overemphasize theoretical learning and discard experiential investigation, neither can we have only investigation and neglect the learning.

As long as practitioners have not yet illuminated the basic root, their enlightened true nature, and their mass of doubt is not yet smashed, then no matter whether their faculties are sharp or dull, all practitioners must work hard at investigating [Chan]. During their investigation they dispense with names and terms and cut off intellectual understanding entirely, so that there is no way out in the four directions and an iron mountain blocks the path. A sword is hanging over the spot between their eyebrows, and the blood spurts up to Indra's heaven. If they keep any verbal concepts, then the poison enters into their hearts and they are throwing dust in their own eyes. Is there any theoretical learning here? When practitioners achieve enlightenment through investigation, they smash the crystal vase and release the hawk that flies to heaven. They embrace heaven and earth and strike the void to make it echo. They penetrate through sound and form so the dragon murmurs in the withered tree.[36] For them at this stage, all the sayings of the Chan masters are just a bowl of noise, and the verbal teachings of the three vehicles [of shravakas,[37] pratyekabuddhas,[38] and bodhisattvas] are just a post for tethering a donkey. At his great enlightenment, Deshan said: "I have fathomed all the abstruse arguments, and they are like a single hair placed in a great void. I have exhausted all contemporary [expedient] devices, and they are like a drop of water thrown into an abyss." You should not put aside investigation and emphasize learning until you have dispensed with names and words and died the Great Death and come back to life after death. Wouldn't it be marvelous if you could be thus thorough? Then, you would have smashed your mass of doubt and clearly illuminated the basic root.

Consider the ancients who said: "The mind of nirvana is easy to understand, but discriminating wisdom is hard to clarify." In the mind of nirvana, there are endless subtleties, and in discriminating wisdom there are infinite difficulties. The enlightenment stories of all the Chan masters are like the interlocking links of a chain, and the teachings of the Five Houses of Chan are like the secret military codes [the commander keeps securely hidden in his own] bedroom. In Chan discourse, the sharp points are concealed in the words and meanings, and even grinding with metal or jade will not reveal them. Existence and emptiness join together, and even a spiderweb or an ant trail cannot get through.

[When it comes to the whole intricate legacy of Chan teachings], how can those who have emptied through all at once and just gotten the "one horn" [of enlightenment] think that they have comprehended it all in a single comprehension and penetrated through it all with a single penetration? To investigate this legacy deeply and accumulate a thorough knowledge of it depends entirely on learning. Those who are not going to be Chan masters may stop here [with the experience of enlightenment]. But those who want to occupy this position will be faced with practitioners asking questions about points that give them doubts and difficulties. They will have to open the way to understanding for monks and nuns and laymen and laywomen. They will have to explicate and interpret for their practitioners the verses and poems and sayings of the classic Chan masters as well as their special comments and the remarks they made on others' behalf and their teaching words. This cannot be done in a confused and perfunctory way. What's more [they will also have to be able to explain] the writings of the Buddhist canon with their vast horizons of meaning and the five compendia of monastic rules with their deep oceans of disciplinary precepts. All of these are included in the precious collections of Buddhist literature: how can they simply be put away and ignored? [There are certain pretenders who have] only the most vague knowledge of all of this but who claim to be Chan masters. They are willfully blind.

They act disrespectful and crazy and arrogantly mistreat people. They have no clear understanding of Buddhist scriptures and are completely in the dark about practical worldly knowledge. If you question them about the teachings of Chan, they prevaricate and equivocate, and if you ask them about the scriptural teachings, they get red in the face and become tongue-tied. If they do open their mouths, they yap like wild dogs and are as ugly as dumb sheep. Yet they wish to assume the robe and whisk [of a Chan master] and occupy the master's seat. They proclaim themselves men of great eloquence to impress and deceive the ordinary people and say they are the heirs of such-and-such stream of such-and-such famous school of Chan. Wouldn't this be enough to embarrass anyone to death?

The *Book of Rites* says: "Their words are uncouth, and their actions have no depth."

When those who try to train patch-robed monks stick rigidly to a single method or teaching, most practitioners do not fully develop their abilities. When those without comprehensive knowledge mold and shape human talents, the multitude of Dharma doors are not used.

When a blind man runs his hands over an elephant, if he has "no nostrils" at all, it goes without saying [that he has no way to judge the elephant's true shape]. Even if his "nostrils" are straight, if he is inarticulate and unlearned, then he may be amply prepared to abide in quietude but he is not able to help other living beings.

A broken jar is not a vessel, and it goes without saying that someone whose personal qualities are not upright cannot be a Chan master. Even if the personal qualities are upright, someone who is lacking in learning may be able to cultivate practice with other people, but he cannot support them and make them stand tall.

In cases like this, though the capacities of the practitioners are set, what's wrong is that the master's forge is not broad [enough to accommodate them].

Those with the most one-sided view defend themselves [and their ignorance] with the [traditional notion] that the Sixth Patriarch [Huineng] was illiterate. Whenever they see practitioners investigating any of the ancient and modern Chan records, they immediately rebuke these practitioners for abandoning the Chan family and running off in confusion. (Section omitted) When they read that the enlightened masters of the past wrote anything, they criticize them as followers of the school of intellectual understanding. These false masters are in effect dismissing the eminent Chan masters who were prolific writers, such as Tiantong, Xuedou, Yongming, Foyin, Mingjiao, Juefan, Miaoxi, and Zhongfeng, as being mere literary masters. Isn't this a ludicrous accusation?!

Selectively Refining Talent

Mingjiao Qisong (1007–1072) said: "Nothing is more honored than the Way, and nothing is more beautiful than virtue." The Way and virtue are the great jewels, both at the worldly level and at the world-transcending level. Fame is not gained through talent alone. It is better to have virtue without talent than talent without virtue. This is true for worldly things and even truer for those who aspire to become buddhas and patriarchs, to escape from birth and death, refine their spiritual illumination, and return to nirvana. As for practice, what should you study?

It might be permissible to rest content with your dullness and hold to your ineptitude if you intend to stay behind locked doors and do little except take care of yourself. But if you intend to be the leader of a Chan community and direct Chan monks, to shoulder the great responsibility of a teaching center and set up the lofty banner of the buddhas and patriarchs, how will you live up to the task successfully and bring glory and greatness [to the calling of Chan master] unless you have ample talent and special abilities that have been refined over a long time?

Thus it is impossible to lead a Chan community without talent, but it is also impossible for someone who relies exclusively on talent. If those who rely exclusively on talent are advanced [to positions of leadership], the damage done will not be slight. Therefore, in nominating talented people [to leadership positions] in a Chan community, account must be taken of their virtue. (Section omitted) The most difficult issue here is that, as people are created, very few have a complete set of talents, while many have one-sided talents, and very few have a balance of talent and virtue, while in many these are out of balance. (Section omitted)

When there are people of excellence in the community who have clearly illuminated both the basic root [of enlightenment] and the guiding principles [of Buddhist theory], people whom the master can hope will turn out to be seedlings [for perpetuating the Dharma], then the master's work of selecting and refining must be even more thoroughgoing and complete. The master must not casually let them go.

In the eastern section of a monastery, proceeding from low to high, [the positions and the duties are as follows]: The "chanting congregation" (*yuezhong*) oversees discipline in chanting and reciting [scriptures]; the "harvest supervisors" (*zhisui*) lead the congregation in their productive labor; the "chef" (*dian zuo*) takes charge of provisions; the "storehouse supervisor" (*zhiku*) oversees the accounts; the "financial prior" (*fusi*) assists in overall management; the "rector" (*weina*) arranges the regulations for the [main] hall; and the "acting priors" (*jianyuan*) and "chief prior" (*dusi*) take charge of temple affairs. (Section omitted)

In the western section [of a monastery], proceeding from low to high, [the positions and the duties are as follows]: The attendant monks, who stay close to the Chan master[, may be assigned particular duties, such as] burning incense, taking care of the robe and bowl, or brewing medicines; the "guest master" (*zhike*) takes charge of registering visitors; the "monk in charge of the baths" (*zhiyu*) sees to community hygiene; the "monk in charge of the canon" (*zhizang*) takes care of the scriptural texts; the "secretary" (*shuji*) oversees written records. There are also the chief monks in the Chan Hall: the "chief of the hall" (*tangzhu*) and the "chief of the rear hall" (*houtang*); at a level above these are the "head of the western hall" (*xi tang*) and the "head monk" (*shuozuo*). The duty of these four chief monks is to assist the Chan master in keeping discipline and teaching the Buddhadharma. They help to train the Chan congregation and receive those who come to learn. Thus their responsibility requires much preparation.

An ancient saying goes: "There is no way to distinguish whether the blade is sharp unless it runs up against knotty gnarled roots and joints." Even if there are talented people in a Chan community, if they are not given experience in these responsible positions, how can their capacity for virtue be shaped and refined, and how can their knowledge and abilities be expanded and consolidated? They may not be crude and impetuous, but they will give free rein to their habits. They may be kept under control, but they will have no ability [for independent action]. If people like this are put in charge of a Chan community, how can they help but ruin things and split the community apart?

Moreover, from ancient times, when Chan masters wished to polish and promote the development of their practitioners' capabilities, they always assigned them to responsible posts in the community. Weishan was an ancient buddha, but Baizhang assigned him to serve as the chef. Xuefeng was a great elder, but Deshan made him in charge of cooking rice. Yangzhi and Zibao were storehouse supervisors, and Yangshan and Xuedou were put in charge of guest masters. Yunfeng was in charge of preaching to the laity. Wuzu was the mill supervisor. Miaoxi was supervisor of the eastern section. Bailing was supervisor of the baths. Yuantong was the monk in charge of the congregation. Huishi was overseer of practice. There was Qu'an the harvest evaluator and Guang the head of water supply. Dongshan was attendant in charge of incense and lamps, and Dabo was an attendant. Lushen was one of the lesser chiefs of the Chan Hall. All of our predecessors did this hard work. In every case it was a way to nurture their capacity, to mature their talents, to refine their inherent abilities, and to harden their sinews and bones. It enabled them to bear heavy responsibilities over the long term and serve as solid pillars of the Chan school.

When it comes to the Chan master passing on his position, why should he insist on the chief monk or the head of the western hall and not any of the other positions? If the master expects his successor to bear the responsibility of the teaching center, the successor must be able to temper and train patch-robed monks: only then will he be able to benefit those who come to practice. If the master expects his successor to take charge of the Chan community, the successor must be able to give the shout of enlightenment on the spot to match the situation and continue the wisdom life of [Chan]. If while serving as one of the section chiefs [in the Chan Hall], he has not perfected his hammer and tongs and made his teeth and claws poisonous, then when he is elevated to hold a Chan master's whisk and bring a glorious reputation [to the teaching center], his inadequacy will be obvious as soon as he occupies this position and starts to carry out its imperatives.

Alas! In recent times we see Chan centers where the masters pay no attention to training and tempering practitioners and are in a hurry to accept people indiscriminately as "successors." As soon as a patch-robed monk enters the gate, the so-called master passes on his bequest in a careless, perfunctory way. This monk may be enrolled in a responsible position in the community, but this is not done according to his qualifications. (Section omitted) Not only is this a blatant error under heaven, but [such a phony] is deceiving himself. The Chan school is at the point of irretrievable collapse [due to this practice]. What can practitioners take as an example [if so-called masters are not genuine]?

Being Scrupulous and Strict with Passing
On the Succession

My account of training and tempering practitioners has already been set forth above. (Section omitted) Anyone who receives this tempering and training can develop insight. Every person can develop insight, but not necessarily every person can be given the master's bequest [and recognized as a successor]. (Section omitted) Nevertheless, to say that all people who have had one experience of insight are qualified to be given the master's bequest reflects incomplete knowledge.

For practitioners to arrive at the point where they are worthy of being given the master's bequest, they must have the eye for the Way that can abide by the guidelines of the masters of the Chan school, the virtuous conduct that can set a standard for humans and gods, the learning that can provide guidance to those who come after them, and the teeth and claws to capture patch-robed monks. Only then can they be entrusted with the mission of appearing in the world as Chan masters and given the responsibility of helping other people. It is like a seal transmitting an impression: if the impression of the seal is faithful and accurate, then the Chan school can rely on it. Since it is the Dharma Ending Age, fully qualified successors are hard to discover, and special vessels of the Dharma are hard to find. It is necessary [for the Chan master and his potential successor] to live together for a long time, so that the master gets to know all about how the potential successor's mind works. Although a promising practitioner may not be capable of the unique eye that transcends the school, if he is [free from inconsistencies and] is not "square on the bottom and round on the top," he is sure to have several particular skills. If he is fairly close to the guidelines, then the master may sanction him.

He cannot be a Chan master [in overall charge of a Chan monastery], but he can be a master in charge of sitting (*jingzhu*). He still needs to have a clear eye for the Way and an upright character and be equipped with the bones of the buddhas and patriarchs. He must be honest and self-contained and not "trespass on the seedling crops of other people." Only then can he fulfill this role. This is definitely not something that low, ignorant, perverse, misguided types should get involved in. (Section omitted)

Mazu produced eighty-four enlightened masters, each of whom became the leader of a Chan school. All of them were proper vessels of the Dharma. Later, those who became great talents were Yunmen, Dongshan, Fayan, Fenyang, Huanglong Huinan, Zhenjing Kewen, Wuzu of East Mountain, Yuanwu, Miaoxi. The charts list more than ninety people to whom Miaoxi gave his bequest. Yet no one has ever criticized these Chan elders for giving their bequest excessively.

Those who made a single transmission of the robe and bowl were Chan masters like Fengxue, Yangzhi, Baiyun, Yingan, and Mi'an. Though they offered the "ritual wine"[39] alone (without many Dharma heirs), they had ample ability to take care of the Chan family and not allow it to cease.

No one has ever insisted that cutting off the transmission is the loftiest course of action. If so, then why did the fourth patriarch, Daoxin (580–651), have to take his long journey from Mount Lu to Niutou (Ox Head Mountain) [to transmit the Dharma to Farong there]? Why did Nanyue have to polish the brick [to alert Mazu to the fact that there is more to becoming enlightened than sitting in meditation]? Why did the Boatman have to capsize his boat [to push Jiashan Shanhui to enlightenment]? Why did Fengxue have to weep [to spur on Shoushan to become a worthy successor of the Linji lineage]? Why did Dayang have to give leather shoes and a monk's robe to Fushan to make him seek to become a vessel of the Dharma? (Section omitted)

When it is a flourishing period for Chan Buddhism, buddhas and patriarchs come to the fore and practitioners with the potential of dragons and elephants gather around. There are practitioners whose wisdom surpasses their masters, or who equal their masters. In the broad and great Dharma gate, there is not one master who is not a vessel of the Dharma. In this situation, even when a master gives his bequest to several dozen people, or even to a hundred people, it is not too many. The Teaching has to be opened up and extended, and masters must not fail to do so.

When it is a declining period, masters lack discernment and experience and practitioners run after empty reputations. There are cases where so-called masters give their bequest to several people and not one of them is fit to be a vessel of the Dharma. There are cases where so-called masters give their bequest to several dozen people and not one of them appears in the world as a master in the correct way. They are sheep in tiger's skins, using deception to attract followers. Even if they were to give their bequest to only a single person, it would be wrong.

In this situation, genuine enlightened masters would rather let the transmission be cut off, and go on in lofty solitude, considering this as a way of repairing and rescuing the Teaching. (Section omitted) Even though they do not give a bequest [in the absence of worthy successors], they stand firm like pillars polished in the stream, and they still possess the eye for the Way. Their light shines through for a hundred generations. Can this be called letting the transmission be cut off? At so-called teaching centers where they go beyond the proper guidelines, though the master may give his bequest to many practitioners, [it accomplishes nothing because] if you water melon vines at midday, they will not set fruit. Before long [such a phony "teaching center"] will go to ruin and create a terrible mess. Can this be called continuing the transmission?

In sum, if the Chan master clearly understands the guiding principles of Chan and knows how to train and temper practitioners, then at the first stage it will not be hard for him to produce people [who awaken to the basic root]. After their enlightenment, he will not carelessly let them go off. He will be most conscientious and careful about giving them transmission, and everything will be good fortune for the Chan school. If [the so-called master] destroys the guiding principles and neglects training and tempering his practitioners, then he will err by passing on the transmission indiscriminately to all and sundry. If the master is too cautious [about passing on his bequest], there is the worry that the transmission may be cut off. Both of these errors mean bad fortune for the Chan school.

Even so, the enlightened master enters into weeds [of ignorance and delusion] to look for people for the sake of the buddhas and patriarchs and to open the eye of enlightenment for humans and gods. It is better to be too cautious with the transmission than to give it indiscriminately [to all and sundry]. It is better to have a few genuine successors than many false ones, and not to let noxious weeds be mixed in among the good plants. If the master follows this course, then the life of wisdom is sure to be great and glorious forever.

It is for this reason that I have made the effort to set forth this account of training and tempering Chan practitioners and, as a final word, that I end it with an admonition to be careful with the transmission. Emphasizing the guiding principles, being diligent in training and tempering practitioners, and being conscientious and cautious with the transmission—in the contemporary world these three things are never heard of and difficult to practice.

PART THREE

THE ESSENTIALS OF CHAN PRACTICE

by Master Xuyun (Empty Cloud)
(1839-1959)

Translated by Guogu

Prerequisites for Beginning Chan Practice

THE PURPOSE OF INVESTIGATING CHAN

THE PURPOSE OF INVESTIGATING CHAN is to illuminate the Mind and see your self-nature.[1] You must eradicate the mind's impurities so as to personally perceive the true face of your self-nature. The mind's impurities are wandering thoughts and attachments; self-nature is the wisdom and virtue of the Tathagata. Sentient beings are replete with the wisdom and virtue of buddhas; they are not two and not separated from one another. If you can leave behind wandering thoughts and attachments, then you will attain this wisdom and virtue that is within you. This is buddhahood. Otherwise you remain an ordinary sentient being.

It is because you and I have been, for limitless *kalpas,* wallowing in birth and death, defiled for a long time, and unable to immediately cast off wandering thoughts that we cannot perceive our intrinsic nature. For these reasons, the first prerequisite of investigating Chan is to eradicate wandering thoughts.

How do we eradicate wandering thoughts? Shakyamuni Buddha taught much on this subject. His simplest and most direct teaching is the word *stop,* from the expression "Stopping is *bodhi.*" From the time when Bodhidharma transmitted Chan teachings to our Eastern Land, after the Sixth Patriarch [Huineng], the winds of Chan have blown far and wide, shaking and illuminating the world. Among the many things that Bodhidharma and the Sixth Patriarch taught to those who came to study with them, none is more valuable than the saying "Put down the myriad entangling conditions; let not one thought arise." Putting down the myriad entangling conditions simply means to put down *all* conditions. So this phrase "Put down all conditions and let not one thought arise" is actually the foremost prerequisite of a Chan practitioner. If you cannot fulfill this requirement, then not only will you fail to attain the ultimate goal of Chan practice but you will not even be able to enter the gate of Chan. How can you speak of practicing Chan if you are entangled by worldly phenomena, wallowing in the arising and passing of your thoughts?

PUT DOWN THE MYRIAD
ENTANGLING CONDITIONS

"Put down all conditions and let not one thought arise" is a prerequisite for the practice of investigating Chan. Now that we know this, how do we accomplish it? The best practitioner, one of superior abilities, can in an instant put to rest all [deluded] thoughts forever, arrive directly at the realization of the unborn, and instantly experience *bodhi*, without being entangled by anything.

The next best kind of practitioner uses principle to rid himself of phenomenal appearance and realizes that self-nature is originally pure; vexation and *bodhi*, samsara and nirvana—all are false names that have nothing to do with self-nature; all affairs and things are dreams and illusions, like bubbles or reflections.[2]

My physical body that is composed of the four elements, the mountains, rivers, and [all that exists on] this great earth—these are all contained within my self-nature, like bubbles on the surface of the ocean, arising and disappearing, yet never obstructing the [ocean's] fundamental essence. Do not be captivated by the arising, abiding, changing, and passing away of illusory phenomena that give rise to pleasure and aversion, grasping and rejecting. Give up your whole body as if you were dead, and the six sense faculties, [six] sense objects, and [six] sense consciousnesses will naturally disperse. Greed, hatred, ignorance, and craving for affection will be destroyed. All the physical sensations of pain, itchiness, agony, and pleasure—hunger, cold, satiation, warmth, glory, insult, birth and death, calamity, prosperity, good and bad luck, praise, blame, gain and loss, safety and danger—will no longer be your concern. Only this can be considered true "putting down [of all conditions]." When you put everything down forever, this is what is meant by "Put down all conditions."

When the myriad conditions are renounced, wandering thoughts will disappear on their own accord, discrimination will not arise, and attachment is left far behind. In this instance of nothing arising in mind, the brightness and clarity of your self-nature manifests completely. Only at this time will you have fulfilled the necessary conditions for investigating Chan. Then, further hard work and sincere practice will enable you to illuminate the Mind and see into your true nature.

EVERYONE INSTANTLY BECOMES A BUDDHA

Many Chan practitioners ask questions about the Dharma. The Dharma that is spoken is originally not the true Dharma. As soon as you try to explain things, the true meaning is lost. If you realize that this Mind is originally the Buddha, then at that very instant there is nothing more to do. Everything manifests its perfected state. All talk about practice or attainment is demonic deception.

Bodhidharma's "direct pointing at the Mind and seeing into one's nature and thus attaining buddhahood" clearly instructs that all sentient beings are buddhas. Once pure self-nature is recognized, you can harmonize with the environment yet remain undefiled. The Mind will remain unified throughout the day, whether walking, standing, sitting, or lying down. This manifests the already perfected buddha. At this point there is no need to put forth effort and be diligent, let alone act in a certain way or be pretentious. Nor is there a need to bother with explanations or discursive thinking. Thus it is said that to become a buddha is the easiest, most natural task. Moreover, it is something you can control, without seeking help from outside. All sentient beings in this vast land can instantly realize buddhahood if only they desire to avoid transmigration of four forms of birth and the six realms of existence in this long *kalpa*, tumbling in the sea of suffering without end. Buddhahood can be attained if you desire the four virtues of nirvana (eternity, joy, self, purity) and wholly believe in the sincere words of the Buddha and the patriarchs, renounce everything, and think neither of good nor bad. All buddhas, bodhisattvas, and patriarchs have vowed to exhaustively save all beings; this vow is not a boast, nor is it groundless, making some sort of grand vow or empty remark.

The Dharma is exactly such. It has been elucidated again and again by the Buddha and the patriarchs. They have exhorted us with the truth and do not deceive us. Unfortunately, sentient beings are confused, and for limitless *kalpas* they have been wallowing in birth and death in the ocean of suffering, reborn here and reborn there, without any control of their endless transmigration. Confused with inverted views, they turn their backs on awakening and embrace the worldly dust [of their senses], like pure gold in a cesspool. Because of the severity of the problem and the degree of their defilement, the Buddha compassionately, without any choice, expounded eighty-four thousand Dharma doors [methods] to accord with the varying karmic roots of sentient beings, so that sentient beings may use these methods to cure themselves of eighty-four thousand habits and illnesses, which include greed, hatred, ignorance, and craving for affection.

INVESTIGATING CHAN AND
CONTEMPLATING MIND

Our sect focuses on investigating Chan. And the purpose of investigating Chan is to "illuminate the Mind and see one's own self-nature," which means to thoroughly investigate and comprehend our original face. This investigation is also called "clearly realizing one's Mind and thoroughly perceiving one's intrinsic nature."

Since the time when the Buddha held up a flower [and Mahakashyapa realized awakening] and Bodhidharma came to the East, the methods for entry into this Dharma door have continually evolved. Most Chan adepts before the Tang and Song dynasties became enlightened after hearing a word or phrase of the Dharma, and Dharma transmission from master to disciple was merely a convergence of Mind to Mind; there was no actual Dharma. Further, questions and answers in daily life were only extemporaneous occasions to untie entanglements, much like prescribing the right medicine for the right illness.

After the Song dynasty, however, people did not have such good karmic capacities as their predecessors. They could not carry out what had been said. For example, practitioners were taught to "put down everything" and "not think about good and evil," but they could not put down everything; if they weren't thinking about good, they were thinking about evil. Under these circumstances, the patriarchs had no choice but to use poison against poison, and taught practitioners to investigate gong'an [and huatou].[3]

When you begin observing a huatou, even if you must begin with a lifeless phrase, you must grasp it tightly, without letting go of it even for an instant, like a mouse trying to gnaw its way out of a coffin. The mouse must focus on one area and it must not stop until it gnaws through the coffin. In terms of huatou, the objective is to use a single thought to eradicate ten thousand thoughts. This method is really a last resort. Just as if someone had been severely poisoned and there was no other way to get the poison out and cure the patient except to open up the body.

The ancients had numerous gong'ans, but later on practitioners started using huatous. Some huatous are: "Who is observing this corpse?" "What is my original face before my parents gave birth to me?" In recent times, many use "Who is reciting Buddha's name?"

In fact, all huatous follow the same format. There is nothing uncommon, strange, or special about them. If you wanted to, you could observe: "Who is reciting the sutras?" "Who is reciting the mantras?" "Who is prostrating to the Buddha?" "Who is eating?" "Who is wearing these clothes?" "Who is walking?" "Who is sleeping?"

They're all the same. The answer to the word *who* derives from one's Mind; Mind is the source of all words. Thoughts arise from the Mind; the Mind is the source of all thoughts. Innumerable dharmas[4] are born out of the Mind; Mind is the source of all dharmas. In fact, huatou [literally meaning "source of words"] is the source of thoughts. And the source of thoughts is the Mind. To put it directly, the state of mind before any thought arises is huatou.

Hence, we should know that observing huatou is contemplating Mind. Your "original face" before your parents gave birth to you is the Mind, and observing the huatou "What is my original face before my parents gave birth to me?" is contemplating Mind.

Self-nature is Mind. When one "turns inward to hear one's self-nature," one is turning inward to contemplate Mind. In the phrase, "perfectly illuminating pure awareness," the "pure awareness" is Mind and "illumination" is contemplation. Mind is buddha. When one recites Buddha's name one contemplates buddha. And contemplating buddha is contemplating Mind.

Thus, observing the huatou, such as observing "Who is reciting Buddha's name?" is contemplating Mind. That is, "illuminating the pure awareness" of your Mind, or illuminating the buddha of your self-nature. Mind is nature, is pure awareness, and is buddha. It has no form, no characteristics, no fixed location; it cannot be grasped and as such is intrinsically pure. It pervades all Dharma realms; it does not exist or enter; it does not come or go. The Mind is the intrinsically self-manifested, pure dharmakaya Buddha.

You practitioners should first shut down all six sense faculties and observe the place where thoughts arise and take care of this "source of words," or huatou; observe it until you perceive your pure Mind separated from all thoughts. Advancing further, your practice must be seamless, without any interruption, and your mind must be refined, quiescent, and luminous. Continue until the five *skandhas*[5] are empty and your body and mind become quiescent. There will be nothing for you to do. From that point onward, activities of walking, standing, sitting, and lying are all performed in stillness. In time your practice will deepen and you will see your self-nature and become a buddha. Suffering will be extinguished. Master Gaofeng (1238–1295) once said: "You must observe the huatou like a sinking roof tile plummeting down into a pond ten thousand feet deep. If in seven days you are not enlightened, you have permission to chop off my head!" Fellow practitioners, these are the words of one who has already reached the other shore. His words are true; they are not boastful words that deceive us!

Still, why is it that in our modern times, although there are many practicing huatou, few actually reach enlightenment? This is because practitioners today have karmic capabilities inferior to those of practitioners of the past. Also, practitioners today are unclear about the principle and path of huatou practice. Some practitioners sojourn from east to west and north to south to practice [under different masters] until they die but still haven't penetrated even one huatou. They don't know the meaning of *huatou* and are unsure what would be considered "observing the huatou." All of their lives they only attach to the words and labels, exerting their efforts [not on the "source" of words but] at the tail end of words. (Section omitted.)

Huatou is precisely the One Mind. This One Mind that is within you and me is not inside, outside, or in the middle. And at the same time *it is* inside, outside, and in the middle. Like the stillness of empty space, it pervades everywhere.

When using the huatou, you should not raise it upward (that is, focus on it in your head region) or suppress it downward (that is, psychologically force the huatou to sink to the lower body). If you raise it upward, you will arouse scattered mind. If you suppress it, you will drift into drowsiness. These approaches are contrary to your mind's original nature and are not in accordance with the Middle Way.

Practitioners are distressed by wandering thoughts. They believe it is difficult to subdue wandering thoughts. Let me state it clearly: don't be afraid of wandering thoughts, and do not waste your energy subduing them. All you have to do is recognize them. Don't attach to them, don't follow them, and don't try to get rid of them. As long as you do not continue wallowing in them, wandering thoughts will naturally depart by themselves.

Lectures on the Methods of Practice in the Chan Hall

INTRODUCTION

All of you come to ask me for guidance. This makes me feel ashamed. Everyone works so hard—splitting firewood, hoeing the fields, carrying soil, moving bricks—and yet from morning to night you have not forgotten the thought of cultivating the Way. Such determination for the Path is touching. I, Xuyun, am ashamed for my inadequacy on the Way and my lack of virtue. What I say cannot really be called "instructions"; I will use only a few sayings from the ancients in response to your questions. As for cultivating the Way, there are four prerequisites:

Deep conviction in [the law of] cause and effect

Strict observance of precepts

Immovable confidence

Commitment to a Dharma door (method)

NECESSARY KNOWLEDGE IN CHAN SITTING

All activities of everyday life should be subsumed within the practice of the Way. Is there anywhere that is not a place for practicing the Way? Originally there is no such need for a Chan Hall. And "seated meditation" is, of course, not necessarily Chan. So-called Chan Hall and Chan sitting are designed for us sentient beings with deep karmic obstructions and shallow wisdom.

When one sits in meditation, one must first know how to attune one's body and mind. If they are not well regulated, then a small problem will turn into an illness and a big problem will result in demonic entanglements. This would be most pitiable! Walking and sitting meditation in the Chan Hall are designed to harmonize your body and mind. Aside from these there are other ways to attune the body and mind. I will briefly elaborate them.

When you sit in the cross-legged position, you should sit naturally and upright. Do not intentionally push the waist forward. Doing so will raise your inner heat, which later on may result in having sand in the corner of your eyes, bad breath, uneasy breathing, loss of appetite, and in the worst case, vomiting blood. Nor should you arch your back and lower your head. Doing so can easily cause drowsiness and dullness. Especially do not lean your back on something [in meditation], which can cause you to vomit blood later on.

If you are aware of the onset of drowsiness or dullness, keep your eyes wide open, straighten your lower back, and gently move your buttocks from side to side. Drowsiness and dullness will naturally vanish.

If you exert too much effort in your practice and become agitated, you should put everything down, including your efforts to practice. Rest for a few minutes, and gradually, after you feel more comfortable, you may take up your method and practice again. If you don't do this, then as time goes on you will develop an anxious and hot-tempered character, or, in the worst case, you could go insane or fall into demonic states.

There are many states one may encounter in Chan sitting, which are too many to speak of here. But as long as you do not attach to any of them, they will not obstruct you. There is a secular saying: "If one is not astonished by the weird, the weird will vanish of its own accord." Even if you encounter or perceive an unpleasant state, do not concern yourself with it and have no fear. If you experience something pleasant, do not concern yourself with it and do not give rise to fondness. The *Surangama Sutra* says: "If one does not entertain the idea that one has attained a holy state, then whatever state one has experienced is a good state. On the other hand, if one interprets what is experienced as something holy, that will attract demons."[6]

APPROACHING THE PRACTICE AND DISCERNING THE HOST FROM THE GUEST

How should one approach practice? In the *Surangama Sutra*, the Honored One Kaundinya spoke to the assembly the words *host* and *guest*. This is where beginners like us must start our practice. He said, "A traveler who stops at an inn may stay overnight or get something to eat. When he is finished or rested, he packs and continues his journey, for he does not have time to stay longer. If he were the host, he would have no place to go. Thus, I reason, he who does not stay is called a guest because not staying is the essence of being a guest. He who stays is called a host. Again, on a clear day, when the sun rises and the sunlight enters a dark room through an opening, one can see dust floating in empty space. The dust is moving but the space is still. That which is clear and still is called space and that which is moving is called dust because moving is the essence of being dust."[7] *Guest* and *dust* refer to deluded thoughts, whereas *host* and *space* refer to self-nature. That the permanent host does not follow the guest in his comings and goings illustrates that permanent self-nature does not follow the sudden arising and perishing of deluded thoughts. Therefore it is said that with no mind to encounter the myriad things, how can one be obstructed by the surrounding myriad things? The nature of dust is to move of its own accord, but it does not obstruct the [otherwise] empty space; this is likened to deluded thoughts that rise and fall by themselves, but do not hinder the "suchness" of self-nature. Thus it is said that if one's mind does not arise, there will be no problems with the myriad things. In such a state of mind, the "guest" naturally will not follow deluded thinking. If you understand "space" and "dust," deluded thoughts will no longer be hindrances. It is said that when one recognizes [the problem], there will be no resentment. If you can approach and try to understand the practice in this way, it will be unlikely that you will make serious mistakes [on the Path].

HUATOU AND THE DOUBT SENSATION

The old ancestral masters pointed directly at Mind and [revealed that] seeing the [self-] nature is attaining buddhahood, like First Ancestor Bodhidharma's "calming of mind" and the sixth ancestor's [Huineng's] exclusive teaching on "seeing self-nature." All that was necessary was the direct seizing and acceptance of Mind, nothing else. There was no such method as observing the huatou. More recently, however, masters saw that practitioners would not throw themselves into practice with total dedication and could not perceive and actualize their self-nature. Instead, these people only play games, mouthing words of Chan, showing off other people's treasure and imagining it to be their own. For this reason, later patriarchs were compelled to set up Dharma doors and cloisters and devise specific expedients to help practitioners, hence the method of observing the huatou.

There are many huatous, such as "All dharmas return to one,

where does the one return to?" "What is my original face before my parents gave birth to me?" and so on. The most common one, however, is "Who is reciting the Buddha's name?"

What is meant by *huatou*? *Hua* means the spoken word[s]; *tou* means the head or source, so *huatou* means that which is before the spoken word[s]. For example, in the huatou "Amitabha Buddha," the *hua* consists of the words, and [the *tou* is the head. Therefore,] the huatou is that which precedes the conception of these words. So the huatou is that moment before a single thought arises. Once the thought arises, it is already the "tail end" of the *hua* [not its "source"]. That moment before thought arises is "nonarising." The state when your mind is not distracted, not dull, not attached to quiescence, or has not fallen into an experience of nothingness, is called "nonperishing." From one moment to the next, single-mindedly and uninterruptedly, turning inward and illuminating this state of nonarising and nonperishing is called observing the huatou, or taking care of the huatou.

To observe the huatou, you must first generate the doubt sensation, which is like a walking cane for observing the huatou. What is meant by the doubt sensation? For example, you may ask, "Who is reciting the Buddha's name?" Of course, everyone knows that it is oneself who is reciting the name, but do you use your mouth or mind to recite? If it is your mouth, then after you die and your mouth is still there, how come you are unable to recite Buddha's name? If it is your mind, then what is the mind like? It cannot be comprehended or apprehended. Thus, because you don't know, you give rise to a subtle questioning mind centered on this "who?" In fact, this [questioning mind] should never be coarse; the subtler the better. At all times and in all places, you should single-mindedly take care of this thought of questioning and maintain it continuously like a fine stream of water. Do not give rise to a second thought. When this thought of doubt is present, do not disturb it. When this doubt is not present, gently bring it forth again. Beginners will find that it is more effective to gain strength from this method when you're sitting than moving about, but you should never make such discriminations [between stillness and activity]. Regardless of whether your practice is effective or whether you are still or active, just wholeheartedly and single-mindedly use the method.

In the huatou "Who is reciting the Buddha's name?" the emphasis is on the word *who*. The other words serve to provide a general context, just as in asking, "Who is dressing or eating?" "Who is moving their bowels and who is urinating?" "Who is trying to be rid of this ignorance and who is arguing with others?" "Who is it that's aware and having feelings?" This "who" is the most immediate and easiest way to arouse the doubt sensation, regardless of whether you are walking, standing, sitting, or reclining. There's no need for further conceptualization, speculation, or contrivance. Hence, huatous involving the word *who* are wonderful methods for investigating Chan. However, you should not take the huatou "Who is reciting Buddha's name?" and merely recite it like a buddha's name; nor is it right to use reasoning to find some kind of answer to the question, thinking that this is what is meant by the doubt sensation. Some people uninterruptedly recite the phrase "Who is reciting the Buddha's name?" but they would gain more merit by reciting Amitabha Buddha's name![8] Others let their minds wander, speculating this and that, believing that this is the doubt sensation. Little do they know, these people will only end up with more deluded thinking. This is like desiring to go upward but ending up going downward instead. You must be aware of this problem.

The doubt that is generated by a beginning practitioner tends to be coarse, intermittent, and irregular, which does not truly qualify as a state of doubt sensation. It can only be called thoughts. Only after the wild mind is gradually tamed and one has more control over one's thoughts can the process be called *can* (pronounced *ts'an*), which means to investigate or look into. As one's practice matures, when the questioning naturally continues without effort and one is not conscious of one's sitting or aware of the existence of a body or mind or environment, continuing like this without interruption, only then can it be called the doubt sensation. Realistically speaking, the initial stage, where you are using the method alongside engaging in wandering thoughts, cannot be considered cultivation. Only when true doubt arises can your practice be called genuine cultivation. This moment is a crucial juncture, and it is easy for the practitioner to deviate from the right path:

At this moment your mind may be clear and pure, experiencing an unlimited sense of lightness and ease. However, if you lose the clear illumination of mind—clarity without confusion is wisdom; undisturbed illumination is stillness—you will fall into a subtle state of mental dullness. If there is a clear-eyed person around,[9] he will be able to tell right away whether the practitioner is in this state and hit him or her with the incense stick,[10] dispersing all the practitioner's clouds and fog. Many people become enlightened this way.

Or at this moment the mind may be clear and pure, empty and vacuous. If the doubt disappears, then you may fall into a state of oblivion.[11] This is what is meant by the expressions "the precipice of withered trees" and "a rock soaking in cold water." When you reach these states, it is crucial to bring forth your awareness and illumination [of the doubt]. However, this is different from the initial stage of your practice, where the doubt was coarse. Now it has to be extremely fine—a single thought, subtle and unassuming, clear and quiescent; at the same time it should be still, aware, and ever knowing. Like the smoke from a fire that is about to go out, it is a narrow stream without interruption. And when your practice reaches this point, it is necessary to have a diamond eye; there will be no need to purposefully bring forth or generate [awareness and illumination] anymore. To do so would be like putting a head on top of your head.

Once a monk asked Chan master Zhaozhou (778–897), "What should one do when not one thing comes?" Zhaozhou replied, "Put it down!" The monk asked, "If not a single thing comes, what does one put down?" Zhaozhou replied, "If you cannot put it down, then take it up." This dialogue refers precisely to this kind of situation. The true flavor of this state, however, cannot be described. Like someone drinking water, only the drinker knows how cool or warm it is. If a person reaches this state, he will naturally understand. If he is not at this state, no explanation will be adequate. It is like the saying "To a sword master you should offer a sword; do not bother showing your poetry to someone who is not a poet."

TAKING CARE OF HUATOU AND TURNING INWARD TO HEAR ONE'S OWN SELF-NATURE

Someone might ask, "How is Guanyin [Avalokiteshvara] Bodhisattva's method of turning inward to hear self-nature considered investigating Chan?" I have previously explained that taking care of huatou is simply and single-mindedly, from one moment to the next moment, to shine the [mind's] light inward and illuminate "that which is not born and not destroyed." To turn inward is to illuminate; "that which is not born and not destroyed" is the self-nature. When "hearing" and "illuminating" follow sound and form in the worldly stream, hearing does not go beyond sound and seeing does not go beyond form. However, when one turns inward and contemplates self-nature against the worldly stream and does not pursue sound and form, then he or she becomes pure and clear. At that time "hearing" and "illuminating" are not two different things.

Thus we should know that taking care of the huatou and turning inward to hear self-nature does not mean using our eyes to see and our ears to hear. If we use our ears to hear or our eyes to see, then we are chasing sound and form. As a result we will be affected by them. This is called flowing with the worldly stream. If we practice with a single thought of abiding in that which is not born and not destroyed, not chasing after sound and form, with no wandering thoughts, then we are going against the stream. This is also called taking care of the huatou or turning inward to hear one's self-nature. This is not to say you should shut your eyes tightly or plug up your ears. Just do not generate a mind of seeking after sound and form.

EARNESTNESS ABOUT LEAVING BIRTH AND DEATH AND GENERATING A PERSEVERING MIND

When investigating Chan, the most important thing is to be earnest with regard to [the question of] birth and death and to generate a persevering mind. If there is no earnestness about leaving birth and death, then one cannot generate the great doubt and practice will not be effective. If there is no perseverance in one's mind, the result will be laziness, like a man who practices for one day and rests for ten. The practice will not be pervasive. If you can generate persever-ance, when great doubt arises, all the dustlike vexations will come to an end by themselves. When the time comes, the melon will natu-rally ripen and drop from the vine.

I will tell you a story. During the Qing dynasty in the year of Gengzi (1900), when the eight world powers sent their armies to Beijing, Emperor Guang Xu (r. 1875–1908) fled westward from Beijing to Shanxi Province. Every day he traveled tens of miles. For several days he had no food to eat. On the road a peasant offered him sweet potato stems. After he ate them, he asked the peasant what they were because they tasted so good. Think about the emperor's usual awe-inspiring demeanor and his arrogance! How long do you think he could continue to maintain his imperial atti-tude after so long a journey on foot? Do you think he had ever gone hungry? Do you think he had ever had to eat sweet potato stems? At that time he gave up all of his airs. After all, he had walked quite a distance and had eaten stems to keep from starving. Why was he able to "put down" everything at that time? Because the allied armies wanted his life, and his only thought was to save his life! But when peace prevailed and he returned to Beijing, once again he became proud and arrogant. He didn't have to run anymore. He no longer had to eat any food that might displease him. Why was he unable to "put down" everything at that time? It was because the allied armies no longer wanted his life. If the emperor always had an attitude of running for his life and if he could turn such an attitude toward the practice of the Way, there would be nothing he could not accomplish. It's a pity he did not have a persevering mind. When favorable circumstances returned, so did his former habits.

Fellow practitioners! Time waits for no one; once it passes it will never return. It is constantly looking to take our lives, so it is more frightening than the allied armies. Time will never compromise or make peace with us. Let us generate a mind of perseverance immediately in order to escape from birth and death! Master Gaofeng Yuanmiao (1238–1295) once said, "Concerning the practice, one should act like a stone dropping into the deepest part of the pool—ten thousand feet deep—continuously and persistently dropping without interruption toward the bottom. If one can practice like this without stopping, continuously for seven days, and still be unable to cut off one's wandering, illusory thoughts, and vexations, may I, Gaofeng, plunge into Avici Hell [and stay there] forever."[12] He continued by saying, "When one investigates Chan, one should set out a certain time for success, like a man who has fallen into a pit a thousand feet deep. All of his tens of thousands of thoughts are reduced to one—to escape from the pit. If one can really practice from morning to dusk and from night to day without a second thought, and if one does not attain complete enlightenment within three, five, or seven days, I shall be committing a great lie for which I shall have my tongue pulled out for cows to plow on forever."[13] This old master had great compassion. Knowing that we would probably be unable to generate such a persevering mind, he made these great vows to guarantee our success.

MASTER XUYUN

ENLIGHTENMENT AND PRACTICE

Master Hanshan [of the Ming dynasty] (1546–1623), once said:

There are practitioners who get enlightened first and then start their cultivation, and those who practice first and then get enlightened. However, there are two kinds of "enlightenment": through understanding and through experience. If a person realizes Mind by following the teachings of the Buddha and the patriarchs, it is considered insight through understanding. One with such an experience will have only a conceptual understanding. In all circumstances she or he will still be powerless. The mind of the practitioner and the environment are divided and are not one. Therefore, she or he may experience many obstructions. It is called simulated prajna and does not come from genuine practice.

On the other hand, those who become enlightened through practice stick to their methods in a straightforward manner until they force themselves into a place where "the mountains and rivers have completely exhausted." Suddenly their last thought drops away and they thoroughly realize Mind. It is like seeing your own father at a crossroad—there is no doubt [as to who he is]. It is also like drinking water; only the person drinking knows if it is warm or cold. There is no way to express it to another. This is real practice and enlightenment. Afterward the practitioner will still have to, on the basis of her or his experience, merge his Mind with the external environment. He will still have to get rid of strong karmic barriers of this life and deluded thinking and emotional attachments, leaving only the True Mind of a single taste.[14] This is enlightenment by experience.

Concerning true enlightenment experiences, there are deep and shallow ones. If one works on the root [of the problem], destroys the nest of the eighth consciousness and overturns the dark caves of ignorance, then one heads directly for enlightenment, without [relying on] any other Dharma. Those who achieve this have extremely sharp karmic roots and experience deep enlightenment. Those who practice gradually experience shallow enlightenment. The worst case is when someone attains little and is satisfied. One should not take illusions, like shadows created by light, for enlightenment. Why? This is because one who does has not destroyed the root of the eighth consciousness and their actions will be contrived. The experiences these people have are manifestations of their own consciousness. Believing such [an illusory state] to be real is like mistaking a thief for your son. An ancient said, "Because cultivators of the Way do not recognize the real and have taken old consciousness [as real], they transmigrate through innumerable kalpas of birth and death. Ignorant people take [consciousness] for their true selves."[15] Therefore, you must pass through this barrier.

On the other hand, there are those who experience sudden enlightenment and cultivate gradually. Although these people have experienced deep enlightenment, they still have not suddenly purified their habitual tendencies. [At this point] it is necessary, on the principle of one's enlightenment experience, to generate the power of introspective illumination to experience the environment and check the mind. If they can fuse with 1 percent of external appearances, then they will have gained 1 percent of their dharmakaya. By eliminating 1 percent of their deluded thoughts, 1 percent of their fundamental wisdom will manifest. All of this will depend on the strength of their practice, which must be seamless and without gap. To practice in the midst of activities is to derive power from it.[16]

We can see that whether we are enlightened or not, or whether our enlightenment is through understanding or experience, we have to continue our practice and sincerely follow it through. The difference is that those who are enlightened first and then cultivate are like old horses that do not go down the wrong road; it is much easier than for those who cultivate first and then get enlightened. Those who are enlightened through experience are grounded and are unlike those who gain insight through understanding, which is shaky and superficial. It is just that those who are enlightened through experience are more likely to derive power from their practice. The elder master Zhaozhou (778–897), at the age of eighty, began his sojourn [visiting various teachers]. For forty years he applied himself wholeheartedly, without any scattered mind, observing the word *wu* (nothingness). He is a great model for us all. Do you doubt that this elder master had yet experienced enlightenment [in all of those years]? His example reminds us not to be satisfied with little accomplishments and not to be so proud of ourselves.

There are those who, after reading a few sutras or Chan discourse records, say things like, "Mind is buddha!" and "[The Mind] exhausts the three periods and ten directions." Yet their words have nothing to do with their own personal lot. They firmly believe that they are ancient buddhas who have come back again. When they meet people, they praise themselves and say that they have attained complete, thorough enlightenment. Blind followers will even brag for them. This is like mistaking fish eyes for pearls! They do not know the difference between the real and the false. They mix things up and cause havoc for everyone. It not only makes people lose faith, it also gives rise to criticism [of the Dharma]. The fact that the

Chan school is not flourishing in recent years is mainly because of the faults of these unruly people. I hope you all can genuinely put forth your efforts in the practice. Do not be pretentious. Do not speak about Chan with empty words. Your task is to genuinely investigate Chan and attain solid enlightenment. In the future you can propagate the Dharma like "dragons and elephants"[17] and shoulder the burden of spreading the teachings of Chan!

INVESTIGATING CHAN AND RECITING BUDDHA'S NAME

Those who recite Buddha's name often criticize those who investigate Chan, and those who investigate Chan often slander those who recite Buddha's name. They seem to oppose each other like enemies, as if wishing the other would die. This, indeed, is a terrible phenomenon in Buddhism. There is a secular saying that goes something like this: "A family in harmony will succeed in everything, whereas a family in decline is sure to argue." When there is fighting among brothers, is it no wonder that others laugh at us and look down on us?

Investigating Chan, reciting the Buddha's name, and other methods are all teachings of Shakyamuni Buddha. Originally the Way is not two. It is only because of the different conditions and karmic dispositions of sentient beings, like giving different antidotes for the different illnesses, that various methods and Dharma doors are taught. Later on, many great masters divided the Buddha's teaching into different sects according to different interpretations. But because the needs of people differed at different times masters propagated the Dharma in different ways.

If an individual practices a method that fits his character, then that method will be the wondrous Dharma door that can lead him to the Way. Actually, there are no superior and inferior Dharma doors. Furthermore, Dharma doors are interconnected; all are perfect and without obstruction. For example, when you recite Buddha's name to the point of single-mindedness, without any distractions, is this not investigating Chan? When you investigate Chan to the point of no separation between the investigator and that which is being investigated, is this not reciting the true characteristic of the Buddha? Chan is not other than the Chan of purity, and so-called "Pure" [Land] is not other than the purity within Chan. Chan and Pure Land are mutually enriching, and they function together. It is only people who are biased and attached, giving rise to sectarian views, that praise themselves and slander others. Such people are like fire and water; they cannot exist together. They have misunderstood the profound meaning of the patriarchs who divided the [Dharma] into different schools and teachings. These people have unintentionally transgressed the heavy offense of slandering and endangering the Dharma. Is this not sad and pitiable? I hope that all of us, no matter which Dharma door we practice, understand the buddhas and patriarchs in their principle of nondiscrimination and nonopposition, and refrain from divisiveness. We should have the mind of helping one another so that we may save this ship which floats amid dangerous and violent waves.

THE TWO KINDS OF DIFFICULTY AND EASE WITH PRACTITIONERS' EXPERIENCE

Those who cultivate the way, according to the depth and shallowness of their practice, have two kinds of difficulty and ease. The first kind of difficulty and ease is associated with beginners, while the second kind corresponds to advanced practitioners.

Difficulties for Beginning Practitioners

The common symptoms of the beginner's disease are the inability to put down wandering thoughts and habitual tendencies; the depth of their ignorance; the obstruction of arrogance and jealousy;

the tendency to greed, anger, stupidity, and craving; the laziness for work but craving for food; the liking for stirring up right and wrong between self and other. All of these fill their big bellies. How can beginners come in accordance with the Way?

There are other kinds of people who are born into wealthy and noble families. Unable to forget their habits and stains from the world, they cannot endure the least bit of difficulty or withstand any hardship. How can these people practice the Way? They have not considered the status of our original teacher, Shakyamuni Buddha, prior to leaving the household life.

Then there are those who are somewhat well-read but do not understand that the problems posed in the discourse records of ancient worthies are actually for testing practitioners' levels of understanding. These people think they are smart. Every day scrutinizing the recorded sayings and writings, mouthing about Mind and Buddha, interpreting the words and letters of the ancients, talking about food but not eating it, counting the treasure of others but not owning it themselves, they think they are extraordinary people and become incredibly arrogant. But when these people become seriously ill, they will cry out for help, and at the end of their lives they will panic and become bewildered. At that time what they have learned and understood will be useless, and it will be too late to regret.

There are other people who misunderstand the saying "Originally we are buddhas." These people say that the original self is already complete and that there is no need for practice. All day long they loaf about with nothing to do, following their whim, wasting their time. These people call themselves "one who is beyond models and forms" and follow only "causes and conditions." In the future these people will suffer greatly.

Then there are people who do have their minds set on the Way but do not know how to exert themselves in practice; they are afraid of wandering thoughts, and since they are unable to "get rid" of them, day in and day out they are vexed, complaining about and lamenting their heavy karmic obstructions. Because of this, their minds set on the Way backslide. Or there are those people who want to battle till death with their wandering thoughts. Furiously they tense up their fists and push out their chests and eyes. It seems like they are involved in something big. Ready to die in battle against their deluded thinking, they not only cannot defeat deluded thinking but end up vomiting blood or going insane.

There are those who fear falling into emptiness. Little do they know that demons have already arisen in their minds; they can neither empty their minds nor get enlightened. And there are those who seek after enlightenment, not knowing that seeking enlightenment and wanting to attain buddhahood are all grave deluded thinking. One cannot cook sand hoping to eat rice. They can seek until the year of the donkey[18] and they still won't get enlightened. Sometimes people become elated when occasionally they sit through a couple of peaceful sittings. These situations are like a blind turtle whose head happens to pass through a small hole in a piece of wood floating in the middle of the ocean. It is not the result of real practice (but mere luck)! In their elation these people have added another layer of obstructions.

There are those who dwell in false purity during meditation and enjoy themselves there. Since they cannot maintain a peaceful mind within activity, they avoid noisy places and spend their days soaking in "stale water." There are numerous examples of this. For beginners, it is very difficult to find entrance to the Way. If there is illumination without awareness, then it's like sitting in stale water waiting to die.

Even though this practice is hard, once you find entrance to the Way, it becomes easier. What is the easiest way for beginners? There is nothing special other than being able to "put it down." Put what down? Put down all of those vexations that arise from ignorance. Fellow practitioners, once this body of ours stops breathing, it becomes a corpse. The main reason we cannot put it down is because we place too much importance on it. Because of this, we give rise to the idea of self and other, right and wrong, love and hate, gain and loss. If we can have a firm belief that this body of ours is like a corpse, not cherishing it or looking upon it as being ourselves, then what is there that we cannot put down? If we can put it down, then anywhere and anytime, whether walking, standing, sitting or sleeping, whether in motion or still, whether resting or active, internally and externally, all will be cold and still, with nothing else but the single doubt of the huatou. And if we peacefully and uninterruptedly continue without a moment of extraneous thought, then like a long sword extending into the sky, if anything comes in contact with the sharp edge, our doubt will extinguish it without a trace or sound. Why would there be fear of wandering thoughts? What could disturb you? Who will be there to distinguish between movement and stillness? Who would be attached to existence or emptiness? If there are fears of wandering thoughts, then you have already added another layer of wandering thought. If you feel you are pure, then you are already defiled. If you are afraid of falling into emptiness, then you are already dwelling in existence. If you want to become a buddha, then you have already entered the demon's path. Therefore, if you know how to practice, then carrying water and gathering firewood are not separate from the wonderful Way; and hoeing and planting fields are all Chan opportunities (*chan ji*). Practicing the Way is not limited to sitting cross-legged throughout the day.

Difficulties for Advanced Practitioners

What difficulties are encountered by seasoned practitioners? Although some have practiced until the emergence of genuine doubt and possess both awareness and illumination, they are still bound by birth and death. Those who have neither awareness nor illumination fall into false emptiness. To arrive at either of these situations is truly difficult. After reaching this point, some practitioners cannot release themselves; standing at the "top of a ten-thousand-foot pole," they are unable to advance. Some people having progressed to this stage, and being skilled in practice, encounter nothing they cannot resolve, so they think that they have already severed the fundamental ignorance; they believe that their practice has reached home. Actually, these people are living in the wave of ignorance and do not even know it. When these people encounter a situation that they cannot solve—where they must be their own master but cannot, they just give up. This is a pity.

There are others who reach the genuine doubt sensation, gain a little wisdom from the experience of emptiness, and understand a few ancient gong'an cases, and then they give up the doubt sensation because they think they are completely enlightened. These people compose poems and verses, act arrogantly, and call themselves virtuous men of the Way. Not only do they fool themselves, they also mislead others. They are creating bad karma.

In other cases there are those who mistake the teaching of Bodhidharma: "To isolate from external conditions, to internally still the mind, make the mind like a wall—this is the method to enter the Way." Or the Sixth Patriarch's "Not thinking of good or evil, at this time what is your original face?" They think that meditating like a withered log and a large boulder is the ultimate principle. These people take the illusory city as their treasured palace,[19] the temporary guesthouse as their home. This is the reason behind the gong'an case of the old woman who burned down the hut to reprimand the monk.[20]

What is the easy way for these advanced practitioners? Do not be proud and never give up the practice. Your practice should be seamless without any gap. In the midst of this subtle, seamless practice, you have to be even subtler; while practicing in a cautious and attentive manner, you have to be more careful. When the time comes, the bottom of the barrel will naturally drop off.[21] If you cannot do this, then find a virtuous teacher to pry off the nails of the barrel and pull out the joints!

The great Hanshan[22] of the Tang once wrote:

On the peak of the highest mountain,
The four directions expand to infinity.
Sitting in silence, no one knows him.
The solitary moon illuminates the cold spring.
In the spring there is no moon.

The moon is high in the sky.
Though I'm humming this song,
In the song there is no Chan.

The first two lines of this song reveal that the appearance of real nature does not belong to anything. The whole world is filled with bright and pure luminosity without any obstructions. The third line speaks of the essence of true suchness. Surely, ordinary people cannot comprehend this. Even the buddhas of the three periods do not know where Hanshan's "I" abides. Therefore, no one can know the Path. The three lines beginning with "The solitary moon illuminates the cold spring" are an expedient example of the level of Master Hanshan's practice. The last two lines are mentioned because he is afraid that we will "mistake the finger for the moon." Thus he especially warns us that words and language are not Chan.

CONCLUSION

I have said too much and have interrupted your practice. These words are like entangling vines (the more one pulls, the more they tangle together). Whenever words are spoken, genuine meaning is absent. When the ancient worthies received their students, they either used sticks on them or scolded them. There were not so many words! However, the present time cannot be compared with the past. One has no choice but to point a finger strenuously at the moon. Still, who is it that points? Who is the moon? Investigate!

There Is Not a Thing That Cannot Be Accomplished
RECORDED BY MASTER LINGYUAN (1902–1988)

Xuyun: What method are you using?

Lingyuan: Reciting Buddha's name and investigating Chan. Both Chan and Pure Land are practiced.

Xuyun: How can you be investigating Chan when you are reciting Buddha's name?

Lingyuan: Although I recite the Buddha's name, in my consciousness there is this doubt about who is reciting Buddha's name. So even though I'm reciting Buddha's name, I'm also investigating Chan.

Xuyun: Are there wandering thoughts or not?

Lingyuan: When the correct thought (that is, method) is brought forth, often wandering thoughts are there along with it. However, when the correct thought is put down, there wondering thoughts are also absent; there's only a sense of purity and freedom.

Xuyun: This purity and freedom is laziness, like a rock soaking in cold water! If one practices like this even for a thousand years, it is still useless. You must bring forth the correct thought with a bold and persevering mind; investigate till the end and really see through just who is reciting Buddha's name. Only then you break through; you must practice with great determination.

Lingyuan: I have heard that you entered *samadhi* for eighteen days in Chungnan Mountain. Was there a mind that entered [the *samadhi*], or no mind that entered that *samadhi*?

Xuyun: If there is a mind that enters *samadhi*, then that is not in *samadhi*. If there's no mind that enters *samadhi*, then one is like a statue made out of wood or mud. Place the mind at one point and there's not a thing that cannot be accomplished.

Lingyuan: I want to be like you, grand master, and enter *samadhi;* please teach me.

Xuyun: Then you must watch the huatou.

Lingyuan: What do you call this huatou?

Xuyun: *Hua* is just wandering thoughts, like talking to yourself [when you're meditating]. So you must illuminate the state before wandering thoughts arise and examine what is your original face. This is called observing the huatou. If wandering thoughts have already arisen, you must still bring forth the correct thought, and the specious thoughts will perish by themselves. If you follow the wandering thoughts, sitting meditation will be useless. However, if you bring forth the correct thought [of using the method] but you're not earnest enough, the huatou will still be powerless; wandering thoughts will surely arise. When practicing, one needs to have a bold and persevering mind as if your parents have [just] died. An ancient worthy said, "It's like guarding the emperor's palace, closely guarding on the top of the palace wall." Another said, "If you haven't endured the bone-chilling winter, how do you expect to smell the fragrance of plum blossoms?" (Comment by Lingyuan: These words [of the ancients] were always said by the grand master in seven-day retreats.) If there are neither wandering thoughts nor the huatou, then sitting there with an empty mind is like a rock soaking in cold water. One can sit for countless aeons and still be useless. If you want to investigate Chan, then this is the only way. If you don't want to do it this way, then don't investigate Chan. One has to have this bold and persevering mind, like a single person fighting off ten thousand enemies—going straight forward without retreat and without letting loose. Reciting Buddha's name should also be like this; reciting mantras should also be like this. The earnestness of your mind of birth and death will increase day by day. If you can be like this, then your practice will progress.

PART FOUR

ATTAINING
THE WAY

from Retreat Talks by Master Sheng Yen

Translated by J. C. Cleary *with* Guogu

Preparing to Practice

GIVE YOUR BODY TO THE CUSHION

THIS IS THE FIRST MORNING of a seven-day intensive Chan meditation retreat. In Japanese Zen this is called *sesshin,* which comes from the Chinese *shexin,* meaning "to collect one's mind [into a continuous meditative stream]." Very simply, that's what we're here to do.

Some of you are attending retreat for the first time. For some this is an unfamiliar place. The noises of New York City never stop. Therefore it is normal to feel nervous or anxious. My best advice is to just relax.

For seven days you will also have your body to contend with. Most of you will suffer from leg and back pains. You may get tired or sleepy. Again, relax. Your body and your mind will adjust quickly if you do not resist. Make a firm commitment to focus, to leave thoughts of past and future outside these doors. You can and certainly will return to your issues after the retreat, but right now thoughts about them will hinder your practice.

At all times keep your mind on your method of practice. When wandering thoughts appear, do not follow them; simply recognize them and return to the method. Know that once you identify a wandering thought for what it is, you are no longer on that thought. If you can do this, I guarantee you will have no anxiety over wandering thoughts.

Decide now not to be concerned with concepts or physical sensations, both real and imagined. Just focus on the method. That is easier said than done, but if you can do it, time will fly. On the other hand, preoccupation with your thoughts and your body will cause the time to drag, and you'll experience a lot of discomfort.

Do not expect to gain anything. Forget any expectations you may have about practice. The practice itself is your goal, and by being here you have already achieved that. Continue to make it a reality. How effective would a worker be if the only thing he or she thought about was the check at the end of the month? So do not think about what you'll get by being here, or where you'll be after the retreat. Just focus on your purpose, which is to meditate.

So, this first day's theme is to relax your body and your mind. Take to heart the saying "Give your body to the cushion and your mind to the method." If you do that, the rest will take care of itself.

WHAT IS YOUR *BODHIMANDALA*?

I hope during this retreat that you will refrain from using your ears except to hear my instructions, refrain from speaking except during interviews, refrain from looking around except when walking or working. At all times, keep your eyes as you would while meditating, and that is to keep clear and wakeful, not to satisfy curiosity.

To cultivators of Chan, I give three guiding principles. First, relax your body and mind. Second, settle upon a practice method as soon as possible. Third, do not concern yourself with how well you are doing. If you follow these guidelines, your practice will be smooth and fruitful.

When you sit in meditation, relax your body from your head to your belly and to your legs. Your mind must not be tense or hurried, and always keep a patient attitude. If you sink into torpor or become scattered, or if your method is not going smoothly, just relax your body and your mind. Tensing will only add to your afflictions and waste time. Remember though, the purpose of relaxing is to further your practice, not to take it easy.

To relax and know that you are relaxed—this is the first step in cultivating practice. Relaxing starts with taking the correct posture and then sitting peacefully as if you have no concerns at all. So, if you discover that you are tense, first check your posture, then relax your mind.

The practice methods we commonly use are breath counting, reciting a buddha's name, investigating gong'an (Jap., *koan*) or hua-tou (Jap., *wato*), and silent illumination, or *mozhao* (Jap., *shikan-taza*). If you have been practicing a specific method, whether for a short time or many years, try to stay with it. Do not be casual about switching.

The third guideline is not to gauge your own progress. If your practice goes well, don't be elated. If it is not going well, don't get discouraged. Just be sure that you are practicing in accordance with the Dharma.

Starting this morning, before you sit, bow to your cushion and ask, "What is my *bodhimandala,* my place of practice, my site of enlightenment?" After sitting, adjust your posture so that your whole body is comfortable and as it should be. It is not necessary to sit in the full-lotus position—the main thing is to be stable. After your posture is correct, do not pay any more attention to your body; just keep your mind on your method.

If you do all of these things you will be practicing Chan.

PRINCIPLES FOR CULTIVATING PRACTICE

On retreat we need to observe the Chan principles for living, which are orderliness, cleanliness, tranquillity, and harmony.

Always maintain a sense of proper order and purity, whether in the Chan Hall, the dormitory, the dining hall, or the bathroom. Being orderly means being aware of the correctness of your environment—your personal space, your sleeping quarters, the dining room, and your meditation cushion. If you do this, when you return home you will surely have a more heightened awareness of order. Without being aware of yourself and your surroundings, how can you be aware of others?

In the Chan Hall, place personal articles between your mat and your neighbor's, not in front of or behind your mat. At the end of the sitting, properly fold your lap towel and place it squarely on the cushion, which in turn is placed squarely on the mat. As you pass through an area, pick up and dispose of any trash.

At the dining table, eat in silence and with full attention. Afterward, rinse your cup and bowl with a small amount of water, then drink the water, leaving behind no food particles. Place your drinking cup in your rice bowl and any fruit peelings or napkins into the cup; utensils go to the right of the cup. Use your napkin to wipe the table where you are sitting, leaving the tabletop spotless, as if it had not been used. Only then can we say that the meal has been finished. This mindful attention to eating is intimately related to Chan life and Chan practice—after all, if we eat in a disorderly way and leave a mess, what can be said of our minds?

If you are aware of the orderliness and cleanliness of your surroundings, you can be more aware of your inner mind. To purify your mind is no small task, but when your awareness functions in orderly surroundings, your mind can reflect that and become more tranquil. Tranquillity also means being silent and smooth in your motions. No matter what you are doing, be calm, careful, peaceful, and quiet. This way, even with a lot of people moving in a confined space, there will be order and tranquillity.

Do not harbor contradictions or antagonisms in your mind. If you cannot harmonize your inner mind, neither can you harmonize with those around you. If you resent your environment and find fault with others, your mind will surely lose its inner balance. Thus an ancient worthy said: "Be ever mindful of your own faults as you sit quietly, and when you are talking freely do not speak of the faults of others." Enmity and strife are not the way to harmonize: tolerance, persuasion, and explanation are better.

Chan practitioners must first do a good job on themselves. If there are no internal contradictions, then you will certainly be able to harmonize with yourself and with others.

THE TWIN PILLARS OF
CONCEPTS AND METHODS

Chan relies on the twin pillars of concepts and methods. Unless both are firmly in place and working together, your practice will lack a firm foundation. Without cultivating practice, studying Buddhist concepts is just an intellectual exercise; on the other hand, practicing the methods without understanding the concepts can lead you astray. Empowerment comes with clearly grasping the concepts and methods and using them to cultivate practice. So please attend to the Chan master's instructions, correct your concepts, and practice your method.

One basic concept is to offer your body and mind to the life of practice. This overcomes self-centeredness and all of its consequences. However hard you practice, cultivating from a self-centered stance can only result in more afflictions for yourself and others. Practice requires three kinds of "putting aside." First, putting aside the self; second, putting aside thoughts about goals; and third, putting aside past and future.

"The self" refers to the notion of "I" that we have as a result of possessing a body and a mind. "Goals" refers to the benefits of Chan practice, especially enlightenment. "The past and future" refers to our mental projections of things that no longer exist and things that do not yet exist. These three attitudes—belief in a self, desire for benefits, and being hostage to past and future—compose the central core of the personality and the essential elements of self-worth. They are the roots of misfortune, bringing with them affliction and bondage. Not putting them aside means that the most important result of Chan practice—enlightenment—will be beyond reach. To experience the benefits of Chan, you have to put these attitudes aside, at least temporarily.

Methods are the tools you use to correct yourself, to regulate your conduct, your speech, and your mind. Basically, we rely on the five precepts and the Eightfold Noble Path to correct our physical, mental, and verbal conduct. On retreat we also use sitting and walking meditation, prostration, and work to regulate bodily conduct. We restrict speech and chant scriptures to regulate our verbal conduct. We practice concentration, recite the Buddha's name, and investigate huatous to regulate our mind.

The mind is the most difficult to regulate—for this we use correct knowledge, correct mindfulness, correct concentration, and correct energetic progress. Day after day we monitor ourselves. From moment to moment we need to be aware of thoughts coming and going. Whether or not they are delusions, we must be aware of them. If a thought arises in a crude, careless way, after it disappears we must alert ourselves: "What was I just thinking?" If we can persevere, we will enjoy correct mindfulness all the time.

There are many methods to keep the mind correct. During everyday life you should practice like this: "Where is my body? Where is my mind? What are my hands doing? Does my mind know what my hands are doing? What is my mouth saying? Does my mind know what my mouth is saying?" An essential principle of Chan practice is not to let the activities of body, mouth, and mind become separated.

AN ISLAND OF TIME AND SPACE

When practicing on retreat, isolate yourself. First, drop everything from the past and everything related to the future. Create an island of time that separates you from before and after these seven days. Refrain from reading, writing, talking, and making phone calls. So far as the outside world is concerned, you did not exist before and you will not exist afterward. You are living on a virgin island with no knowledge of anything outside.

Unless you think like this, you will be dragging along a huge tail, carrying a lot of baggage, and it will be very painful. You will have come not to meditate but to indulge in false thinking. If any outside thoughts occur, tell yourself: "I was born on this virgin island. These outside thoughts have nothing to do with me."

Second, isolate yourself from others. Within this island of time, create an island of space, which only you inhabit. There is only one person on your cushion—you. Give your body to the cushion and your mind to the method.

If people walk by you or sit beside you, this has nothing to do with you. If someone behaves strangely, if someone runs in and does cartwheels, or if your back itches, you still respond the same way: "This has nothing to do with me!" There is a saying, "Fundamentally there is nothing in the world to be concerned about, but people make trouble for themselves." If the outside world does not influence your mind, nothing can disturb you.

Third, isolate yourself from your previous thought and from your succeeding thought. Good or bad, do not be concerned with them. Just take the present thought and tie it to the meditation method—that is what's most important. The past is gone, the present is dying, and the future is not yet. Regret, satisfaction, worries, expectations—these are all delusions; do not waste a second on them.

PRACTICING IN A GROUP

The advantage of practicing Chan on your own is that it is very free; it can be adjusted and arranged according to your mental and physical condition and your particular needs. The drawback is that for people who lack the ability to cultivate themselves and the mental power of self-control, it can be easy to lose track of the guidelines.

Practicing Chan in a group can be with or without a teacher, but both require guidelines for collective practice. The teacher has three functions: first, the teacher explains the concepts and methods of Chan to the group as a whole; second, based on the correct knowledge of the Buddhadharma and experience of Chan, the teacher gives specific meditation instructions and corrections to the group; third, the teacher works with practitioners individually or collectively to resolve difficulties that arise.

Some practitioners become aware of problems they are having and bring them to the attention of the teacher for help. In cases where students do not recognize their own problems, the teacher needs to recognize the student's problems, bring them to light, and provide help and correction.

Everyone who comes to retreat has a unique physical and mental condition. If the teacher's instruction is the same all the time, it might be of help to some, but that is almost like listening to a tape. There will be no way to address people's individual problems or prescribe the right "medicine" for them. For all of these reasons, receiving proper instruction is a necessary part of the retreat process.

Impermanence

THE FOUNDATION VIEW

On the practice path, there is no achieving undeserved success. Someone on retreat asked me, "Of the nine levels of meditative concentration, the highest is the *samadhi* in which sensation and conception are obliterated. How is this cultivated?" This is the *samadhi* of total extinction, the holiest of the four fruits of the Hinayana path, the so-called Lesser Vehicle. However, if you have yet to achieve the four absorptions (*dhyanas*) and the eight *samadhis*, how can you think of cultivating the ninth level? This is like building the top floor of a house before the foundation is in.

To learn Buddhism, you must start from the foundation view of impermanence. What is impermanence? It is suffering, it is emptiness, it is no-self, it is the absence of intrinsic identity. These are basic concepts of Buddhism and Chan. Impermanence is inherent in the cycle of birth and death. Our bodies, our minds, and our surroundings are impermanent. There is nothing that does not change. Some people say, "The changing moment itself lasts forever," but this view is alien to Buddhism. Buddhadharma holds that all mental and physical phenomena are impermanent, perpetually coming into being and extinguishing. Buddhadharma requires that we understand this.

When I asked a prominent gentleman why he entered Buddhism so late in life, he said that when his mother and elder brother died in quick succession, he felt a deep loss. Impermanence had touched him at the most painful point in his life. If we fail to reflect on impermanence, we are living a dream, because we really do not know what life holds for us. Someone who has never peeked through death's door and taken a look inside might feel immortal.

When I was young, I respected old Buddhist teachers. I also felt sorry for them because they were not far from death. Now my turn to be pitied has come! Impermanence is painful when we cannot get what we seek or we seek to hold on to what we have.

In the Three Kingdoms period following the Han dynasty in the third century, the general Cao Cao (pronounced *ts'ao ts'ao*) wrote this verse:

Human life in the world—
How much happiness can there be to it?
Happiness is like the morning dew,
And when it vanishes, how much we suffer!

Not a Buddhist, Cao Cao still had an insight that accords with Buddhadharma.

There is an intrinsic link between impermanence as suffering and impermanence as emptiness. Our environment and all phenomena in it exist only temporarily. They are like reflections of the moon on the water—empty, illusory forms. Not knowing that emptiness means impermanence, we cling to phenomena and bring suffering upon ourselves.

If we understand that life is impermanent, full of suffering, and void of intrinsic reality, our problems will mitigate and we will know a thing or two about "no-self." One student told me, "It's no use trying to avoid the inevitable, and it's no use pursuing what is not in one's karma. What I can get, I work for; what I can solve, I solve. The rest, I let go. If I can't let it go, I just accept it. My mind has become much calmer." Studying Buddhism has been very useful to him.

The *Diamond Sutra* speaks of formlessness. It points out that the four forms of self—oneself, others, living beings, life—are all derived from the idea of an independent, intrinsic identity. Because of this, "you" and "I" and "other living beings" are put in opposition. "Life" refers to the movements of "you," "I," and "living beings" in space and time. Foregoing this false self, you can witness formlessness, see your real nature, and open up to enlightenment.

Don't imagine that after a few retreats you will be enlightened. It's possible, but as long as the self form still rules and egocentrism is solid, how can you see your true nature?

Some people think: "I am selfish and clinging, but once I'm deeply engaged in the practice, the master just has to shout or hit me at the right moment, and then I'll be enlightened!" I really don't have this ability. Selfish clinging is deep-rooted and intimately linked to one's life. To overcome it, you must do the work yourself. All I can do is point out the way. "Where water goes, a channel forms." When the necessary work has been done, success will come; then all it takes is a light tap, and selfish clinging can suddenly be removed.

It is true that Chan espouses sudden enlightenment, but if I told you to stop discriminating and abide nowhere, could you do it? If you could, you would be suddenly enlightened. If not, every stirring of your mind is discrimination and clinging. If people who claim to be enlightened are still living with affliction and attachment, what's the difference between being enlightened and not being enlightened?

First, learn to abide nowhere. Abiding means holding on to your senses, your conditioned perceptions, and your preconceived ideas. Seeing, hearing, perceiving, and knowing—in reality they encompass the whole of spiritual, mental, and physical life. Clinging to any of this means there is abiding. Where there are concepts of self, there is abiding, and there is form. This is not no-self.

Abiding nowhere means having no discriminating thoughts. If you can refrain from discriminating, then you have no thoughts. If you have no discriminating thoughts, then you abide nowhere. If you abide nowhere, then you can be formless. If you can be formless, you will then see your true selfless nature.

The meditation method that we teach is an orderly process for helping you step-by-step until you reach the state of having no discriminating thoughts. We have thoughts all the time. When our scattered and chaotic mind is strong, these thoughts are illusions, the mind of affliction. After using the meditation method properly and consistently, you will gradually detach from the afflictions of greed, anger, ignorance, arrogance, and doubt.

Perhaps some people think that meditation is also a form of attachment. This is true, but it is not an attachment that brings affliction. On the contrary, it can relieve affliction. The meditation method is the Way.

To genuinely benefit from Buddhism, there is no other route except to walk on solid ground and start building from the foundation of understanding impermanence.

You can't enter the realm of enlightenment by just imagining it.

You must exert the patience it takes to meditate. The records of Chan, such as the *Record of the Transmission of the Lamp in the Jingde Era* and the *Five Lamps Meeting at the Source,* show that there are hardly any cases of great penetration and great enlightenment except through practice. Thus we have the admonition "If you don't endure the cold that pierces your bones, how can you smell the fragrance of the plum blossoms?"

You can't come to retreat as a caterpillar and in a few days go fluttering off as a butterfly. You must start with the basics, whether in concepts or in methods. It would be arrogant to claim attainment where there is none. If you seek followers but are not qualified, you will endanger them and yourself. To seek to rise but to fall instead is very unfortunate indeed.

BE MINDFUL OF IMPERMANENCE

When I was a child time passed slowly—I had to wait so long to be a year older. When I became an adult, time passed very quickly. Now I have lived sixty-three years in vain, and time flies ever faster. The Buddha spoke of impermanence, and the Chan patriarchs spoke of sudden enlightenment. If you do not study Buddhadharma, you will not know impermanence, and if you do not cultivate practice, you will not know sudden enlightenment.

When Shakyamuni Buddha first turned the Dharma Wheel at Deer Park, he taught impermanence. Before entering nirvana he reminded his disciples that "whatever is born must perish." Birth, death, and impermanence characterize worldly existence; it is only in the liberation of nirvana that birth and death perish. If you do not practice toward genuine realization, how can you escape the delusive snares of the demons of impermanence?

Every day, in the evening session, we recite Bodhisattva Samantabhadra's warning:

This day has passed.
Our lives too are closing.
Like fish in shallow water,
Joy will not last.
Let us work with pure effort,
As if our heads were aflame.
Be mindful of impermanence.
Beware of idleness.

Life is too short, and time passes too quickly; if we do not value the time and work as hard as we should, we will miss our chance. If we are alert to the brevity of life, we will not waste our precious time afflicting ourselves and others, dealing in affirmation and denial, benefit and harm, gain and loss. As you practice Chan, if every thought is imbued with a sense of impermanence, you will transform delusion into mindfulness.

There are people at this retreat who have practiced Chan for twenty or more years without losing faith—this is rare and precious, and there must be a profound reason. Many have stayed in temples and Buddhist centers and have gone to one or more intensive retreats a year. But did they practice every single moment during that time? In their ordinary lives most meditate an hour or so a day; otherwise they are busy with their lives, their families, their work; busy with delusions, afflictions, and boredom. What does it mean, then, to say that someone has practiced for twenty or more years?

During a seven-day retreat, even though you are in the Chan Hall from morning to night, please clarify for yourselves how much of this time is actually occupied by delusions, oblivion, and scattered thoughts. How much of this time is spent in wholehearted meditation? If you truly understood that the time you actually practice is really not that much, you would determine not to slacken and to begin making energetic progress.

So I ask all of you, before sitting, first bow to your cushion, your *bodhimandala*. At the same time say to yourself: "I vow to use all of my time on meditation." After you sit, make another vow: "I vow to put my whole being into my practice." In this manner, you will develop mindfulness and understand impermanence.

UNDERSTANDING IMPERMANENCE

When I was young, it seemed forever between birthdays; now each year flies quickly by. I turn around and twenty years are gone! From the perspective of cosmic time, a life is shorter than the blink of an eye. Buddhism teaches that all phenomena—all things seen, heard, thought, or experienced—are impermanent, arising and perishing in a fragment of time. When Shakyamuni Buddha first turned the Dharma Wheel at Deer Park, he expounded the doctrine of impermanence. During every evening service, we recite, "Be mindful of impermanence; be careful of idleness." The canon of Buddhism is full of admonitions about impermanence.

The time you have to practice is precious, fleeting. Once gone, it can never return. If you maintain a clear awareness of impermanence, you will not waste time engaging in vexing thoughts like jealousy, arrogance, or pointless criticism of others and self. Not only does this harm you, it also harms those you come in contact with. Therefore, keeping this mind of impermanence, you will work harder and practice better, and you will benefit yourself and others.

When you are drowsy during practice, think of impermanence—you will realize you have no time to waste sleeping; when distracted by a scattered mind, remember impermanence—you will realize there is no time to waste on scattered thoughts. Coming to retreat is a rare opportunity; make the best of it.

If you have been on many retreats and think you've been practicing seriously for years, this is self-delusion. If you consider one or two hours of daily meditation and a yearly retreat as continuous practice, you're mistaken. Most of your practice time, including now, you are lost in vexation, wandering thoughts, and drowsiness. Is this true practice? Great Chan practitioners never let their minds stray far from impermanence, and when not meditating, they use the teachings of the Buddhadharma to help themselves and others.

When you truly realize that life is impermanent and time is short, you will be able to practice consistently and hard. From now on, prostrate to your cushion, your *bodhimandala*, before sitting, to remind yourself of this. Vow to be diligent. After you sit down, make another vow not to anticipate the bell. Plunge wholeheartedly into the practice. You must do this, because life *is* impermanent and time *is* short.

While being mindful of impermanence, continue to relax your body and mind. It sounds inconsistent, but you must have an alert and diligent yet relaxed attitude. Tension will exhaust you. If you relax to the point of falling asleep, kneeling on the hard floor for a few minutes should wake you up. If merely drowsy, open your eyes wide and stare at the wall while you continue to meditate. That will help drowsiness subside.

Because our sense of time in daily life is slow, maintaining a mind of impermanence is difficult. We become complacent and think we have all the time in the world. Retreats equip us with knowledge and experience of impermanence that can only enhance our daily lives. Understanding impermanence does not mean taking license to do whatever we want, since "it is all going to end soon anyway." On the contrary—because we understand impermanence, we know we have no time to waste in idleness, especially in practice. I once met a man with only a few months to live who accomplished several years' worth of practice in those remaining months. If you can develop a similar attitude and apply it to practice, your progress will be quick and smooth.

Faith

THE MIND OF FAITH

Without a mind of faith, there is no practice. First, believe that you have good karmic roots. Buddha said, "To attain a human form is rare," and you have already attained that. Buddha said, "To hear the Buddhadharma is rare," and you have already heard it. Buddha said, "To practice the Dharma is difficult," and you have already begun to practice. Buddha said, "To meet an illuminated teacher is rare." An illuminated teacher is one who holds the correct views of Buddhadharma and has tasted at least some of the fruits of realization. I do not claim to be illuminated, but I am a teacher and I can give you some guidance.

Like the buddhas of the past, we should believe that we ourselves are sure to become enlightened. We must also believe that the Dharma expounded by the Buddha is genuine and true, that he would not deceive us. All the methods and ideas I teach on this retreat are based on the Buddhist teaching, the Buddhadharma. Ever since the time of the Buddha, the Sangha has transmitted the Dharma; therefore we believe in the Three Jewels—the Buddha, the Dharma, and the Sangha. If you believe in the Dharma, you must also believe in the Buddha and you must also believe in the Sangha. The Sangha includes the generations of illuminated teachers who transmitted the teachings of the Dharma, first expounded by the Buddha.

Your teacher should have a correct view of the Dharma, an illuminated mind, and the skill to guide others. If you accept the guidance of this teacher, he or she is your illuminated teacher. If not, even an illuminated teacher cannot help you. The Sangha includes generations of enlightened teachers from the Buddha onward, as well as the monks and nuns who upheld the Three Jewels, who practiced and spread the Dharma to help sentient beings. Your teacher, in fact, represents the Three Jewels.

"Without faith, a person cannot stand." Faith in the Three Jewels can come only from faith in yourself. The Dharma Jewel was expounded by the Buddha Jewel and transmitted by the Sangha Jewel. Without faith in the Buddha, there is no Dharma to learn; without faith in the Sangha, you cannot be taught the Dharma. Therefore, start with believing in yourself; next, believe in the Three Jewels. Thus it is evident that faith is the basis for practice.

Be prepared to accept a painful course of training. Only if you experience this pain can you become the most developed type of human. "If you don't endure the cold that pierces your bones, how can you smell the fragrance of the plum blossoms?"

On this retreat the environment, the necessities of life, and the practice methods have all been provided. Despite such great fortune, you must still train your own body and temper your own mind. Your legs, back, and feet will ache; you may feel numbness, discomfort, itching. Meditating all day, you will feel confined; you will feel discouragement and doubt. These sufferings may continue throughout the retreat. It may not be until near the end that your body and mind will adjust and things will go comparatively well.

Nevertheless, don't be anxious; don't expect disaster. Just give your body to the cushion and your mind to the method. Ignore wandering thoughts or anything else and you will be at peace. Thus you will quickly put aside problems of body and mind and not constantly struggle with affliction.

Now let us prostrate three times in homage to the Buddha. In doing this, you respectfully accept and uphold the Buddhadharma. Before sitting, always bow to your cushion, your *bodhimandala*, where you will consummate the work of the Way.

FAITH IN YOURSELF

There are many kinds of karmic obstructions—barriers that prevent us from improving our Chan practice. Among the most difficult to overcome are greed, hatred, pride, and self-pity. Greed and anger often spring from the same source—when we can't get what we want, desire can change to hatred. Pride and self-pity are like that too. When others don't share our high opinion of ourselves, very often we turn to putting ourselves down. It is the same negative energy, directed outwardly in one case, inwardly in the other. The root of these obstructions is lack of faith in oneself. Without faith in yourself and your abilities, you feel no recourse but to expect others to benefit you with their effort. This opposes the law of karma, wherein you reap what you sow.

If you can arouse humility and repentance, you will have a more receptive mind. With a receptive mind you will meet good teachers and be helped by them; your karmic obstructions will lighten. The instant your concept of self changes for the better, your ability to receive help will also increase. The best example of faith in oneself is the Buddha. After many years of practicing without finding liberation, Shakyamuni resolved to find the way. Armed only with his faith in himself, he attained liberation under the Bodhi Tree. His legacy is yours to inherit and embrace.

LEVELS OF FAITH

If you have practiced Chan for a number of years, there is no question that you have developed a mind of faith, otherwise you would not have persevered. But for those new to Chan, your faith in Buddhism or in your teacher may still be uncertain.

To follow and benefit from Chan, you need to believe that its concepts and methods are the most realistic and correct, that they are useful, and that the Buddhadharma has value. If you also have a

Chan teacher who is reliable and trustworthy, then you will have the foundation for a mind of faith—a Chan mind. If you practice with sincerity the principles and methods given by your teacher, the benefits of Chan will accrue.

There are several levels of faith. At the lowest level is blind faith—believing in something without understanding why. Next is admiring faith—knowing a belief or teaching is true but still seeing it as something lofty and out of reach. Then we have faith based on understanding—when reason and logic tell you to accept a teaching, and you act on it. Finally, there is experiential faith—when your experience confirms the theories and methods. Each succeeding level is a more secure basis for grounding one's faith; each succeeding level increases one's faith.

Learning to practice Chan is not unlike learning other skills: you must endure countless episodes of refining and polishing before the new skills are perfected. If you are determined to advance boldly and without fearing failure, you will establish a firm and solid mind of faith, one that grows with your practice.

Principles of Chan

THREE PRINCIPLES OF BUDDHISM

Buddhist practice rests on the three principles of discipline (*sila*), concentration (*samadhi*), and wisdom (*prajna*). Discipline includes precepts for living and for preparing oneself to commit to the Way by making vows. Concentration, or *samadhi,* broadly construed includes the meditative methods, but Chan patriarchs have said that *samadhi* is none other than the mind. It follows that cultivation of *samadhi* through meditation will lead to a clear, stable mind.

It is generally accepted that the cultivation of concentration leads to the third principle, wisdom. Other spiritual disciplines view wisdom in a different light. Their levels of deep meditative absorption lead to wisdom, insight, and mental stability but not to liberation in the Buddhist sense. The wisdom that Buddhism speaks of refers directly to the experience of buddha-nature.

In the *Platform Sutra,* Sixth Patriarch Huineng says that *samadhi* is *prajna* and *prajna* is *samadhi.* The essential theory states that there is no truly abiding self because nothing is permanent. When one practices *samadhi,* one directly experiences impermanence and opens the gate to *prajna.* Thus *prajna,* or wisdom, is the fulfillment of the complementary relationship between theory and practice. When *samadhi* accords perfectly with *prajna,* this is Chan wisdom.

The simple method of watching the breath is, in fact, contemplating impermanence. Breath, body movements, numbers, all continuously change from moment to moment. During meditation it is equally important to contemplate the impermanence of wandering thoughts, which continuously arise and perish. The idea of self is generated by thoughts, or rather from attachment to these thoughts. Once we experience their ephemeral nature, we also experience the ephemeral nature of the self. Thoughts have no independent existence, and neither does the self that identifies with them.

Practitioners of outer paths interpret *samadhi* as nonmovement of the mind, but even in that state there is still one thought. When even one thought remains, there still exists attachment to self. The experience of impermanence is even more important than trying to halt the thinking process. If we maintain an awareness of the impermanence of thoughts, we will see there is no self that attaches to these thoughts. We will be able to directly perceive each one as lacking a self-center. This in itself is wisdom.

Concentration and Wisdom Are One Essence

To practice Chan we begin with afflicted mind and learn to discipline it. We then concentrate the mind to unify it, and eventually we perceive the true nature of mind and realize enlightenment, which is the essence of Chan.

Discipline corresponds to the spirit of the Buddhist precepts that guide personal behavior. It also corresponds to the habits of normal daily living—maintaining an orderly, clean, tranquil, and harmonious environment.

Concentration means using methods of Chan to rein in and pacify the mind. The *Platform Sutra* of Huineng says that *samadhi* itself is *prajna*. This means that wisdom and concentration are not separate things. Apart from the mind, there is no *samadhi* and no *prajna*.

The third and paramount principle of Buddhist practice is wisdom. Wisdom is the direct experience of phenomena as precisely emptiness—the realization that self and all objects of the mind are empty and that emptiness is not separate from form. This understanding arises from a state free of afflictions and deluded thoughts.

Worldly methods of concentration do not free us from afflictions, and worldly wisdom does not lead to liberation. Only the union of *samadhi* and *prajna* in Chan or Buddhist wisdom, with its power to reveal our true nature, can bring release and liberation. Release and liberation are two aspects of one essence. Thus *samadhi* and *prajna* accord with each other. They are different yet one and the same, neither two nor one.

Wisdom means clearly understanding that all compounded things are impermanent and realizing that all things have no independent self. When you practice Chan, you contemplate the body and its actions and you see that they are impermanent; you observe thoughts coming and going and you see that they are impermanent. You know they have no fixed existence, no self, and thus you witness their empty nature. This is engendering wisdom through contemplation. Therefore selfless wisdom is the great concentration that comes from being free from affliction.

Concentration in Chan is not a state where there are no thoughts in the mind—the mind is not just blank. In Chan we avoid dwelling on forms and we merge with the suchness of everything, which is called buddha-nature (*tathagata-garbha*). The ordinary mind attaches to phenomena, and thoughts are stirred up by the forms they follow. The enlightened mind is neither moved by phenomena nor stirred by forms; it functions freely but abides nowhere. Not stuck at the level of discrimination and affliction—this is the pure mind of wisdom, responding to the myriad things and giving each its due.

Sudden enlightenment may be abrupt, but it is not easy to attain. It is terribly naive to believe it can happen without genuine cultivation. Without the methods of Chan guided by practical wisdom, one will practice blindly or be misled by wayward ideas.

In Buddhism there is worldly knowledge and transcendent knowledge. There is also the boundless wisdom (*samyak sambodhi*) of the buddhas of the highest attainment. This is the stainless, formless wisdom of the buddhas. Chan practitioners on the Path rely on this supreme source and the guidance of ancestral Chan masters. We take the words of the buddhas and Chan masters as our guide on the Path and as a mirror of our own minds. We feel secure in relying on these methods. With them we investigate our true nature and resolve the great questions of impermanence, the nature of mind, and enlightenment.

No Enlightenment without Discipline

As we have said, practice according to the Buddhadharma consists of none other than the three impeccable studies of discipline, concentration, and wisdom. Right now I want to talk more about the meaning of discipline. Discipline means not doing what you should not do and not failing to do what you should. From the point of view of karma, your actions have consequences and you will earn retribution. From the point of view of practice, negative actions create mental chaos, and a chaotic mind cannot attain wisdom. In this state you would just be another sentient being trapped in ignorance. Discipline is the basis for achieving mental balance and stability and therefore is a prerequisite for liberation.

On retreat we have rules of conduct. They include silence, eating vegetarian meals, separation of the sexes, and not concerning oneself with others. This discipline is a foundation on which to build practice while on retreat. Energetic practice therefore implies upholding discipline. I have asked you to give your body to the cushion and your mind to the method. If you have not at least tried to do this, isn't this a violation of discipline? If you work at it day by day, in the end you will succeed. We say the mind is a "mind monkey" or "thought horse" because, like monkeys and wild horses, the mind is very difficult to tame and control. Enlightenment is not possible in a state of scattered mind. Only when you collect your attention again and again from wandering and achieve a peaceful and focused state will you have a chance of attaining enlightenment. This is taming the "mind monkey" and reining in the "thought horse."

Many people go on retreat to get "enlightened." Someone asked me, "Shifu, please help me experience enlightenment." But if I could give you enlightenment, would this be my enlightenment or yours? I can teach you Buddhadharma, but awakening to the knowledge of the buddhas requires your own cultivation and realization. There is hope of opening the wisdom eye, of "breathing through the same nostrils as the buddhas of the past, present, and future," only when you stop the deluded mind and shatter the self-referential view of body, mind, and world.

To become enlightened, you must uphold discipline and intensively cultivate meditative concentration. Some people may say, "That way is gradual enlightenment; I want sudden enlightenment!" Since I have been directing retreats, I have met too many people who are in a great hurry to find enlightenment. When I ask why, many say they think their problems will vanish once they become enlightened. I tell them that the more they hurry, the longer it will take to become enlightened.

Some people even demand of me: "Are you enlightened?" "Was it sudden or was it gradual?" "Did you do it on your own or did someone help you?" To all such questions, my answer is not to answer. If I say I am not enlightened, you will ask me what I use to guide people. If I say I am enlightened, there is nothing I can tell you that you can hear or see.

But I can tell you this: None of the ancestral teachers of Chan, going back to Shakyamuni Buddha, achieved sudden enlightenment without practice. After he left home Shakyamuni Buddha practiced for many years. On the other hand, the 120-year-old Subhadra realized enlightenment after hearing just one sutra by the Buddha. This may seem to have been very easy, but Subhadra was a great Brahman who had practiced for decades before becoming a disciple of the Buddha. Sixth Patriarch Huineng also seems to have gotten enlightened without practice. In reality his mind was very steady and clear ever since he was very young. His work was so pure and single-minded it is no mystery that he became enlightened suddenly.

Practicing the Buddhadharma gives you no undeserved advantage. If it did, the law of karma would be violated. Those who think this way have very wrong notions of causality, and some are nihilists who even deny cause and effect. In the Middle Way practice you get only as much as you put in. That's why the perfection diligence is so important.

Chan practice cannot be faked, and it cannot be watered down. All the way through it's like two hard objects colliding. The results you get are proportional to the effort you put in. On the path to enlightenment, no one gets by with trickery.

Some think that Pure Land is a shortcut—just recite the Buddha's name and you get reborn in Amitabha's Western Paradise. The other day someone told me he wanted to become a monk. I asked him why he didn't just go to a Pure Land temple and recite

Amitabha Buddha's name. He said, "If I died and went to the Pure Land, I don't know how long it would be before I could return." I asked him, "Don't tell me you are so reluctant to leave this world." He replied, "It's not that, it's just that I cannot bear to see the sufferings of sentient beings. By the time I went to the Pure Land and practiced until I reached the stage of no falling back, then returned here on the boat of compassion, who knows how many times this world would have perished?" This kind of compassion is really moving! Still, for people whose faith in their own power is not strong enough, relying on Amitabha's power to deliver them to the Pure Land is realistic.

Pure Land practitioners whose faith and vows are correct are likely to be more devoted, more compassionate, more giving, and wiser about the workings of karma than some so-called Chan practitioners. Chan people are frequently selfish and small-minded, eager to escape reality. They have been harmed by misreading ideas from Chan books and led astray by the word *enlightenment.* They have yet to give rise to the bodhisattva's altruism, which seeks enlightenment for the sake of all sentient beings. Some want me to help them gain enlightenment as soon as possible, after which they say they will certainly support me. This is opposite to the principle that selfishness must be put down before one can be enlightened. With such thinking, they are not even practicing the Small Vehicle of the Hinayana, not to mention the Great Vehicle, the Mahayana.

Therefore we need to first establish the correct view. We must walk on solid ground and work hard at the three studies of discipline, concentration, and wisdom.

Discipline in Buddhism can mean observing the five precepts, but on the Mahayana Way, it also means following the bodhisattva precepts. To give rise to the aspiration of enlightenment but not to serve all sentient beings is to deviate from the bodhisattva precepts. To uphold them, you should make it your essential duty to benefit sentient beings.

Concentration in traditional Buddhism refers to the nine stages of concentration (or *samadhi*), ceasing mental activity, avoiding becoming detached from desires, and entering into peaceful extinction of the deluded mind. Concentration in Mahayana Buddhism means that the mind is undisturbed by internal states or external objects, so that even as you respond to the sentient beings with compassion and wisdom, your mind is unfettered. You may have no afflictions when in concentration, but if they return when you come out of concentration, you are not yet liberated. Thus, in the Mahayana, the Sanskrit word *samadhi* means much more than mere concentration; it is a state where your mind is peaceful and stable at all times and in all places. It is like a clear mirror, reflecting images without waves of affliction. This requires scrupulous practice, and while meditation is the main means of cultivation, all the circumstances of life are used to refine the mind.

I urge you now to make an absolute determination to put aside the scattered and seeking mind. Discard illusions one after another as they arise. Don't be upset by scattered thoughts—just immediately return to the practice and all will be well. If you maintain discipline and practice concentration, in the long run your attainment gets more and more profound. Eventually, selfless wisdom is sure to appear, and that is the true enlightenment.

REINING IN AND PACIFYING THE MIND

In Chan we practice toward self-mastery so that we will no longer be subject to external circumstances and to the comings and goings of internal afflictions. To help you with this, I give you two key principles: reining in the mind, which means bringing your mind back from clinging to external objects, and pacifying the mind, which means settling your mind that is floating about here and there.

In Japanese the seven-day Zen retreat is called *sesshin,* a translit-eration of the Chinese *shexin. Sesshin* has two meanings: one is "gathering in"; the other is "unbroken continuity." Thus the goal of *sesshin* is to gather in the mind from its illusions and attachments and to make it a steady stream of no-delusion-arising. Without reining in the mind, you are a wandering ghost, chasing the mind's ceaseless waves and currents.

Pacifying the mind also has two meanings: one is calming the mind that is awash with afflictions and vexations; the other is liber-ating the mind from all discriminatory thought, thus achieving no-mind. When your mind is settled, it is relaxed, at peace—this is meditative concentration. When there is not even a mind that can be pacified, you attain true mastery and see your buddha-nature— this is the discovery of the selfless mind that abides nowhere.

Unable to pacify their minds, ordinary people feel fear, worry, sorrow, hopelessness, and other negative emotions. As Chan practi-tioners we have concepts and methods that help us reach the goal of gathering in and pacifying the mind.

At a higher level, no-self is not even having a mind that can be pacified. All phenomena, whether mental or external, arise and per-ish in less than the blink of an eye. Inhabiting the false realm of delusion, they are characterized by impermanence. When we truly understand impermanence, we will see that there is no abiding self; we will not be blown around by the winds of circumstance.

The methods of pacifying the mind are twofold: direct and indirect. The direct method of pacifying the mind is simply to put down all illusions. You practice mindfulness, reflect, and become aware of mind itself. Then the false mind will dissolve like a petty thief in the dark. The indirect method is to use the techniques of Chan: breath counting, reciting the Buddha's name, investigating gong'an or huatou, and doing prostrations are all effective methods. Take your troubled mind and expose it to the method. After long practice, you will discover the realm where there is no mind to be pacified.

False thoughts are like willow fuzz drifting in the air—they stick like lint to whatever they can. So if you let the willow fuzz stick to your method, the agitated mind will also become pacified.

NOT LETTING POISONS ENTER YOUR MIND

In his *Exhortations on Investigating Chan,* Master Boshan said, "The various poisons entering the mind result from being disturbed by deluded thoughts." There are three stages of practice in which the mind cannot be poisoned by deluded thoughts:

First, when you are fully engaged in practicing Chan, deluded thoughts are displaced by the method itself; even if they arise, they have no opportunity to take shape.

Second, when the enlightened state appears before you, deluded thoughts do not arise and the miscellaneous poisons are cut off until the mind returns to the ordinary state.

Third, upon realizing complete and great enlightenment, the crazy chaotic mind comes to a stop and the various poisons can no longer disturb the mind.

Aspects of Chan Meditation

TO BECOME RIPE AND EXPERT

When you learn a method of Chan meditation, you should use that method to go from being raw and naive to being ripe and expert. This cultivation of sitting meditation, we call practice. If you have questions, ask a knowledgeable teacher. If the teacher cannot help, you must rely on yourself to make the proper adjustments to your practice or to your mental state. Practice does not mean relying on your teacher to tell you everything. When you begin, your practice will not be very pure or thorough. After practicing for some time, relying on the wisdom of others before you, you will be able to add to and guide your own practice. You will then become completely pure, content, and thoroughly proficient.

RELAXING

In the course of the seven-day retreat, I may teach several meditation methods, but with just two goals in mind: the first is to help you relax your body and mind; the second is to help you pacify and stabilize your body and mind.

In reality these two goals are aspects of the same thing. If you can relax, you will be stable and at peace, and if you are stable and at peace, you will relax. But the place to start is relaxing. You could say that peace and stability are the result of relaxing. If you can relax your body and mind, your vexations are sure to be reduced, your pressures and burdens will be lightened, and your capacity for wisdom will be enhanced. With mind and body relaxed, your attention will be concentrated, your body functions will be balanced, and your mind will be calm and peaceful.

People sometimes recite the Buddha's name and transfer the merit to others in order to create good karma for sentient beings. While this is useful, its effect is indirect. However, if we can relax our bodies and our minds, and as a result change our words, actions, and disposition, this will be more directly useful to ourselves and to others.

Strenuously seeking good things and avoiding bad things will create a lot of tension. So avoiding both of these extremes can go a long way toward relaxing our bodies and minds in daily life. There is a karmic reason for every occurrence in our life. Therefore, as you encounter each one, deal with it calmly and serenely. Thus it is easier to be relaxed. This is an example of practice and daily living exemplifying Chan.

MEDITATING ON THE BREATH

Meditating on the breath is a method for concentrating the mind. There are in general two approaches to meditating on the breath. One is to pay attention to the breathing process itself. In this method, you place your mental focus entirely on observing the length of the breath or on the subtle movements of the abdomen. In some practices the focus is on the passage of air through the nostrils. In maintaining such awareness, do not attempt to control the rhythm of your breath or your moving abdomen. Simply be aware of the relationship between breath and your point of focus. Although this method can make you feel stable and comfortable, it is difficult to move beyond that point.

That is why I usually advise the second approach, counting breaths. This requires that you count your breath in cycles of ten. When you start, on the first exhalation, mentally recite the number one. Maintain your awareness on the number until the next exhalation, and then count two. Do this silently up to ten, and then begin again. When counting, do not concentrate on your abdomen or the length of your breath. Instead, breathe normally, and when exhaling, focus on the current number. While you are counting, wandering thoughts will come up. The advantage of this method is that you will quickly notice their intrusion and be reminded to return to the count. When you notice that you have lost count or are scattered, return to your breath and begin at one again. Do this for the entire sitting period.

Ordinarily you count the out-breaths, but some people prefer to count their in-breaths. For most people the out-breath is longer, but others take a slower in-breath. You should count whichever breath is the slower one. Sometimes you are so scattered you cannot even get to ten or you repeat a number or you count past ten. If this occurs without improvement, try the following alternative: first count even numbers backward from twenty to two, changing numbers with each exhalation; then count odd numbers backward from nineteen to one. Since it requires more concentration, this method may help to lessen scattering

Here are some important practice points: First, after settling into the correct posture, relax. Tension, whether physical or mental, is a detriment to practice. It leads to resistance, which causes exhaustion, and you cannot concentrate if you are tired. Second, disengage your mind from any concerns other than the practice method before you. You will have wandering thoughts anyway, but if you determine to concentrate on the method, this will help dispel scattering. Third, be patient. Do not anticipate or push for results. Simply persevere. The practice itself is the result. That is the Chan attitude.

Give your body on the cushion and your mind to the method! This is the foundation for effective meditation.

STAGES OF MIND TO SELFLESS WISDOM

The teachings of Chan enable us to clearly understand the need to put aside self-centered ways of acting and thinking. But the teachings alone are not enough. We also need techniques to put the teachings into practice. So concepts and methods work together in Chan to help us practice. First we need concepts to redirect our attitudes; then we need meditation methods to put the ideas into practice.

Now I will discuss the stages your mind can pass through to arrive at selfless wisdom. When you first take up the method, the mind is like a caged monkey whose eyes and ears are focused outside. Your task is to take this chaotic monkey-mind and focus it on the meditation method. This is easier said than done, but having taken up the method, you are at least in the first stage. Take your scattered mind and place it on the method. Allow the chaos to gradually diminish, but you should not actively hope that stray thoughts will lessen, as this hope itself is a delusion.

When you become aware of a wandering thought, just return to the method—patiently bring the method to bear, time and time again. Start the sequence all over from one. Don't think of this as a defeat, don't regret it, and don't blame yourself. Realizing that you had a stray thought shows that you are engaged, and you should feel encouraged by that.

The second stage is quieting down the confusion in the monkey-mind. Figuratively, we get the monkey to cover its eyes and ears; though the mind is still restless, it is at least blind and deaf to the outside, reducing the disturbance of external objects. The more you focus on counting the breath, the less room there will be for outside thoughts. Even though you still have illusory thoughts, there aren't as many as before. The breathing is there, and though illusory thoughts come and go, the counting is not interrupted.

In the third stage you leash the monkey-mind to a post so that it cannot dash back and forth in confusion in the cage. It must obediently stick to the meditation. This means that you just consistently return to the method when stray thoughts come up. The counting continues naturally without interruption, and there are some illusory thoughts, but they pass in a flash and you don't remember them.

In the fourth stage of unified concentration, not only is there no involvement with external objects, even internal objects are abandoned. The mind monkey has finally quieted down and, in fact, is nowhere to be seen. There are no miscellaneous thoughts at all, other than your counting and your mental activity is concentrated solely on the meditation method. The counting of the breaths is continuous—every strand in place. You will feel very comfortable and very happy—your mind will be unburdened, and you may not even be aware of your body.

At the fifth stage, awareness of the breath is still there, the sense of self is still there, but the counting has stopped. It's not that you deliberately stopped it, but your breathing is so rarefied that there's nothing to count—you're still doing meditation work, but the counting is gone.

At the sixth stage the body and the mind, the internal self and the external surroundings, are all still there, but they are no longer seen as separate. Body and mind are unified, internal and external are unified, the previous thought and the successive thought are unified. The unification of the thought stream occurs when all thoughts are connected to the same content—the method itself. At some point, however, thoughts will neither arise nor disappear; there is no before or after and no feeling of time or space. You have entered the precious oneness of stable meditative absorption.

But this is not enlightenment. When both internal and external are emptied out at once, when oneness is shattered, then selfless wisdom appears. When there is no internal or external and no clinging to the in-between, this is enlightenment.

These are typical stages you can pass through on the way to unified concentration, but while meditating, you shouldn't think about what stage you're in. If you do, that puts you right back in the first or second stage.

Which stage is your monkey-mind in right now? Are you focused outside the cage? Are you still putting up a struggle, not leashing yourself to the method? If so, you must give up the struggle and put aside the myriad thoughts before unified concentration can appear. Only then will the burden of your body and mind diminish and eventually melt away.

Therefore, to meditate to the point where scattered thoughts become fewer and fewer, first we rein in our six sense faculties—eyes, ears, nose, tongue, body, and mind. The eyes don't see, the ears don't hear; sensations of the body and other faculties don't react to stimuli. Because stray thoughts are news brought in through the sense faculties, after they are shut off, all sorts of internal false thoughts will subside. As they gradually lessen, the mind will gradually stabilize. At that point it is easier to recognize your own character and tendencies, what sort of person you really are. The more we truly understand ourselves, the more we can make our moral character sound and whole.

Now I ask you all to pay keen attention to understanding and practicing this method and to match your practice with this monkey-mind analogy.

THE FULL MOON OF AWAKENING

The things we teach are many: sitting postures, movements, ways of walking and prostrating, guides to contemplation and energy. These are all for tempering and harmonizing the body as well as retrieving a mind lost in illusion.

For beginning meditation, we teach contemplation by breath counting. This means breathing naturally and putting the power of your attention into counting your breaths. It does not mean that you focus on breathing itself, whether coarse or fine, deep or shallow, fast or slow. Mentally count every breath out, starting with number one, continuing to ten, and then starting over again at one. Generally you just count exhalations, not inhalations. Breathe naturally. Do not try to expel all the air in your lungs, as this is unnatural, nor should you inhale too much, as this will produce a bloated feeling.

If at any time you feel that you are trying to control your breathing or are having difficulty breathing, stop counting breaths and just focus on your breath moving in and out. An example of controlling your breathing is when you continue exhaling after the count is completed. This can cause unnatural changes to your breathing rhythm.

If counting breaths causes breathing difficulties for you, instead count invocations of the name of Amitabha Buddha or Guanyin

(Avalokiteshvara) Bodhisattva. (For example, "Amitabha Buddha, one, Amitabha Buddha, two, and so on. This method allows your breathing to occur naturally and of its own accord.)

When your scattered thoughts are reduced somewhat and your mind is steadier, you can use the huatou method and continuously work on sayings such as "Who am I?" "What is *wu* (Jap., *mu*)?" or "Who is reciting the Buddha's name?"

Using a huatou is not just being mindful of the saying—you must strive to learn its meaning. You must recite the saying and fill your mind with it as if penetrating its meaning were your life's goal. When you put effort into this practice, it is quite possible that you will constantly come up with answers. These answers may be your own, you may have read them in books, or you may have heard them somewhere. In reality, they are not all genuine answers. Whatever answer occurs to you, you must tell yourself: "This is not it; I need to inquire further." Time after time you must discard the answers you come up with; you must pursue your inquiry without interruption. Only with this kind of effort will you be able produce the doubt mass that can energize you to push aside the clouds and see the full moon of awakening. Whatever method you use, do not hope to achieve quick results. Remember that using the method sincerely and properly does not guarantee anything else. The practice is itself the goal.

Chan practitioners must have faith in the Three Jewels—the Buddha, the Dharma, and the Sangha. The Buddha experienced and transmitted the Dharma. Without the Buddha, there would be no Dharma, and without the Sangha, there would be no community to uphold, cultivate, and transmit the Dharma. Therefore we can only enter the realm of Chan after we have complete faith in the Three Jewels.

Besides having pure faith in the Three Jewels, you must also have faith in yourself—that you have good karmic roots for studying the Dharma and that you are able to practice Chan. Do not underrate yourself or harbor doubts, otherwise you will give up when you run into difficulty. That you have come to retreat for seven days is a good sign that you do have faith in yourself.

OBLIVIOUS AND SCATTERED MIND

Most of you have adjusted to the pains and discomforts of sitting, but there are still some who can't dispel an oblivious or scattered mind. Oblivious means that your mental energy is deficient; scattered means that your mind is drifting without focus. Early in the retreat, sinking into oblivion was probably due to tiredness from your hectic outside life. But if you follow my advice to make progress energetically and meditate like a fine stream, you will be able to preserve your energies. Making progress energetically just means persevering in your efforts without giving up. If you are doing this but still sink into oblivion, there are three possible causes:

First, your posture is incorrect: you are letting your neck droop; you are lowering your head, bending your waist, or failing to keep your back straight. Bad posture will make your breathing sloppy and without power—this could create a shortage of oxygen and bring on torpor. The correct posture is to keep your waist straight, without thrusting out your chest. Align your spine, your neck, and your head, like a puppet dangling on a string. The head should be neither raised nor lowered, the lower jaw tucked in. If you can sit like this, you won't be short of breath and you will be more alert.

Second, when you sit for a long time, as if you were a dead log, and do not experience "good" states, your mind will fatigue. You're sitting there like a hen in the same old nest, on the same old egg; there seems to be no hope of hatching a chick, so you might lose faith to some degree and become lethargic.

Third, if you are not clear about the methods of Chan, or have no confidence in them, you will be unsteady about how to practice. This can make you lazy and cause you to sink into oblivion.

If none of these causes explains your problem, most likely you have become subconsciously lazy and negligent. At such a time, it is best not to sit in the standard crossed-legged way but to kneel on the floor, with your hands joined and your eyes open wide and looking straight ahead. You may feel a bit refreshed, but after a while your knees may hurt a little. If you can tolerate it, this may help you preserve mental clarity.

A scattered mind is somewhat different from an oblivious one. When you are scattered, you cannot use the meditation technique with any power. It could be due to psychological or physical factors. If your scattered mind perturbs you to the point of being unable to meditate, then you should go outside the Chan Hall and do walking meditation or do prostrations before the Buddha statue. Proceed slowly as you walk or prostrate and focus very clearly on your physical movements and your sensations. Be clearly aware of the rising and falling of your thoughts. When your energy gradually becomes more relaxed and you feel less scattered, resume your sitting.

The method for dealing with scattering is expressed in the classic admonition "Do not fear thoughts arising, just fear that you will be slow to awaken to them." If you become aware of your mind becoming scattered and confused, then you have already pulled back. Just immediately return to the method and let correct mindfulness reassert. Just keep doing this. Don't worry about scattering and confusion: put your attention on the meditation method and you will be fine.

Two of the hardest things to overcome in meditation practice are scattered mind and oblivious mind.

Scattered mind is drifting from one disconnected thought to another, without focus. When the mind is scattered, your practice is at best spotty, with intervals of confusion and wandering thoughts. At the extreme, the method has been displaced completely and you are completely scattered. Scattered mind is usually caused by an improper understanding of how to use the method. Other contributing factors are mental fatigue and laziness. If scattered mind frequently occurs, the first thing to do is relax your body and mind. In other words, take a rest. Consciously put the method aside and take a break. If laziness is the root of your problem, you'll be completely immersed in your wandering thoughts and not even realize that you've lost the method. For practice to be useful, once you realize you've lost the method, you must will yourself to return to it.

Oblivious mind is lethargic and deficient in awareness. Because the mental and/or physical energies are flagging, the mind cannot hold on to the method. This can even result in falling asleep. Scattering and oblivion can occur simultaneously and even feed off each other. Understanding the three basic aspects of any practice method can help you overcome both scattering and oblivion. These three aspects are contemplation, awareness, and attention focus. Contemplation means that you are actively using a meditation method. Awareness means that you know you are using the meditation method. Attention focus means that if you stray off the method, you will immediately realize it and quickly refocus your attention.

To use an analogy, if contemplation is like walking down the road in a concentrated, attentive manner, then awareness is in knowing that you are doing this; you are observing yourself walking. Attention focus occurs when you notice that you have taken a wrong turn, or your pace slackens, and you immediately refocus your attention on walking correctly. Whichever meditation you use requires these three principles: contemplation, awareness, and attention focus. Keep them in mind as you prepare to practice and they are bound to help you sit better.

ILLUMINATION WITHOUT EFFORT

To achieve a concentrated state of mind when you sit, you must pass through three levels. The first is called "picking it up," which means to return to the method over and over. In other words, if gaps or interruptions occur, you just keep returning to the method. The second level is contemplation, which occurs when there are no gaps in your method and it goes smoothly and continuously. If your contemplation continues on a smooth course without interruptions, you may reach the third level, illumination. It is the clear awareness that you are practicing the method. Of the three, illumination is most important.

When you are working smoothly on all three levels, you are truly using the method correctly. During such times, speaking of scattered mind is irrelevant, since there will be no scattering. Working on all three levels will also help you to overcome drowsiness. Sometimes, however, the best thing to do is rest. As of now, most of you should be concerned with the first level, namely, taking up the method. Don't be swayed by tempting thoughts. Just continuously bring yourself back to the method.

Whichever method you use—counting the breath, huatou, *shikantaza*—point your attention inward; the light of awareness needs to reflect back to illuminate the mind. Therefore, while meditating you should know whether you are dull, scattered, or really on the method—this itself is cultivation.

In breath counting, for example, you will naturally be aware that you are counting your breaths. It is not a direct awareness but peripheral, indirect, unintentional. This awareness is illumination. It should be present no matter which method you use. I should make clear that illumination is not concentration. Concentration demands energy, but illumination is effortless. It rises of its own accord as a natural part of the method. It is like a mother who is busy while her child plays nearby. Although not watching the child directly, she is always aware of the child. After you have spent considerable time practicing a method, illumination will be so strong that you will no longer be aware of external stimuli. You will be close to that level beyond awareness of space and time, where thoughts are minimal and the body ceases to be a burden. This is effective practice indeed.

CENTERING

When we engage in practice, whether standing or sitting, mindfulness requires that we be properly centered. This starts with having your center of gravity below the waist. When sitting in meditation, if you feel your mind and vital energy (qi) dissipating, make a conscious effort to place your center between your buttocks and the cushion. If you feel pressure in your head or blockage in your chest, you should put the feeling of the center on the soles of your feet.

The position of the hands when sitting should be just below the navel. The curved left palm should rest on the curved right palm, the thumbs touching to form an oval. This will enable the mind to concentrate and settle down. It will also cause the sense of the body's center to naturally follow the hands and settle below the waist.

When standing in the Chan Hall or before the Buddha shrine, listening to a lecture, or speaking with your teacher, the same principle applies: locate your center below your waist or on the soles of your feet. The difference is with the hands. When standing, the right palm should be placed over the left palm. This will keep your mind and your vital energy focused.

Finally, be sure to relax the muscles at the point where you have placed the feeling of the center.

CLEARING THE FOGGY MIND

Someone asked me: "I have practiced breath counting to the point that I did not know whether or not I was breathing and the count wasn't there anymore. When I suddenly discover that I am still breathing, ten minutes or more have gone by. Is this entering *samadhi*? Was I still on the method, or did I lose it?"

This situation can be good, or it can indicate problems. When your breathing slows down to the point where your mind is very pure and there are no stray thoughts anymore, naturally there will be no way to find a number to count. This state of affairs means that you are still on the meditation method. If you were an expert rider galloping astride a powerful horse, the rapport between you and the horse could be so close that the two of you are like one and you forget each other; of course this is a good situation.

I have mentioned before that the essential points of practicing a method are contemplation, awareness, and attention focus. When "horse" and "rider" merge, the power of awareness is very strong and you don't need contemplation or attention focus because the three of them are already going forward together.

But it can also happen in counting breaths that you become lazy and scattered and you content yourself with a spacious feeling of peace. Or perhaps you're just not getting enough oxygen. It is also possible that your bodily strength is lacking and you are tiring. At such a time you are not aware of any scattered thoughts, your breathing is very rarefied and weak, and there is no way to keep count. Your mind seems to be plunged into a thick gray fog. This is not entering *samadhi;* this is slipping into oblivion. You are not in deep sleep but dozing off at a shallow level. Naturally, this is not doing Chan work.

Still, don't concern yourself with whether this is good or bad. As soon as you discover yourself slipping into dullness, immediately return to the meditation method—this is the attention-focus principle. Quickly move your eyeballs, your head and neck, and both shoulders a few times very lightly. Then take three deep breaths to mobilize your energy and take up the method again.

Some people are practicing gong'an or huatou, using the whole of their bodies and minds, and even the whole of the universe, throwing themselves into the question. The result can be that they feel as though they were in a thick fog. Is this the feeling of the doubt mass? There is a clear difference between the feeling of being in a fog and the experience of the doubt mass. Fogginess indicates confusion about your mental state and your practice method. You just feel that there is something covering your mind's eye and you don't know what it is.

On the other hand, generating the doubt mass does not mean harboring suspicious doubts in the ordinary sense. Rather, it means that you know very clearly that you are asking an extremely serious, extremely important question, and you hope to find the answer. But it is also like bumping into a silver mountain or an iron wall—no one answers, and there's nowhere to get a grip. But you truly believe that the answer is in the question you are investigating. At this moment you have cast your whole body and mind, and even the whole universe, into the gong'an or huatou. You are so immersed in it that there is no more distinction between inside or outside, body or mind, host or guest. This is called the doubt mass; when it shatters, enlightenment appears before you. If the doubt mass disperses before being shattered, then you will need to take up the method again. I should mention that pouring all of your energy into the question is appropriate during times of intensive Chan cultivation but is usually not appropriate for ordinary life.

When you are immersed in a gong'an or huatou, you may feel that your mind is like a fly that has fallen into a glue pot and is thrashing around desperately. Instead of a mass of doubt, all you feel is a mass of confusion. At such a time you are not actually doing Chan—rather, you are sunk in oblivion and illusions and your mind is like a dense fog. When you become aware of this, immediately massage your neck and the muscles around your eyes with soft gentle movements. Open your eyes wide and look clearly in front of you. Then you can put your attention back on the meditation method.

INVESTIGATE ONE SAYING

The ancient Chan masters often advised their disciples to investigate a single gong'an or huatou throughout their life, even after enlightenment. The idea was to devote one's practice to a single question, to inquire into it continuously, to come to grips with it, and finally to resolve it. For example, "Who is reciting the Buddha's name?" or "What is my original face before I was born?" or just "*Wu?*" Such is the power of a single question that it can cut through the snare of affliction and break the cycle of birth and death. In one single gong'an or huatou one can find peace and realization, unstained by the slightest defilement. With this practice, wherever you are, you put your complete attention on the question and dig into it. This is called "investigating" Chan.

When you practice gong'an or huatou intensely, there should arise a feeling of doubt, because your mind is ceaselessly asking itself a question that needs an answer. Because illusory thoughts may interrupt your investigation, you hold steadfastly to the question and pursue it with all of your might. However, you have to really come to grips with it. Just mechanically asking the question, without really looking into it, will not generate great doubt. Trying to find a rational answer will lead you totally astray—the question will not yield to conceptualizing.

The key is to generate doubt, which does not mean skepticism in the usual sense. This doubt comes from the conviction that the issue before you is of the greatest consequence and you have nowhere else to turn for the answer. This kind of doubt comes from a very strong faith in Buddhism and the method of Chan. So your doubt keeps you digging into the question: "What is the answer? I want to know right now, I have to know, I must know—ultimately, what is this?" This is the feeling of doubt in the Chan sense.

Suppose you are investigating "*wu.*" You ask yourself, continuously and with energy, "What is *wu?*" or just "*Wu?*" After a while it is like being given a solid iron ball and told that if you can crack it open, you will find inside a lifetime of peace and security, absolute freedom, and all forms of skillful means. If you fail, you will bring disaster upon yourself and end up at a dead end. Wouldn't you be eager to take this iron ball of *wu* and find some way to penetrate it? There is nobody who can do it for you, so all you can do is keep on asking, "What is *wu*?" We know, of course, that there is no iron ball and there is nothing behind *wu*. There is only the Chan method of investigating the nature of mind. It can move you forward in your practice, but you need to hold on to *wu* day and night, questioning it without a break. This is the feeling of doubt.

Concentrating this way, day after day, will also rein in and pacify your mind. One day it is sure to result in "parting the clouds and seeing the sun." Suddenly one day you will discover the real substance of this iron ball, which is the totally flavorless but marvelous *wu*. Whether you open it up or not, it's all the same, and when your doubt dissolves, you will open into enlightenment.

Here there is a question. If you know from the start that in any case it is *wu*, why not just let it go and be done with it? We have the Chan saying "Great doubt, great awakening; small doubt, small awakening; no doubt, no awakening." In other words, if you do not arouse the feeling of doubt, you cannot penetrate into the meaning of your question. From this we know that great doubt is a tool to energize your determination to crack open the iron ball and reach enlightenment.

SILENT ILLUMINATION

The method of silent illumination is also known in Zen as *shikantaza,* from the Chinese *zhiguan dazuo.* In the West this has also become known as "just sitting." If this method is used incorrectly, you may as well make tea by soaking stones in cold water. Misusing it can also amount to escaping into the demon cave to weave dreams of unconcern. The practitioner who does not understand this method can become like an old turtle buried in an ancient well for centuries. Suddenly one day it is dug up and comes back to life, but this turtle is still a turtle—it hasn't changed into a phoenix! One surmises that all of this time the old turtle was not really cultivating practice, because "just sitting" is not the same as "having nothing to do."

To avoid the fate of the turtle, it is important to understand the proper use of this method. In silent illumination your mind focuses on the awareness of your body sitting in meditation and nothing else. Therefore, correct posture is critical. Do not focus on parts of the body, but be aware of the totality of the body as a unity. Your body parts may have different feelings and sensations, but be aware only of the whole body. Your awareness of you just sitting there should fill your mind. If your awareness falters, check and correct your posture, then resume being aware of your sitting, and its sensation, as a total unity.

While you are practicing just sitting, be clear about everything going on in your mind. Whatever you feel, be aware of it, but never abandon the awareness of your whole body sitting there. *Shikantaza* is not sitting with nothing to do; it is a very demanding practice, requiring diligence as well as alertness.

If your practice goes well, you will experience the "dropping off" of sensations and thoughts. You need to stay with it and begin to take the whole environment as your body. Whatever enters the door of your senses becomes one totality, extending from your body to the whole environment. This is silent illumination.

From this it should be evident that it is not a matter of having nothing in your mind but, rather, that "you are thinking of what does not think." You mind is fully alert but not stuck on forms. As Chan master Hongzhi Zhengjue (1091–1157) explained in his *Inscription on Silent Illumination:*

> In silence and serenity, words are forgotten;
> In clarity and luminosity, all things manifest . . .
> Only this silence is the supreme speech, and this illumination,
>   the universal response.

If in illumination silence is lost, then distinctions will be
perceived . . .
If in silence illumination is lost, then murkiness will lead to
wasted teachings.

In the *Platform Sutra* the Sixth Patriarch said: "While you are in
samadhi, prajna is in *samadhi,* and while you are in *prajna, samadhi* is in *prajna.*" Silence is *samadhi,* and illumination is *prajna.*
When *samadhi* and *prajna* are not two separate things, this is silent
illumination.

Let's talk now of another turtle. In the sutras there is a parable
of a turtle pulling in its feet, head, and tail when in danger. This
metaphor refers to reining in the six sense faculties in order to dis-
entangle the web of false thoughts they engender and to still the
mind. The sutra says, "The four elements join to form the body, and
the entangling shadows of the six sense objects become the forms of
the mind." The six internal sense faculties take as their object the six
external sense objects, engendering the mind of false thought of the
six consciousnesses. If you take the six sense faculties and gather
them back in from the six sense objects, the false mind has no
entangling objects to which it can cling.

This is good Chan practice, but it does *not* mean abolishing the
function of the six sense faculties. Otherwise you are like the turtle
buried in the well. In this kind of Chan, when the eyes see a beautiful form, there is no craving, and when the eyes see an ugly form,
there is no loathing—the sense faculties acknowledge the corresponding sense objects but without any false thoughts arising. The
six sense faculties and the six sense objects are in contact, but discrimination, attachment, and affliction do not manifest. This is the
also the case when silent illumination functions in the midst of
daily life.

Being silent in this sense means not being subject to the entangling web of delusion; illumination means being clearly aware of the contents of the mind. It surely does not mean not using the six sense faculties, and it surely does not mean not using the mind.

FOUR KINDS OF PROSTRATION

Among the methods for practicing Chan are the four kinds of prostration in homage, each with its own purpose and meaning, depending on the state of your mind. Otherwise they are externally similar.

First is prostrating for influence and response. You prostrate in the hope of receiving a response from the buddhas and bodhisattvas, or from the spirits who protect the Dharma. For example, you seek such things as health and long life, family harmony, success, wealth, intelligent offspring, happiness and prosperity for your descendants, security in your worldly endeavors, or for everything to go as you wish.

Second is prostrating to offer respect. In this kind of prostration we are showing respect, reverence, and gratitude to the Three Jewels. It comes forth from the inner heart and mind without any thought of wanting help. This kind of prostrating is also done to one's Dharma teacher, but it is for the benefit of the student, not the teacher.

Third is prostrating in repentance. This kind is done to repent for past deeds or thoughts for which we are ashamed. This form requires humility and a genuine vow to correct our faults. It is impossible to do this if, even as your head touches the floor, you regard yourself as above others. Without sincere remorse, repentance bowing is like putting on a new suit of clothes when your underwear needs washing. If your repentance is genuine, you may find spots on your new clothing, but that is good. It means you are aware of your faults. However, do not indulge in self-pity, which is negative and refers back to the self. When done with the proper attitude, repentance can restore your mind to wholeness; it can make you more honest with yourself and more receptive to others.

Fourth is formless prostration, which is described in the *Platform Sutra* and is a very pure form of practice. It is difficult for beginners to immediately arrive at formlessness, since this implies thorough understanding of impermanence. So we start with form and progress through stages until we get to no-form, or formlessness. Similarly, to get to no-self, we start with the self. From there we contemplate emptiness until we gradually move to the level of no-self. We do the same with nonattachment, beginning with contemplation on attachment and working toward our goal.

Formless prostration is based on contemplating the Four Foundations of Mindfulness: mindfulness of body, mindfulness of sensation, mindfulness of mind, and mindfulness of dharmas. Whichever we contemplate, we begin with form and end with formlessness. We can consider these four foundations in the context of the three stages of formless bowing.

In the first stage you consciously direct your body to prostrate. From movement to movement, you control the body. While prostrating you remain extremely clear about your movements as well as the sensation. Already you are contemplating the first two foundations—mindfulness of body and sensation. The third foundation, mindfulness of mind, is also involved, because clarity and awareness are the mind itself. Since your body movements are carried out slowly, your thoughts should also be fine and subtle.

In the second stage you know you are prostrating and you feel it, but your body is moving without directions. You no longer have to control its every motion. Somewhat like a bystander, you are now a witness to your own actions. Who is prostrating? The body is prostrating. At this stage there is no longer the thought of "I am prostrating." It is just happening and you are just watching.

In the third stage others may see you prostrating, but you are no longer witness to your own action; this is attaining formlessness. Body, mind, and sensation are fused, without separation. When learning to ride, at first there is a rider and a horse, with separate wills wanting to go their own ways. As a result, the ride is rough. With experience, rider and horse become one, so that the ride becomes fluid and uninterrupted.

This is the stage of formlessness, but it is not yet no-self. When you perfect the third stage, there are no influences whatsoever. You are affected by neither internal nor external conditions. Of course, you must always begin with the first stage. If you cannot even reach the initial level of calm, subtly moving mind, then it will be impossible to progress to the next stages.

If conditions are ripe, it is precisely at this point that the earth-shaking state of enlightenment will appear suddenly right in front of you.

This meditation method gets its name from the lack of any object to the prostrating. It is not done for any purpose except to attune the mind; it is therefore "formless." It is somewhat distinct from repentance prostration, another form of meditation. When doing formless prostration, don't think about which way you are facing or which buddha you are bowing to. Just put your attention on every movement of your body. The movements should be just like a slow-motion film. Slowly, very slowly, you bow. When you join your palms together, your eyes are looking at the tips of your fingers, and then as you are prostrating, your attention is placed on the palms of your hands. Pay attention to the movements of your hands, the movements of your legs, and the movements of your feet.

As you bow, don't flex your head toward your chest; keep the same alignment of head and body as in sitting meditation. Bend from the midsection, not your back. Bend your knees and kneel down, but don't let your head fall forward. Bow with your head and back in a straight line. Touch the ground with your forehead, not with the crown of your head. Otherwise you will get dizzy or hurt your head.

Pay attention to the movements and feelings in every joint in your body, in every muscle and bone, and in every inch of skin. Concentrate, relax, be natural—there should be no tension anywhere. Prostrate with your body supple, your breathing smooth, your muscles relaxed, and your nerves calm. Don't fall to the ground like a log. You should lightly float toward the ground like a tuft of cotton or a snowflake. When you get up, you should be like a sponge slowly expanding. The floor may be cement or wood, but you should feel that it is as soft and comfortable as a Persian rug. Your body should be as light and free as a cloud floating in the sky.

There are three meditative levels of prostration: As indicated above, at the first, you clearly realize you are prostrating and are clearly cognizant of every movement. At the second level, you direct your body, but that body is not your own. It is as if you were an onlooker directing somebody else in prostration. It is like driving a car: the car is not your "self," but it follows your directions. At the third level, the directing has become very purified and spontaneous, and you are just looking on with your mind at this person doing prostrations—you don't have to use your mind to direct your body. You clearly see the body in motion, but even though it is prostrating, your mind remains motionless. When you reach this stage, you will be very light and peaceful and comfortable, and there will be no burdens on the body or the mind.

WHEN THE MEDITATION WORK
IS THOROUGHLY FUSED

When you sit in meditation, your mind typically passes through stages of relatively deeper concentration. In the first stage, stray thoughts are numerous, and even when you notice them, there is no awareness of their origin and extinction—they are just there. At this point you are still not really putting your whole mind on your method. At the next stage, when you become aware of the rise and fall of stray thoughts, you are engaged—in other words, really using the meditation method. In the third stage, you really don't see thoughts being born and extinguished; there aren't any because your mind is totally on the method. Now you are meditating very well indeed.

When you meditate, you may hope to reach the third stage, but the probability is not too great, especially if you anticipate it. When wandering thoughts arise, be neutral in your feelings—do not be angry or irritated—just immediately return your mind to the method. "Moment-to-moment birth and extinction" means that once wandering thoughts are born, they will spontaneously melt away. If you don't oppose or worry about them, they will just fade away.

What is most important is to begin again. Every wandering thought is also an opportunity to begin again, because by the time you notice it, the thought is already dying and the next one has not been born. Therefore, each present "now" is a new beginning.

Here is an analogy: When a mountain climber ascends a dangerous cliff, he must not look too far ahead or behind or else he may lose his footing. If this should happen, he has to grab the ropes he has secured with the pitons and immediately pull himself back to the spot from which he slipped. Then he can continue his ascent. So, for the climber, every step must be held fast, every step is a new beginning. Meditation is like this.

Each rising and falling thought is a movement forward, and each new beginning is another step in completing the meditation work. When you use a method the first time, your thoughts will often stray. As you gain experience, you will become aware of passing thoughts without losing the method. So, approach it in this manner: the first thought is on the method, and so are the second, the third, the thousandth, and so on. If you sustain this without a break, that is called "meditation work closely continuous." When there are no thoughts, there is only the method. When even the method is gone, you reach the stage where "the meditation work is thoroughly fused."

Obstructions

KARMIC OBSTRUCTIONS

There are many reasons why some practitioners do not experience the benefits of Chan, but I'll mention just three. One is not having a good teacher, another is not knowing how to relate to the teacher, and the third is having a teacher who doesn't know what your problems are and can't help you.

From this it might seem that the student's failure to make progress lies with the teacher, but in fact the problem usually arises from karmic obstructions within the student. A piece of jade embedded in a rock must certainly encounter a clear-eyed craftsman before it can become a precious jewel, but if the rock is just a rock, even an expert craftsman cannot turn it into a jewel.

The basic condition of your own body and mind, and your karmic roots and merits, will determine your progress. If you have prepared by learning the Dharma and practicing energetically, and have the zeal to spread the Dharma, you can be enlightened even without a first-class teacher. Like ripe fruit, you will fall from the branch with the slightest breeze. However, [for your experience] to be confirmed, you still need a teacher who has received transmission [who is enlightened and is capable of recognizing it in others].

Thus, between such a teacher and an adept student, constant, direct teaching is not necessary. These students, whose obstructions are few and minor, can be helped by just a few simple words from the teacher. It is to students who are somewhat "green" that a teacher needs to give much time and detailed instruction. They are like chicks when the mother returns to the nest. As much as she loves them, they still need to bestir themselves and open their mouths to get fed. Realizing this, such demanding students should be humble, sincere, and diligent.

The teacher is like someone who holds the key to the treasure chest. Just giving the key to an adept student is like delivering the whole treasure. After the student has received this benefit, he will feel very grateful to the teacher and to the Buddhadharma. At the other extreme are some who, while rebuking the teacher, have no idea what to do with the key. They are blind to their own obstructions.

Most people are between these extremes but still have obstructions. What are obstructions? They are nothing but affliction bred of egocentrism and surrounded by a "Great Wall" of defensive mechanisms. Though obstructions are related to one's karmic residue, they can still be changed for the better or even removed.

Certainly mental blocks like suspicion, arrogance, low self-esteem, cravings, anger, and wrong views are all familiar to Chan practitioners. If they are willing to constantly reflect on their own negative mind-set, they can effect gradual improvement and reduce these mental barriers. If you can vow to forget yourself and your problems for the sake of the Dharma, you can change these barriers into no barriers at all.

The best approach for removing obstructions is to arouse repentance. We can do this by making vows and by practicing single-mindedly and with energy. This is a good formula for self-correction. Once your concept of self is healthier, karmic barriers will be reduced. Your compassionate vows and your zeal to seek the Dharma will bring you into contact with a good teacher who will find in you a responsive and eager student. When your meditation practice opens up, your forward motion can be rapid. At this stage, while obstructions may still exist, they will not impede you. Then the benefits of practice will surely come.

Karmic obstructions are the cause-and-effect entanglements we have created over countless lifetimes, which we carry into the present. They leave us no way to be independent and free; they pursue our every thought-moment, and as our thoughts succeed one another, the obstructions follow as shadows follow forms. Where our body and mind go, our karmic obstructions go. Karmic obstructions are also realities created by our mental and physical actions in the present life. Many seek to practice Buddhism, but their bodies and minds don't obey and the circumstances of their lives won't let them. Finally, karmic obstructions depend on a person's age, status, level of prosperity, and character, but this connection is not necessarily fixed. Some people have to leave lay life before they can practice Chan, while others practice Chan fairly well in ordinary life.

While external obstructions are a problem, the most serious ones exist in the inner mind. With a mind of repentance and vows, you can learn to practice well, and if you arouse the *bodhi* mind, you have set out on the bodhisattva path.

EXTERNAL VERSUS INTERNAL OBSTRUCTIONS

One major source of obstructions is external, from the environment. Obvious examples are family or livelihood, which can get in the way of practice. The other major source of obstructions is internal, from within oneself.

Of the two, external obstructions are comparatively trivial—they are more easily overcome. I knew a monk who returned to lay life and began working; he then abandoned his practice because he felt overwhelmed by work. On the other hand, I know a layperson that has an equally demanding job, and he says that, in fact, the job encourages him to practice better. Even if the jobs were similar, why should they have opposite effects on two different people? The answer is that the environment is only a minor aspect of one's obstructions. The more difficult obstructions are created by the mind.

Keeping a humble attitude helps us to practice anywhere, anytime, whether in the Chan Hall or in the workplace. This comes to pass simply by radically reducing opportunities for strife, conflict, and the side effects of egotism.

Also, if you maintain the impetus to generate *bodhi* mind, everyone you meet will be a recipient of your compassion as well as a source of help. Not just every person but every situation. One situation may cause aversion in one person yet be an opportunity to practice to another. It depends on your attitude.

We practice Chan to transform ourselves, not to change the environment. Once we are transformed, the environment, as an extension of ourselves, transforms as well. Thus we can positively influence all we encounter.

HOW SOON ENLIGHTENMENT?

People want to know how long it takes to become enlightened. The answer is a second, an hour, a year, a lifetime, many lifetimes. In ordinary matters, someone might achieve in an hour what takes another a week. One person, with a single phrase, might save a million people, whereas another might not help a single person in a lifetime. Rather than waste time and energy speculating, practitioners should give thought to their level of diligence and their karmic obstructions.

Obstructions have been accumulating since time without beginning and carried in our minds through life after life. The bad as well as the good karma that we have created is carried within our minds. Ceaselessly, thought after thought, we carry these karmic debts and credits, and we continue to attach to ourselves. This is what drives us on. Our obstructions to practice should be the focus of our concern, not how long it takes to become enlightened.

WHY PRACTICE REPENTANCE?

We practice repentance to remove karmic obstructions that impede us, to learn compassion, to develop a mind of enlightenment, and to purify our mind so that we can move forward on the Way. To truly repent your misdeeds, your negative thoughts, and your negative words, you must first experience remorse—the contrition and humility that come with regretting things you have done or neglected to do. To give rise to remorse you must introspect and look into the three factors that create karma—your thoughts, your words, and your actions. If you do this honestly, you will realize that in the past your egocentrism has caused suffering to yourself and to others. With this realization will come better understanding of yourself, and the motivation to change.

Introspection is not easy; it is rare that we can recognize our own faults. Being self-centered, we usually blame others or the environment and see ourselves as victims. This leads to conflict with others, which increases mutual vexations. Swamped by our own delusions, we truly live in an ocean of suffering. Buddhadharma teaches us that through enlightenment we are liberated from the ocean of suffering and arrive at the other shore of wisdom. Therefore, practicing well requires constant introspection in order to see oneself clearly. From the subsequent sense of remorse comes genuine repentance. Being unable to recognize one's own faults shows deeply rooted self-centeredness. We all have traits of greed, hatred, arrogance, and destructive self-criticism, to one degree or another. If we hold strongly to our ways, it will be difficult to give rise to humility, without which there is no remorse and no repentance. To move forward there must first be self-recognition, which you can only accomplish yourself.

Karmic obstructions can stifle progress in many ways. One way to overcome such obstructions is to find a good teacher, but don't expect your teacher to be a mind reader. You must actively seek help and advice when you need it; otherwise you make one more obstruction, a wall separating you from your teacher.

Those with heavy obstructions require a lot of work and attention, and their progress is slow. Often such people end up faulting or criticizing the teacher. On the other hand, someone with few karmic obstructions can be helped easily. Just a few words from the teacher can propel him or her forward, and the student usually feels deep gratitude.

PRACTICING REPENTANCE

So much of our energy is invested in building defenses to protect ourselves and reject others. If we open our minds to this with humility and shame, we can learn remorse and repent our self-centeredness. Thus we can live a more harmonious and peaceful life. Therefore, we practice repentance prostration to alleviate negative karma and cleanse our minds. To open our minds, we need the introspection of Chan. Through it we can gain a clear understanding of both our good qualities and our shortcomings. With this intimate knowledge comes greater faith in ourselves, enabling us to interact with others and the world with more tolerance and harmony.

Therefore, begin with introspection. Look into your life, past and present, and try to recall things you have done, said, and thought that have brought suffering to others and to yourself. The purpose is not to provoke guilt or recrimination but to face up to these things and to understand how they led to your present predicament. Through this process you can experience remorse and repentance. This will purify your mind, allowing you to move forward on the luminous path of Chan toward compassion and wisdom.

So please reflect as you prostrate. First recall your childhood. Try to remember all the things you said and did that hurt others and, consequently, yourself. Then do the same for your youth, early adulthood, and so on until the present. Look deeply into your heart; see what is there.

Normally we don't know how to resolve the conflicting feelings that come up with self-reflection, how to deal with the turmoil from long-buried memories. Therefore we avoid self-reflection. But now is the time and opportunity to do just that—to recognize our shortcomings, to feel cleansing remorse. This is a chance to purge negative emotions and have a pure mind again. This is also a chance to rely on faith in yourself, which, along with faith in the teacher and faith in the Way, is the bedrock of Buddhism. Repentance is a good way to cleanse your mind and increase faith in yourself.

PUTTING ASIDE THE SELF

Our sense of self can have a large scope or a small scope; it includes the "small" self of the individual ego and the "great" self that identifies with all of existence, with absolute truth and divinity. For Chan practitioners, even the great self is not free of the taint of ego and attachment and should therefore be transcended. This is easier to understand in theory than in practice, but through Chan we can directly experience putting aside concepts of self.

When we observe the breath, we realize that our lives exist only from breath to breath, that selfish clinging is just a thread connecting one thought with another. When we stop breathing, our lives are over; in like manner, when our thoughts dissolve, there is no real basis for clinging to them. As we observe the breath with a pure mind, our sense of self recedes, and this can be liberating—we directly experience the self as illusory.

While meditative concentration is useful for reducing the tyranny of self, we also need repentance. The ordinary mind is ruled by arrogance, self-abasement, suspicion, jealousy, anger, hatred, and so on—all projections of the self. To the extent that we cling to these feelings, we cling to self. Without purifying our minds, it is easy to accept small attainment as enough or to be discouraged by little attainment. When we resolve some of our karma, we can make energetic progress and persevere through suffering. Thus we prepare the mind-ground to practice the six perfections: generosity, discipline, patience, diligence, meditation, and wisdom.

"There are eighty-four thousand Dharma doors, and all lead to the great citadel of nirvana." Any genuine entry point to the Buddhadharma can liberate us. Breath counting and repentance arouse the mind of enlightenment, thus motivating practice. Reciting a huatou and practicing silent illumination are like golden keys to the Dharma doors. They are also yours to use.

REPENTANCE PROSTRATIONS

When you sit poorly because of wandering thoughts and physical problems, these are all obstructions, the karmic residue of past actions. Buddhadharma is meant to release you from your bonds, but as soon as you hear the teachings, they go into your brain, become obstructions, and end up as suffering. I have explained the Chan methods very clearly, but some still can't use them effectively. It is as if a wall erected by demons surrounds your mind, obstructing your vision, allowing you no exit. Beyond lies a broad highway to liberation, but if you manage at all to set foot outside the wall, you step on excrement everywhere. These karmic obstructions have been there since time without beginning.

You have not committed any great evils in this lifetime; still, one obstacle after another confronts you. None of this is outside your mind. Failing to practice, your awareness of this will be dim, but paradoxically, the more you practice, the higher the barriers, the greater the afflictions. But this heightened awareness is good; it shows that you are practicing effectively. In this situation you must practice repentance prostrations.

Repentance prostration is like formless prostration, but you focus on seeing your shortcomings and arousing a sense of remorse. When you prostrate in repentance, if you bob up and down like a chicken pecking at grain, with the mumbling of a distracted mind, it may not be totally useless, but it will not be very effective. You must be candid and sincere, and you must not hide from yourself the ugliness and evil that you have to face. After several days of practice, you should have the courage to confront your darker aspects.

Everyone wears a mask of goodness. This is fine—at least you have a sense of morality and shame. It gives people the courage to go on living. But when we practice Chan, we have no place to hide anymore; we lay ourselves bare and look deeply and unsparingly at ourselves.

Repentance means facing yourself, past and present. Practicing Chan is like stirring up an old cesspool. You must release the years-old stench of egocentric clinging. The more you can dissipate the odor, the purer you will become. The only fear is that you can't bear the unpleasantness and that you will not be resolute. That would be a pity!

As you prostrate, focus on your defects. What you are ashamed of within yourself and what you are ashamed of in front of others—those are your defects. Some think there is nothing that would make them ashamed in public, but is this possible? We are sentient beings with a karmic legacy and the traits of human beings. We are mentally wounded, physically scarred. To see how disfigured you really are, you must endure uncovering the scars one by one.

Don't tell me what you find. I don't need to know. Just face yourself and be honest with yourself; relentlessly probe your shortcomings and earnestly repent. Prostrate very slowly.

Open up your heart, confront yourself; use the spur of shame. Only then will you begin to find peace of mind. We judge others. Few truly see themselves as less adequate than others. It is usual to forgive yourself and blame others. This is a loathsome aspect of our personalities.

Whom can you face with a totally clear conscience? Your parents? Your children? Your teachers? Your friends? Can you face yourself with a clear conscience?

Your parents gave you this life; are you wasting it?

Selfishness, arrogance, deceiving yourself and others! How can someone whose mind runs wild think about enlightenment without being willing to first repent?

When we're done prostrating, we can get up and wipe away any tears! Put aside your shame and repentance. Forget what you just experienced. We must be able to examine our defects at any time, anyplace, but we also must be able to stop. After arousing shame and repentance, it's best to return to your practice method. At this time emotions are easily settled and mental energy is not that unstable and impulsive, so it is easier to get into the method. Just give your body to the cushion and your mind to the method.

Attaining the Way

JOY OF DHARMA, DELIGHT OF CHAN

To truly function as a Chan person, you cannot be naive; you need to realize there is a lot to learn and cultivate. Don't be in a hurry to get enlightened, but don't wait for it either. In the beginning it is most important to pacify the mind, to settle it down. And you need to be free, at all times and in all places, from the undue influences of external objects. If you can do this without bothering other people, you will know the joy of the Dharma and the delight of Chan.

In the sutras there is a metaphor about reining in and pacifying the mind: "Guard your six sense faculties the way a turtle hides its limbs, head, and tail." Like the turtle, we must guard our six senses of vision, hearing, smell, taste, touch, and thought from being disturbed by objects.

On the first day, I asked you not to use your six senses—eyes, ears, nose, tongue, body, and mind—for producing illusory thoughts. The six internal sense faculties become attached to the corresponding external sense objects and produce the illusory mind of the six senses—what we call consciousness. When we rein in the mind that is entangled with attachments and return it to its immovable inherent nature, we are pacifying the mind.

When we sit, we go from mind moment to mind moment without straying from the focus of concentration—this is the method of Chan. To relax body and mind, to settle seriously on the method, not to calculate success and failure—these are principles of Chan. Impermanence, no-self, no-thought, nonabiding, formlessness, no-attainment—these are the perspectives of Chan. Please take these methods, principles, and perspectives and commit them firmly to memory and practice them without letting up.

This is all very simple and at the same time very profound. But without practice you will not know its profundity, and neither will you know its simplicity. On the contrary, the simpler something is, the harder it is to penetrate its inner mystery.

ALL ACTIVITIES ARE CHAN

Speech and silence, motion and stillness, walking, standing, sitting, and lying down—these are all practice. In the Chan Hall—sitting, standing, walking, stretching—these are all forms of practice. Outside the hall—eating and drinking, sleeping and arising, working after meals, all places, all moments—these are also practice. When doing tasks that do not require thought, you can recite the Buddha's name or count breaths. When doing work that requires your attention, make sure that your mind and hands work together. Your mind should be where your hands and body are. Washing dishes, leave them spotless. Cutting vegetables, be the knife that cuts perfectly. Splitting firewood, heating water, sweeping the floor, put your whole mind and strength into the task, cleanly and skillfully—this is practicing Chan. Concentrate on your food when eating, chew deliberately, and do not let your mind wander. Going to bed, put aside the four elements of the body and the five aggregates of form, sensation, conception, volition, and consciousness. Forget past, present and future; just have a good sleep. That too is Chan.

PLOWING AND WEEDING

Coming to retreat to accomplish something may be a correct attitude, but for now you must forget all about goals. When working on the farm, you focus on plowing and weeding, not on the harvest. Storms, floods, droughts, and earthquakes are all beyond your control. If causes and conditions and past merit are good, there will be a rich harvest. If not, there may be a meager one or none at all. The farmer's only choice is to put his whole heart and strength into his work; he cannot ensure any results. Yet the very experience of arduous tilling and planting is itself a precious thing.

Therefore we make practice itself a goal we can rely on. Whatever you are doing—eating, meditating, cooking, cutting vegetables—that is both the practice and the goal. Just single-mindedly apply yourself to the task with an even, down-to-earth, balanced mind. With your mind thus free from peripheral issues, you will truly practice Chan.

Good results appear when you don't covet gain and just pay attention to the practice. With this attitude you will surely harvest a bountiful crop someday.

BIG VOW, SMALL VOW

Chan practitioners should not fear failure; through failure we gain experience. No one succeeds in the myriad affairs of a lifetime, but there may be examples of failing in all. The Buddha himself experienced failure before he chose the Middle Way and achieved enlightenment. If you feel, so far, that you have not met your goals on this retreat, you are sure to fail in the time that remains. Drop any ideas of success or failure. Just treasure each present moment, make each second a second of pure practice, and it will be a rewarding time.

Our bodies and minds may veer out of control and our unrealized dreams may dissipate, but those willing to undertake great vows will surely benefit. Vows, taken again and again, remind us of their intent, and we gradually advance toward the goal. We cannot immediately uphold all of our vows, but as our efforts accumulate over time, "where water goes, a channel forms."

For those beginning to arouse the mind of enlightenment, taking great vows might seem futile. But vows give us direction on the Path, and though the destination is distant, it is truly in sight. Used correctly, vows can move us forward. The vows we make can be great or small. Vowing to become enlightened is a great vow; vowing to pacify your mind is a small vow. Before meditating, bow to your cushion and, with serious intent, vow: "I will not leave this *bodhimandala* until my mind is at peace." Though this is a small vow, it resonates with the great vow of achieving enlightenment. Making this vow every time you sit will solidify your intent and your faith, and you will sit long and well.

FINDING YOUR OWN NOSTRILS

This is day five of our seven-day retreat. How quickly time passes! When you practice Chan, however, the sense of time passing can be very relative. If you are really adept at Chan, in just an instant you can overturn the cosmos, shatter heaven and earth, and suddenly see "ten thousand cloudless miles, unstained by a speck of dust." The *Surangama Sutra* calls this the "sudden cessation of the crazy mind." In Chan we call it "illuminating mind and seeing its true nature." But if you are not adept at Chan, time can pass very slowly; and no matter how hard you try, or for how long, you may not even be able to find your own nostrils. So first learn Chan.

HAUL IN YOUR NETS

One of the biggest reasons Chan people have difficulty attaining the Way, or even benefiting from practice, is lack of perseverance. When you travel to a place you have never seen, it can seem to take forever to get there. People who have never seen their true self-nature may feel the same way about enlightenment. Beginners may doubt that they are on the right path, or that the path even exists.

Try to see this last day of retreat not as a kind of ending but as a beginning. By now you should have a better attitude and a better idea of how to practice with few interruptions. We grow on retreats; we increase our faith by becoming more aware of our shortcomings. The more we recognize our faults, the less we will cling to them, and perhaps we'll replace them with better qualities.

It is said that to generate *bodhi* mind and make vows about practice is easier than maintaining a persevering mind. Therefore I urge you to work especially hard today. If the previous days have been difficult, put that aside. Today is a new day. It is important to complete the retreat without slacking. To finish strongly helps to develop the persevering mind. However, do not confuse diligence with tension, which is a self-defeating obstruction. Relax both body and mind. Diligence is uninterrupted but relaxed practice.

A fisherman casts his net hoping to catch fish. Later on he must haul in his net whether he caught any fish or not. That's how he finishes his day's work. To survive, he must not abandon his net. We are fishing for the Dharma, and our practice method is our net. Like fishermen, we too must finish our work and haul in our nets, whether they are jumping with fish or empty. If your net brings in more garbage than fish, this too is useful, as those are the negatives you need to work on. Cultivation is like this. One retreat will probably not resolve all of your problems or correct all of your faults; however, you must complete your fisherman's work. Come to another retreat to cast your net again. With a persevering mind, you will resolve your problems and the catch will be bountiful.

LAY THE LAST TILE

There's only a half day left until the end of retreat. It is six hours until evening service. This is plenty of time to practice. Make every thought and every movement a moment of practice. Make every place a *bodhimandala*—a place for practice. If you can do this deeply, then hereafter, all times and situations are *bodhimandalas,* all thoughts and actions are practice.

Use every second remaining. Every second, stay on your method; be acutely aware of any subtle body movement or thought. By now you should know how to relax body and mind. Then put your whole mind on the method. Don't be angry if you cannot accomplish this in every moment, but do your best from one moment to the next. If you give 100 percent of yourself, that is practicing well. This persevering attitude will serve you well in daily life. Always finish what you start. A house is not complete until the last tile is laid.

CAT AND MOUSE

If you have climbed a mountain, you know that sometimes it goes smoothly, while at other times it is difficult. Meditation is like that. Sometimes things go well, but other times you have negative physical and mental reactions. It is normal to sit well for a while, and later not do so well. Our physical and mental strength are assets that we expend. A car speeds smoothly along, but it still uses up gas. Similarly, you may sit well, using up energy, and later feel tired. So if you sit well for the time it takes to burn a stick of incense, don't expect that your practice will always go that well.

For old hands, experienced cultivators, it is different. Without exerting to the utmost, their meditation is like a fine stream that flows on forever. Experienced travelers know how to conserve their energy and nurture it, keeping themselves sharp. A good martial artist will not overuse his moves or squander his strength needlessly. Old hands are like this. They meditate in a very normal frame of mind, keeping solid and steady, nurturing their strength until it comes forth. They certainly do not let their minds bounce up and down.

More accurately, whether people are old hands does not depend on how long they have been practicing. Being an old hand means carefully studying the methods of practice and using them without wasting physical or mental energy; it means sitting continuously without losing the method. Chan master Dahui called this ability "the place of saving power." People who know how to meditate tie their minds to the practice; people without this skill struggle with illusory thoughts. Tying your mind to your practice means that you are aware that you are meditating, somewhat between consciously and unconsciously. Having discursive thoughts means that you have a stranglehold on the practice; you are tense, strained, and using a great deal of energy, fearing from one moment to the next that illusory thoughts will intrude. Of course they will! If you proceed this way, you will soon collapse from exhaustion. Tying your mind to your practice means that your mind is light and calm and your body is relaxed.

Once a wise cat catches a mouse, the mouse will not escape. The cat is very casual, as if playing with the little beast. The cat may even let it escape a little, then cut its path and recapture it. It doesn't tire itself in frantic pursuit of the prey. Only kittens act nervously, throwing themselves into hot pursuit. Imitate a canny old cat, not a kitten trying to catch a large rat.

When meditating, don't waste your energy, and don't go to desperate lengths. You should feel as if you were waiting at ease for a tired enemy—unhurried and relaxed. Deal with obstacles skillfully rather than blundering forward. I have already told you to isolate yourself from outside concerns, to relax, and to be natural. This is the same principle.

We practice Chan to unfurl our wisdom. Wisdom means awakening, or *bodhi;* it only appears when afflictions drop away. Affliction and *bodhi* are opposites, but they share the same essence. People whose minds are muddy with afflictions, whose emotions are unstable, are blind to *bodhi.*

Some people hope to get enlightened but have not thought about changing their disposition. They complacently assume that all they need is a gift from the teacher—a method for getting enlightened. This kind of person thinks: "All I need is to get enlightened. Then I will have wisdom and no longer have afflictions." This reverses cause and effect! First we should change our disposition and reduce our defiled energy. Only then can we attain wisdom and reach enlightenment.

In the past, people who had no plumbing used cesspools. During the summer a thick layer of excrement would form at the top, and this would, in effect, contain the stench. In the winter the cesspool would freeze over and still not stink. The foul smell would be released only in the spring, when the ice was broken or the layer of excrement was penetrated.

A retreat is like stirring up a cesspool in the springtime. If you keep it sealed, the mess is still contained inside and the noxious vapors get even worse. Thus you need to churn it up again and again, expose it to the cleansing air of practice. So it is a good thing to discover one's defects and illusory thoughts during retreat. The more you know your own deficiencies, the sounder your character can become.

To transform your disposition from a turbid to a clear and pure state, you must take your afflictions and transform them into compassion and wisdom. The milder your afflictions become, the sounder and healthier your mind will be, and this will benefit others. Otherwise, ten seven-day retreats won't do much good. To be really useful to yourself and others, you must take with you the mind of compassion and the mind of wisdom. To reduce afflictions, begin by reducing expectation, seeking, and eagerness for success and gain.

CHAN PRACTICE AND WILL

Take the direct experience of impermanence and infuse it into your life. At all times, remember that you live amid impermanence and that your life itself is impermanent. Indeed, to maintain this awareness is very difficult and takes willpower. A young man came to practice Chan, and he developed the aspiration to leave home and become a monk. In the course of his training he did not gain any power, and being a monk irked him. Recognizing that his preparation was inadequate, instead of sticking with it, he returned to lay life. This exemplifies lack of willpower in Chan practice.

Buddha said, "Control the mind in one place and everything is accomplished." This can also mean that with a strong, determined will, you can cope with anything. To learn Buddhism and become enlightened is a task for many lifetimes. Becoming a monk or nun is not a game, Chan practice is not a passing fancy—it is a lifetime commitment. There is no room for dilettantes or the halfhearted. You must steadily advance over the long haul, through wind, waves, ice, and snow; only you will be able to reveal the beam of light from Spirit Peak. If you are mentally prepared, your willpower will be strong. Anticipating difficulties along the way, you will work through them and make progress.

I have a disciple who is not especially brilliant, but he brings to bear his whole energy whenever he does anything. His advantage is that he has the strength of will to say to himself: "When I set a goal, I will work until it's achieved." Chan students need to emulate this kind of willpower to make progress on the Way.

WHEN BORING IS GOOD

Even seasoned meditators often feel that they are not making progress. Once, on a trip in the American Midwest, I felt the car was going very slow, but when I looked at the speedometer, the car was actually going fast! Why did it seem like this? Because the scenery was very much the same over long stretches, it created the impression of our going slowly. When you are meditating well, you might feel bored by long stretches of the same scenery and be tempted to slacken. This may be a normal reaction, but resist it. In fact, if you find your meditation scenery getting very interesting, you may be losing your method, if you haven't already!

AS CLEARLY AS THE PALM OF YOUR HAND

Inner observation of the mind's direction is awareness—knowing at all times what your thoughts are doing, whether you are focused on the method, lost in illusory thought, or not clear what you are doing. If you can see these conditions of your mind as clearly as the palm of your hand, you are really practicing Chan. If you can ignore your body but observe your mind, if you can ignore external objects but observe the movement of your thoughts, you will soon forget time and space. When you observe your inner thoughts, their numbers will diminish, time will contract, space will expand, and your body and mind will lighten.

When you are counting breaths, you are of course practicing.

Realizing that you are practicing is awareness. You manage to continue practicing even as intentional or random thoughts keep trying to break in. Holding on to the awareness that you are practicing while the practice continues without break—this is practicing Chan. Proceed in this mode whatever method you are using. When you are extremely clear about what you are doing, it's as though you are observing yourself, or someone is observing you. At this opportune time, without tensing, maintain your mental clarity and hold fast to the method. As simple as this may sound, not all can do it. People who don't know how to meditate make a great physical and mental effort to control themselves, but this is misguided and ineffective.

BALANCING ON A FINE POINT

Effective Chan practice requires balancing on a fine point between relaxation and dullness. To practice for more than a few periods in succession, much less days, without tiring, you need to be relaxed, both in mind and in body. Otherwise physical and mental exhaustion will overtake you. On the other hand, while relaxing the body and mind, you must guard against dullness. If you can maintain this balance, the energy that is freed up can be channeled into the method and nourish your dedication to the Way.

After practicing one method a long time, you may become bored and feel you are just spinning your wheels. It is like driving a car across the heartland of America—hour after hour, the scenery seems the same. You aren't even aware how fast you are going. Then, suddenly, you arrive. In the same way, though you may be practicing well, it may not seem like you're making any progress. If, however, you generate the power to go on and on if need be, suddenly you will arrive. So do not give in to boredom; it may actually be a sign you're practicing well.

On the other hand, please recognize that if you get excited when you sense you are making progress, you are in danger of losing the method. Avoid both emotional extremes and simply rely on your determination to continue. Think of yourself as a trailblazer carving a path through wilderness. After you have surmounted obstacles and bypassed dangers on the way to your destination, the path will no longer seem so forbidding. Though obstructions still lurk, your experience in dealing with them will render them harmless.

Your objectives are to learn correct attitudes for practice and to become thoroughly familiar with your method. This requires continuous dedication in a long process. Your gains will be diligence, perseverance, and patience. All of these benefits cannot help but improve your life and your practice.

MEDITATION IS THE ROOT OF LIFE

For true Chan people, their practice is the root of life; when separated from practice, it is as if they are in danger of losing their lives. Therefore the Chan teachers since ancient times have taught disciples to hold fast to their gong'an or huatou as the guardian of their life. You should imagine that you are lost at sea, clinging to a life preserver—how could you dare let go?

Even so, after meditating for a long time and beginning to feel tired and lazy, you may succumb to that feeling, even if you don't want to. As a Chan student, this is the time to mobilize your courage, rededicate yourself, and energize your faith; this is the time to renew your grasp on the lifesaving Chan method. But if you give up the method, you should feel a great sense of shame, a piercing, painful sense of shame. What you need then is to take a vow of great compassion for the sake of sentient beings. This will strengthen your diligence, dispel oblivion and scattered thoughts, and inspire you to wholehearted practice.

INNER AND OUTER PATHS

On occasion you have heard me oppose certain ideas for being off the Buddhist Way, referring to this or that method as being misguided, and even criticize other people within Buddhism. You may think, "Isn't Buddhism supposed to be all-embracing, the most inclusive and interpenetrating of all paths?" I must scrupulously tell you that, while Buddhism is a wide path, you must still "separate inner and outer paths and distinguish between misguided and correct." To choose wisely among the dishes you find on the table of Buddhism, you must be absolutely clear about this distinction. If you attend a banquet prepared by many chefs, some of whom may be misguided or unqualified, at first glance the dishes may all look delicious, but some may not be so nutritious or may even make you ill. It is my job to tell you what "dishes" in Buddhism are nutritious and which may harm you.

Buddhism is sometimes called the inner study because it requires introspection. But this is not necessarily so. People may begin to practice for physical health, psychological health, or spiritual sublimation. In terms of Buddhadharma, each level is "higher" than the one before it. First, a healthy body enables you to do more and be more useful to others. Emotional stability helps you to put resentment and blame aside and to keep peace around you. With spiritual sublimation you become aware that your true self is more important than your individual self-identity; you will be more conscious of your kinship with all beings and that all share the same essence as the one true spirit.

No philosophy, religion, or art goes beyond these three levels. But I must tell you, if you remain stuck at these levels, you are outside the Buddhist Way. When you study Chan, you must definitely transcend these limits to experience ultimate liberation.

Spiritual sublimation is the most perilous. When self-awareness fails, you may see yourself as a supreme adept who has united God and self, and you may have a powerful urge to control things around you. You may think, "Those who join me will flourish, and those who oppose me will perish." This disease is a residue of religious mania, a by-product of religious zeal, very much to be feared, as it can create major disasters for humanity. The reason for the saying "God and the devil are sometimes hard to tell apart" is that misguided spiritual sublimation can give rise to arrogance and the delusion that you can save humanity and the world. People who fall prey to this delusion have to dominate, subdue, and control others, thereby violating their human nature. The result is a cult of personality in which clinging and attachments become even deeper. This is outside the Buddhist Way; it is not Buddhism.

Nevertheless, even though we distinguish between Buddhist and non-Buddhist paths, we should not attack people for following outer paths. Causal conditions for some people are such that they encounter only non-Buddhist paths. Rather, we should use the all-embracing nature of the Buddhadharma to go beyond the non-Buddhist paths and work hard to propagate the Buddha's correct teaching—this is a better way to refute non-Buddhist paths.

FICKLE MIND

Thoughts tend to float and scatter around the mind with no stability. The previous thought floats off as the next one stirs. When you are meditating correctly, one thought follows another like feathers falling on a fan. The succeeding thought is like a feather slowly floating down onto the fan, [where it settles and stops]. However, if the fan stirs like a scattered mind, the movement will send the feather floating off again. This useless chasing of false thought after false thought results in its being easy to sink into torpor. The illusory thoughts of your fickle mind and your impatience drain your energy.

Since the first day of the retreat, I have asked you to keep your center of gravity down low when sitting. Locate it in the soles of your feet or in your buttocks. This is a very important technique. In cultivating their vital energy, martial artists speak of letting the vital energy (qi) sink down into the field of elixir (the *dantian*, the region below the navel). Keeping your center of gravity in the lower body, you will be light on top and heavy at the bottom, like one of those rocking dolls that cannot be knocked over. Then you will feel light and relaxed, as well as solid and stable. Ordinarily people are top-heavy—their brains are full of stuff they can't cope with. This is a source of suffering for themselves and others.

When people are fickle and unrealistic, the Chinese say, "You are light in the bones" or "Your whole body doesn't weigh four ounces." People like this have neither the mind of shame nor the mind of repentance. They may have done wrong to others, or to themselves, and not even realize it. Living in ignorance, they cannot cultivate the Buddhist Way successfully.

If I feel shame, I should repent. I know my present mistakes, I know my past mistakes, and I vow not to repeat them. If I make the same mistakes again, I repent again. Eventually my vows grow stronger, and I will be able to practice according to the Dharma.

ACTING LIKE A GOOD-FOR-NOTHING

During the interviews, I have learned that some people are still very tense, still struggling with their meditation method. There are those who may have sat well for a few sessions, but the good feeling has not come back, and they search for it in vain. They feel pressed for time, and their mental states have become more harried, impatient, and tense.

I've used many metaphors to explain that if you want to arrive quickly, you'll never get there, but many of you are still making trouble for yourselves, looking for pain to suffer. Buddhist practice is polishing your patience and forging your determination. When you demand peace of mind, your mind is not at peace. To deal with these afflictions, you need to "move the firewood out from under the pot." This means not caring at all, acting as if nothing were happening, feeling that there is no harm in being a good-for-nothing. The very process of the meditation retreat is itself the result. All you have to do is sit for seven days: if you do it well, that is a result, and if you do it badly, that is also a result—it's all valuable experience. Don't have your heart set on doing well; just keep your mind on the meditation method. Don't get upset about oblivion or scattered thoughts. Pain, numbness, aches, itches—let it all happen. If the sky falls, pay no attention.

I remind you, please do not tense up. If you relax, at least your body can feel good and your mind can feel stable. If you feel tension and urgency, you'll end up with a bellyful of anger. One of you sat well for a stretch, and his mind seemed to open; he felt very comfortable and content. After that, with every sitting, he waited for his mind to open again, but it didn't. When body and mind are relaxed, comfort and ease will appear. If you are tense, hoping that your mind will open, then you will already have closed it tightly. A retreat is not a contest. There is no score and no medals. Our only concern is perfecting the ability to relax and creating some spaciousness for our mind.

PATIENT ENDURANCE AND DILIGENCE

If you accept the harsher realities of practicing Chan and stick with it, things can go favorably. But if there are conflicts in your mind, serious difficulties can result. I want to offer you two perspectives on practice that may help: patient endurance and diligence.

Patient endurance does not mean gritting your teeth; it means using the normal mind to face your situation. While practicing Chan, your body and mind can react in different ways, causing problems. Aside from symptoms of real illness, these adversities can be managed with patient endurance. A Chan retreat entails much discomfort and little pleasure, but the experience can be savored endlessly. For serious practitioners, their whole life is like this. I am sixty-three and I have been practicing for quite a while. I have known the joy of the Dharma and the delight of Chan, but I have also often seen adversity. To be faced with problems and to deal with them—this is the normal life of practice.

You may have heard that the Chan path is strewn with difficulties, and even on the verge of enlightenment, obstacles may surface, one after another. This is why you must learn patient endurance—to face adversity patiently. Only then can you calmly overcome barrier after barrier. If you develop this attitude during retreat, you can also deal with adversity in daily life. Your mind will be in equilibrium, and nothing can stay in your way.

Diligence means persevering in the practice without giving up. You grasp it tightly, bite into it, stick to it, without letting go. There was a Chan master who described the diligence of working on a gong'an as chewing on a piping-hot sweet bun. Because it tastes delicious you won't spit it out, but because it's too hot you can't swallow it. You roll it around in your mouth, not daring to stop lest it burn you. At such a critical moment, your mind is concentrated and dares not wander off in confusion.

The analogy is not perfect, as the bun will soon cool off, but this relentless focus of energy means employing a method continuously, as if the bun stayed piping hot forever. When your practice method is going well, it can be as delicious as a sweet bun. Then it will not be a strain. You will derive joy from it and exert yourself with true diligence. This does not mean going all out; it simply means exerting yourself without letup. Don't be in a hurry and don't slack off—just practice without interruption. Don't charge ahead impetuously, exhausting your energy. Don't be like a mountain torrent; be a fine stream that flows continuously. A mountain torrent can create a flash flood, but it may also bring a drought in its wake. A fine steam flowing on and on will be more useful and safer to you and others.

REPAYING BENEVOLENCE

The Confucians have a saying: "Remember, no meal comes easily, and a single strand of thread comes only with hard work." This saying carries the idea of repaying benevolence. Now that environmental awareness is in style, we should urgently put this saying into practice. To enjoy the conveniences of modern life while blaming others for the state of the environment is hypocrisy. We must go beyond lip service.

Buddhists should seek simplicity and plainness in their lives: if you don't freeze in winter and are not starving, your material needs have basically been met. When we have good fortune, we should recognize and cherish it; we should nurture it and put it to good use. But often people seek petty advantages, enjoying things made by others and striving for their own convenience. But people with deeper roots will give something in return—this is recognizing and repaying benevolence. Buddhists should not only give something back; even more, they must practice charity and make good karmic connections with sentient beings. Wherever you go, whether or not you benefit from being there, let that place benefit from your being there. This is good practice for the mind of enlightenment and the mind of compassion. To give something back in return for a benefit received is good, but strictly speaking, this is not in accord with Buddhadharma. *Dana*, giving, is one of the six perfections; it means giving without conditions—it is one of the ways of the bodhisattva.

For example, you may make an offering to the Sangha in gratitude for the retreat, but it would be even better if you left with a better understanding of the teacher's intent, with a clearer idea of helping sentient beings. To repay all forms of benevolence, there is nothing better than delivering sentient beings. Since you have received the benefits of Buddhadharma, you must proceed to protect and uphold it, enabling others to benefit from it. This is truly called recognizing and repaying benevolence.

Conscious of earning merit, you attend meditation retreats; cherishing merit, you are frugal with it; nurturing merit with all your mind and strength, you use worldly dharmas and world-transcending Dharma to make karmic connections everywhere.

EXPRESSING GRATITUDE

Knowing how rare and difficult it is to encounter the Buddhadharma, Buddhists should feel gratitude and indebtedness for the benevolence of the buddhas and the enlightened teachers. It is hard for people to acknowledge and appreciate that other people have helped them throughout life. They feel that they have given at least as much as they have received. Others believe that the help they have received from others did not matter, that they would have done just as well without it. Some people express gratitude but there is no real gratitude in the speaker's mind; it is mostly lip service. Attitudes like these are arrogant, self-centered, and vain; they do not accord with the true gratitude we should feel for receiving the precious gift of Buddhadharma.

As Chan practitioners, we should feel grateful for so much as a grain of rice or a drop of water. Beyond feeling gratitude, we should give something in return. However, repaying the benevolence of Buddhadharma can be as hard as making water flow upstream. It's not just a matter of making direct material offerings. If Chan practitioners are able to calm the mind of false thoughts, put it into correct balance, and begin benefiting themselves and others, this is truly repaying the buddhas and the enlightened teachers.

For this form of repayment, please cultivate "observing" and "awareness." Observing means really seeing what we are doing right now; awareness means clearly knowing what we are doing right now. As you cultivate observation and awareness, you will discover how often you say the wrong thing, do wrong deeds, and think wrong thoughts. As you become aware of your shortcomings in these areas, you must also develop the mind of repentance to correct your path.

MAKING OFFERINGS

Prior to partaking in our vegetarian meals, we recite an offering:

We make offerings to the Buddha,
We make offerings to the Dharma,
We make offerings to the Sangha,
We make offerings to all sentient beings.

One could say that this is in the spirit of Chan, and one could also say that this is the heart of Mahayana Buddhism. First we make offerings to the Three Jewels—Buddha, Dharma, and Sangha, because we are grateful to them for giving us the means to practice the Way. We then make offerings to all sentient beings for their contributions to our welfare. Mealtime offerings help us to develop the mind of gratitude and the mind of giving.

Ordinarily we make material offerings, as well as offering ourselves, to the Three Jewels so that sentient beings may be delivered on a broad scale. We transfer things of value for the benefit of all sentient beings. The merit that we receive for this act, we in turn dedicate to all sentient beings. What remains is selfless wisdom and universal compassion. Simply put, we first offer material goods and then transfer the merit to others. This is spiritually effective medicine for diluting egotism and dissolving the illusory self.

The modest fee you paid for this retreat is not to pay for the teacher's time, rent the space, or pay for your provisions. This is material wealth that is pure, given as a donation to the Buddha, Dharma, and Sangha. In the process you create merit. In this situation, I too feel gratitude and try to repay it, and I offer it to all of you, for you to repay the benevolence of the Buddha, Dharma, and Sangha. At the same time, I thank you for giving me the opportunity to make this offering.

At the end of a meal, we recite this verse:

> Our meal is over, and we wish that sentient beings accomplish liberation and fulfill all Buddhadharma.

We express the hope that all sentient beings will also make offerings, accept the Buddhist teachings, and in the future become enlightened. We also affirm that our practice is not for our own sake. So, people of Chan, when you set to work cultivating practice, you must tame and refine yourselves. You must move from seeking to no-seeking and onward from that to cultivate making offerings on a wide scale.

Enlightenment

BENEFITING OTHERS

There is a saying in Buddhism: "It is rare to attain a human form and difficult to encounter the Buddhadharma." We here are very fortunate; we have managed to acquire human bodies and hear the Buddhadharma. We also have the good karma to meet teachers who can guide us in practicing the Dharma. The chance to take part in a Chan retreat is hard to come by, and for this opportunity we should feel great joy. To make use of our good fortune, we should generate the aspiration for enlightenment. This means undertaking the four great vows: to deliver sentient beings, to cut off mental afflictions, to master Buddhadharma, and to attain buddhahood.

The Buddha taught that suffering results from ignorance about the causes of suffering and the means of ending it. The Buddhadharma gives us a way out of this predicament. But when we consider that countless other sentient beings suffer as much as we do, or more, how can we think of our own deliverance as the goal of practice? Therefore we learn Buddhadharma to help us deliver not ourselves but other sentient beings from their suffering. Thus we study and practice Buddhadharma to become enlightened not for our own sake but for the sake of sentient beings. Before Shakyamuni Buddha left home, he had already generated the aspiration for enlightenment. He left home only after he had observed the suffering of sentient beings and had begun the search for a method to help others become liberated from suffering. Not yet buddhas, you perhaps came to this Chan retreat hoping to gain something. If so, such a notion comes from an ordinary self-centered mind, and any benefits you get here would be very limited. But if you do arouse *bodhicitta,* the mind of enlightenment, the benefits will be limitless. How does one arouse the mind of enlightenment? The Buddhist path shows us how. There are two aspects: one is learning the Buddhadharma; the second is cultivating practice. Attaining the first aspect is hard work in itself, but it is not enough; one must put the theory into energetic practice under the guidance of a teacher, and this is even more difficult.

Knowing the teachings of Buddhism gives you an intellectual understanding, but it does not give you an integral connection to the Three Jewels. Only through personal experience can the Buddhadharma truly be useful to you and to other sentient beings. There is a Chinese saying: "Sitting and talking is not as good as getting up and doing." When you know one teaching of the Dharma, you should act in accordance with it; only then do you truly benefit from it. Next you must make it useful for others.

Studying Buddhism requires that we learn its perspectives,

attitudes, and procedures. Everything must accord with the true teaching, the Buddhadharma. The Buddha had the aspiration for enlightenment, and so must we. But when we are taking our first steps, we cannot match the standards of the Buddha, so we must learn step-by-step and travel on the Path for a long time.

AROUSING *BODHI* MIND

The aspiration for enlightenment arises from hearing and studying Buddhadharma and is called *bodhi* mind, or *bodhicitta*. This is the mind's signal to itself that it is ready to abandon affliction, nurture compassion, and cultivate wisdom, which is to say, perceive one's own true buddha-nature. To arouse *bodhi* mind, one first loosens the mind's fixation on craving, anger, folly, arrogance, ignorance, and countless other afflictions that cause suffering and keep one from seeing one's true nature. The mind of a buddha is manifested on the one hand as compassion and on the other as wisdom. However, they are not separate but aspects of the same thing. To seek wisdom for oneself is not the way of the bodhisattva. Arousing the mind of enlightenment should be simultaneous with arousing the mind of compassion. Chan practitioners should not defer vowing to help sentient beings until after being enlightened; doing so would defer the supreme enlightenment of the Mahayana—*anuttara-samyak-sambodhi.*

Conduct is the causal basis for tasting the fruit of supreme enlightenment—one must travel the bodhisattva path, benefiting sentient beings before benefiting oneself. Transforming the ordinary into the compassionate self, you will be in accord with the selfless wisdom of liberation. Shakyamuni Buddha saw that sentient beings suffered from birth, old age, sickness, and death and that the weak are prey for the strong. Out of compassion he resolved to find a way to relieve sentient beings from suffering; he abandoned the sumptuous life of an Indian prince and pursued the Way. His great action is the precedent for all of us—the idea that compassion comes before wisdom.

During our seven-day retreat, at least four times every day we must remind ourselves of the four great vows:

I vow to deliver innumerable sentient beings.
I vow to cut off endless vexations.
I vow to master limitless approaches to the Dharma.
I vow to attain supreme buddhahood.

It is important to note that the vow to help sentient beings precedes the vow to become enlightened. If you work hard at meditation but do not arouse the aspiration for enlightenment, though you wear out a thousand cushions, you are still "sitting by the stump waiting for a rabbit," and it will be an even longer time before you see "your original face before you were born."

CROSSING OVER

The moment you first give rise to the aspiration for enlightenment is the arousing of the *bodhi* mind. Hearing the true vision of the Buddhadharma and being impressed by the grandeur of the Way, you aspire for the first time to become enlightened and to follow the Way of the buddhas. The first tender sprouts of enlightenment spring in your mind and you begin to forge ahead on the Way. Although only a modest beginning, this motivating force drives you on your quest for buddhahood.

The *Flower Ornament Sutra* says:

The aspiration for enlightenment is the seed of all enlightened states, the seed of all the buddhas, because it can give birth to all the phenomena of enlightenment, to all the Buddhadharma.

The *Treatise of the Great Perfection of Wisdom* says:

When bodhisattvas first develop the aspiration for enlightenment and form a causal connection with the supreme path and vow to become a buddha, this is called the mind for enlightenment. For those at the stage of the initial aspiration for enlightenment, the buddhas explain that all phenomena are conditioned. For those who have been studying for a long time and have become attached to good things, the buddhas say that all phenomena are empty and utterly nonexistent.

In the *Sutra on the Stages and Practices of Bodhisattvas*, the chapter "Generating the Mind for Enlightenment" says:

When bodhisattvas first generate the mind for enlightenment, this is the root of all right vows.

When bodhisattvas first generate the mind for enlightenment, this is what they say: "I must find supreme enlightenment and put all sentient beings at peace and bring them to ultimate nirvana with no remainder and to the great wisdom of the ones who come from thusness."

When bodhisattvas first generate the mind for enlightenment, this is called "crossing over," and they number among the bodhisattvas of the Great Vehicle's enlightenment.

After you first generate the mind for enlightenment, you gradually attain to supreme unexcelled perfect enlightenment. Therefore the initial aspiration for enlightenment is the basis for enlightenment. After you have generated this mentality, this mind for enlightenment, you see all sentient beings subject to measureless sufferings and the mind of compassion arises; you want to liberate them. Therefore the initial aspiration for enlightenment is the basis for great compassion.

When the initial mind for enlightenment is strong and solid, it opens the way for two good things to enter: first, skillful means to benefit oneself and develop the mind of enlightenment, and second, skillful means to benefit others and extinguish all suffering.

Good people, you should know that the Chan Hall is called "the place where buddhas are chosen." Once you enter the Chan Hall and you have been chosen and reach the stage of the buddhas, not only will you illuminate mind and see its true nature but you will suddenly awaken and become enlightened. But if you do not first generate the aspiration for enlightenment, you will lack the causal basis for tasting the fruit of enlightenment.

The aim of Chan is to awaken, to enter the ocean of wisdom of the buddhas, and to develop universal compassion. So, good people, the very first aspiration for enlightenment is the most precious. Maintain it and extend it and you are sure to become enlightened. Whenever you discover that you are afflicted by laziness, self-indulgence, inertia, craving, or anger; whenever you become aware that your actions or words are malicious, immediately recall your first aspiration for enlightenment and renew it.

Never forget that first aspiration, abide in it every moment, preserve it wherever you are—you will then not stray from the standards for cultivating the Way; you will make steady progress and not lose heart.

There is a practitioner who always says at the end of every retreat he goes to: "I've begun again." "This time was a real beginning after all." "I've finally gotten to the beginning of the path of supreme enlightenment." Superficially, it might seem like he is marking time and making no progress. In reality, true bodhisattvas learn from experience that they are always generating anew their aspiration for enlightenment, that they are just ordinary people on the Way. If they do not abandon their commitment, they find themselves renewed day after day.

THE MIND OF COMPASSION

The ordinary love that people feel is basically egocentric and brings afflictions that lead to more afflictions. This is not true Buddhist compassion. Even so, Buddhists should learn compassion at this level and progress to a higher expression, which is to help all equally, while the act, actor, and object are all seen as empty.

True compassion springs from selfless wisdom and is not conditioned by relationships; it is everywhere equal—what the *Lotus Sutra* calls "a single rain that brings nourishment to all." Compassion cannot be based on the hope of receiving benefits from acts of kindness. This is acting for one's own sake, not genuine compassion.

Therefore, if you would arouse the mind of compassion, you must boldly advance and energetically practice to cut off delusion and witness the real. Be guided by Buddhadharma and rely on the methods of Chan. Chan is based on the teaching of cause and effect. To center and guide our practice, we must root it in the mind of great compassionate vows and energize it with the mind of great enlightenment. Otherwise we practice blindly, like wandering ghosts floating in the air

Without the mind of detachment, aren't you just an ordinary person? Without the mind of enlightenment, should you call yourself Buddhist? Without the mind of great compassion, are you not, at best, seeking enlightenment for yourself? Lacking any of these, you are not on the Way of the Mahayana. Many on spiritual paths think that to experience "the oneness of all things" is the highest level and that this is the same as Buddhism. In fact, a path that does not recognize the mind of detachment, the mind of enlightenment, and the mind of great compassion is neither Chan nor Buddhist.

Through the vows of great compassion you can give your cooperation, concern, and help to sentient beings whose minds are knotted in pain and affliction. Where are these sentient beings? They are in your own homes; they are people you meet every day. Since ancient times, the enlightened Chan teachers have helped people rein in and pacify their minds in the midst of everyday life. If you can always meet people with the mind of compassion, you will be able to use the mind of wisdom on yourself; this is the work of Chan people on the Way of the Mahayana. To take the vows of great compassion means to wish all sentient beings the ultimate bliss of nirvana. This can only be achieved through guidance from the Buddhadharma. Everyone knows that he or she should engage in some benevolent activity, and this is indeed very good. But it only takes care of the branches. To take care of the root as well, you must use the Buddhadharma to help purify the human mind and to enable people to find true peace and happiness. This is the fundamental Way.

To say "I'll help sentient beings after I get enlightened" is to reverse the root and the branch. When Shakyamuni appeared, he manifested the Buddhadharma with his own enlightenment and afterward dedicated himself to helping sentient beings. Today the Buddhadharma is already there for us. As we reap its benefits, we should also transmit it to others. Most people know that a loving heart is a virtue. When your own child is sick, you suffer and hope for her or his speedy recovery. But when a stranger's child is sick, do you feel the same urgency? When animals are slaughtered for food, are you indifferent? Could Buddhists feel this way? Compassion is not just for close ones; it must extend to all, even the smallest creatures. To be compassionate means, at all times, to act so that sentient beings may attain peace and happiness and to forgo advantage to oneself. In time, egocentrism will diminish and the day your mind is liberated will come closer.

MIND OF DETACHMENT, MIND OF ENLIGHTENMENT

Some people call themselves Chan masters but are still attached to the five desires (the objects of the five senses). They think that even

Shakyamuni Buddha did not detach from the five desires, and they believe that practice can be truly carried out only in the midst of desires. This is a distorted teaching, not Buddhism. Without a mind of detachment, you cannot go beyond the triple world of past, present, and future and be free in the midst of birth and death; you are still controlled by the five desires and moved by sense objects.

Some people think that the mind of detachment is only for the Small Vehicle, while Chan, being Mahayana, has nothing to do with detachment. This is not correct. The mind of Mahayana and Chan occurs only when three qualities are present: ordinary human morality, the detachment of the Small Vehicle, and the bodhisattva's mind of enlightenment. Without detachment as a foundation, you have a mind enamored of the world, a mind of craving and attachment, or else a kind of heroic delusion fraught with arrogance and insanity. Thus, if the mind of detachment is lacking, there can be no mind of enlightenment.

In our materialistic culture, when human desires run wild, there are too many seductive temptations. Detachment is difficult, since it requires giving up the five desires. Without it, you can't even be reborn in the heaven, one of the desireless realms, much less know the holy fruits of nirvana. For people wallowing in the five desires, to aspire to detachment is far from easy. Today there are a lot of people studying Buddhadharma, and many work hard at it. But some just want to learn a little something from a teacher, then go out and peddle it to whomever they meet. They declare themselves Chan masters and run meditation retreats. For such people, to have a genuine mind of detachment is not easy.

But before you can resolve the question of birth and death, you must first have the mind of detachment. To catch a tiger, you must have the courage to enter its lair. When you have this kind of courage, gained through hard work, your faith grows and you will at last experience the power of Chan. You can put your whole being into the practice and become a guardian of Buddhadharma; then you can "cling fondly to nothing" and find your support and refuge in Buddhadharma.

Some people think detachment means rejecting the world, parents, children, everything. True detachment is not aversion and it is not escapism. When Sixth Patriarch Huineng left home, he first made sure his mother was taken care of. Monk, nun, or layperson, detachment does not relieve you of your duties.

As for the mind of enlightenment, surely this means "not seeking peace and bliss for oneself, vowing that all sentient beings will win release from suffering." It means "being an ox or a horse for the sake of sentient beings." This may sound humbling, but oxen and horses carry people, and when the riders reach their destination, so do the animals. "To be a ferry for sentient beings" means to help transport them from this shore of samsara to the other shore of nirvana. When sentient beings reach nirvana, the ferryman arrives too. If we can go back and forth freely between the shores, then basically there is nothing to be called "this shore" and "the other shore"; the mind of enlightenment, the *bodhi* mind, is absolutely liberating. To deepen your grasp of the Buddhadharma, you should first develop the mind of detachment by putting aside clinging and attachment. Next develop the mind of enlightenment by letting go of egocentrism.

CHAN AND ENLIGHTENMENT

Some people who covet enlightenment think that if they are enlightened, they will fully grasp Buddhadharma without any additional effort. Perhaps they think they will be like the young Huineng, who became enlightened when he heard someone quote the *Diamond Sutra*. They imagine that Huineng, who had not read any sutras, received in one stroke all the teachings as if funneled into his mind directly from the source. Do such things really happen? They happen only in mythology or perhaps in the magical arts of some outer paths. In truth, grasping the Buddhadharma invariably requires one's own practice and one's own realization.

Chan teaches sudden enlightenment, but this is not distinct from gradual practice. You practice gradually for years, and suddenly you're enlightened. There is also gradual practice after sudden enlightenment. Some rare people are quick to reach enlightenment because their karmic roots are deep and their basic nature is keen. They do not necessarily have to cultivate anything but can experience enlightenment directly, as did Huineng.

Some people go on retreat because they want someone to attest to their enlightenment or because they want a method for becoming enlightened. So impatient! When Fifth Patriarch Hongren met young Huineng, he knew that this was someone special. But he still sent Huineng to work in the kitchen. While milling rice, Huineng did not hanker after enlightenment; he just milled rice. He did not rush to the Fifth Patriarch to ask for transmission [to confirm his enlightenment]. One day his readiness burst forth and he was able to reveal his realization. So don't be in a hurry. I'm here every day casting my Dharma net! All of you are big fish; it's just that you haven't found my net.

Chan enlightenment does indeed exist, but you cannot attain it in a hurry. It does not matter when you will see the Path open into enlightenment—you just have to keep to it. When you're on a road trip, you don't always have to be asking "Are we there yet?" Just pay attention to your driving, and suddenly you're there. As long as your method is correct and your direction is right and you work continuously, there will naturally come a time when you get there.

Enlightenment is sometimes considered something one "experiences" and "realizes." While there may be problems with this understanding, certainly for all of you the seven-day retreat is something you experience and realize. For Chan practitioners, the process is the result. Thus the reality of retreat could also be called "experiencing the result." But in the records of great Chan teachers from the Tang until the Song dynasties (seventh to thirteenth centuries), they never talked about results or levels of attainment. All they ever said was that someone "had an insight," meaning an insight into emptiness, or no-self. Some people in the Chan records were enlightened a great many times, some only once. Like his Chinese contemporaries, the Japanese Zen master Dogen called this "the bottom dropping out of the bucket," when the traces of the self have disappeared. This is called "the state of enlightenment appearing before you."

Enlightened people seem very ordinary. When I was taking the precepts of a monk on the day of a feast making offerings to ten teachers, the precepts master, Lingyuan, was not there. It was time to start the ceremony and nobody had seen him; we looked all over for him. Suddenly someone said, "There's an old monk eating in the kitchen. Could this be Old Ling?" Everyone ran to the kitchen, and sure enough, it was he. "Old Ling, why are you eating in the kitchen? Everybody's waiting for you so we can start the ceremony!" Master Lingyuan said, "I didn't know. When I told them at the gate that I was here for the feast, they brought me here to eat." This happened because Old Ling wore the tattered garb of a poor monk, not an elegant robe with wide sleeves, and he was carrying a patched cloth bag. He did not look at all like an important monk. Somebody brought him to the kitchen to eat, and he ate with gusto. He did not give it a thought, nor did he say, "I am the precepts master; why am I here in the kitchen?" Thus, truly enlightened people do not think that they are above others. They are not concerned about their own enlightenment at all; they are even more ordinary than other people.

WHO CAN BECOME ENLIGHTENED?

Chan practice has often been defined by the following passage from the Chan classic the *Transmission of the Lamp:*

Illuminating the mind and seeing its true nature, suddenly awakening and becoming a buddha, not establishing any words or language, but directly pointing to the human mind.

This passage has proven to be rather attractive to Chan aspirants, but it is often misunderstood. Many people study a few gong'ans (koans) and read the recorded sayings of the Chan and Zen masters and then suppose that everyone has the qualifications to become enlightened. This is true insofar as all sentient beings inherently possess buddha-nature and therefore can become enlightened—this is the basic teaching of Buddhism. But in the historical records of Chan and Zen, there were not that many people who experienced sudden enlightenment and achieved buddhahood.

Mazu Daoyi, the Chan master who had the largest number of enlightened disciples, had only 139 students who deserved to sit on the *bodhimandala* and enter his chamber for advanced Dharma teaching. According to the records of Chan, the enlightened ones can be counted, but no one knows how many cultivated Chan without achieving illumination. While opening into enlightenment is indeed important, you can still derive great benefit for yourself and others without being enlightened. People in general wrongly believe that the benefits of Chan appear only with enlightenment. Sometimes they seek refuge in the mountains and forests to practice in seclusion, leaving other people to help sentient beings in the meantime. After becoming enlightened, they reason, they will return to work for the good of all sentient beings. This kind of thinking is selfish and demonic. Because their egocentrism is so strong, it is, in fact, not easy for them to become enlightened. There were many reasons for the decline of Chinese Buddhism, but the main reason has been the selfishness of Chan people.

There is no set timetable for enlightenment. Some people can do in an hour what other people do in two days, and for some even two days is not enough. Some people can help ten million with a single sentence, but others cannot help a single person in their entire lives. Therefore, there is no way to use time as a measure of progress in cultivating practice. We must take into account such factors as the students' diligence as well as their karmic obstructions. This being the case, the best way to practice is to forget about when you will be enlightened—to see the practice itself as the goal and the result. With this attitude, you cannot fall into misunderstanding.

THE NOURISHING BREAD OF *BODHI* MIND

Many practitioners believe Buddhist wisdom comes from being enlightened. So then, how does one become enlightened? Enlightenment manifests when one's focus turns radically away from the needs of the self, when greed, hatred, and ignorance no longer manifest. One can accomplish this by learning the Buddhadharma and practicing Chan. Practice is guided by views or attitudes. When one's attitude is correct it is called right view; when it is erroneous it is called heretical view, or outer path. To develop right view, you need to expand your base of awareness from the self to all sentient beings. Egocentrism slowly abates as you develop compassion for others. When self-centeredness no longer arises, wisdom manifests.

The development of compassion is the development of *bodhi* mind. Completely realized *bodhi* mind is *anuttara-samyak-sambodhi* (unsurpassed, altruistic, enlightened mind). To generate *bodhi* mind, you must traverse the bodhisattva path; you must develop compassion by focusing on saving sentient beings. Shakyamuni Buddha practiced for the benefit of sentient beings; he saw the endless cycle of birth, aging, sickness, death, and the preying of sentient beings upon each other. He resolved to find the way to alleviate this suffering. Thus, compassion was the Buddha's starting point.

Every day on retreat, we recite the four great vows. The first is

"I vow to deliver innumerable sentient beings." The last is "I vow to attain supreme buddhahood." The order is important; we develop compassion first and attain enlightenment later. So, if you would truly practice Chan, vow to benefit sentient beings. Sit for their sake. Learn the ways of a healthy mind and help others learn.

Most of us want to benefit from meditation and achieve enlightenment. If a farmer wants a crop of wheat, he has to sow grain, then nurture and harvest the crop. Only then can bread be made. The point is that you have to put in something, expend energy to attain a goal. In Chan we plant seeds in the field of sentient beings to nurture our connection with them. We thus generate compassion, which eventually yields the nourishing bread of *bodhi* mind. This is the path of compassion.

THE GROWTH OF COMPASSION

Newcomers and outsiders often misunderstand Chan Buddhism. People read about stories where Chan people are enlightened upon hearing a single phrase or a sound, or feeling a whack on the shoulder. Some even think that enlightenment can be found by reading books. Especially misleading is the term *sudden enlightenment*. Thus, thinking that enlightenment requires little if any practice, they wait for it to strike like lightning. But in fact, very few people, including disciples of great patriarchs, have become enlightened in the sense of completely transcending their sense of self and seeing their buddha-nature.

For example, Master Mazu had the greatest number of disciples in Chan history, but only 139 of them attained enlightenment. It is recorded that the Song dynasty's Master Yuanwu Keqin brought 18 disciples to enlightenment in a single night. Simple arithmetic tells us that if he kept up that pace, he could help 180 disciples reach enlightenment in ten days, 1,800 in one hundred days! Obviously, it didn't work that way; Yuanwu was not just handing out diplomas. He just had a spectacular night. Still, these numbers are impressive. Then there was Yuanwu's disciple Dahui, a teacher who brought to realization fewer than 25 disciples in his entire career.

Remember, though, that Chan has been around for more than a thousand years, and thousands upon thousands have devoted their lives to its practice. What about the vast majority who did not achieve enlightenment? Was practice a waste of time for them? Should they have given it up? No one should think so for a moment. Everyone derives benefit from practice, to one degree or another. The Chan path itself is the goal of practicing.

Many people believe that the whole purpose of Chan is to get enlightened. Such people would like it if everyone else helped them reach this goal. After enlightenment they would gladly return the favor. Practicing like this for years only creates heavy karmic debts, thus making it even more difficult to achieve enlightenment. Such practitioners have forgotten that the foundation of practice is benefiting sentient beings. The first of the four great vows is to save all sentient beings. Only when we get to the fourth do we vow to become enlightened.

Practicing and generating the mind of enlightenment complement each other. When in your practice you balance these two elements, you and others will benefit. Please keep compassion in the forefront of your mind. If this is difficult for you, developing a sense of humility can be a catalyst for the growth of compassion.

Remarks at the End of Retreat

THE MOST MARVELOUS DAY

Today is the last full day of retreat. That makes it the most marvelous, most solid, most to-be-savored of the seven days. You have worked hard and are already clear about the concepts and methods of Chan, and your body and mind have adapted. You have had problems such as oblivion, scattered thoughts, illusory thoughts, attachments, selfishness, and ignorance. As a result of practice, you should have at least known shame and remorse. Hopefully you have had moments of clarity and peace and gained some insights into yourself. You are already much improved over someone who has no self-awareness. You should at least have become more sincere and more genuine. Most important, you now have the power to face yourself. Let us value this last day. If we can meditate well, every second is worth more than gold. Otherwise time passes in the blink of an eye and even a hundred years of sitting won't be worth excrement. As for the teaching I have given, be content to have listened and used as much as you could.

Remember the following points when doing Chan: relax body and mind but hold on to the method; if you lose the method, just pick it up again; do not think of success or failure—just accept the practice as the goal. Just by letting go, you are making progress. Use the mirror of remorse to reflect on yourself, and the pure water of repentance for self-cleansing. Use the power of the mind of enlightenment to help sentient beings. To attain buddhahood, we must first benefit sentient beings. Use the power of diligent progress to perfect yourselves. The true hallmark of a Chan person is the perfection of compassion and wisdom.

PACIFYING YOUR MIND

We have come to the end. This is the last stick of incense that we will light during this retreat. Put your whole mind and body into your meditation; practice what you have learned one more time. Of course people who engage in illusory thoughts will still engaged in them, and people sunk in oblivion will still be sunk in oblivion. Those who dedicate themselves will clearly understand that their mind often stands opposed to them, that they are not their own master. If you are not your own master while awake, there's no use talking about while you are dreaming; if you are not your own master now, you'll be in a worse mess in your future lives.

When you think you have no problems, problems will abound; when you do and say what you should not, while not doing and saying what you should, that is pitiful; hiding your faults while celebrating your good points is a source of afflictions. Or, if you lack confidence, denigrate yourself, and willingly degenerate, this too is a source of afflictions. To practice Chan, first clearly recognize yourself as you are so that you can affirm yourself and establish self-confidence. At first the mind of faith is hard to establish because you waver between discontent and anticipation of something better. The ancients called this "being in the north in the morning and the south in the evening." Illusory thoughts are simply being in the north during the previous thought and the south during the next thought. You are like grass growing on a wall: when the east wind blows it leans to the west, and when the west wind blows it leans to the east. You are like a wandering ghost floating in space, not knowing the way home.

Someone told me, "I used to drift along not knowing which way to go, but after coming to retreat, I know that the destination is right here. From now on I hope that wherever I am will be the destination." When I heard this, I nearly cried. How sad to drift along for such a long time before discovering the way home. I only hope that every one of you will be able to profit from this retreat in such a way.

In reality, that which does not abide anywhere is everywhere, and there is nowhere that is not a place to pacify your mind. Don't always be like a headless fly darting around in confusion. Realize that to put your crazy mind to rest, here and now is the ultimate. So many people are like mice that don't realize they are already inside the grain bin. They leave their droppings inside and go somewhere else looking for grain to eat. It's perfectly clear that right where you are is your destination, yet you still wander homeless, looking everywhere but where you are.

So now let us put aside all illusory thoughts and sit, saving energy while this last stick of incense burns down.

TREAT MEDITATION EXPERIENCES AS ILLUSIONS

Chan practice really begins when you return home after retreat. Take what you have learned and put it to use. If you practice according to the Dharma, you will not fall into delusion. You may have experienced certain physical and mental phenomena, perhaps the supernormal—this sometimes occurs with hard practice. Don't covet small gains, cling to your experiences, or seek to repeat them. If you cling to them, trying to demonstrate or rely on powers you gained, you will experience great affliction; you can really go wrong and fall into delusion. That is not practicing according to the Dharma. If you just treat meditation experiences as illusions, you will be safe and in accord with the Dharma.

TAKING REFUGE AND PRECEPTS

After an intensive retreat, body and mind seem to have been cleansed by a good bath. During these seven days we have been purifying the karma of body, speech, and mind, and though we are still not totally pure, we are working in that direction. Now we must consider taking a step further, and take refuge in the Three Jewels of the Buddha, the Dharma, and the Sangha. The Three Jewels are the guides for our practice, the goal of Buddhist life. Some people seek enlightenment and claim to rely on the Three Jewels but do not uphold the Three Jewels at the level of phenomena. In other words, their words and actions belie their claim. How can their nihilistic views help them reach the formless Three Jewels of inherent nature? This is very contradictory.

The Dharma was expounded by the Buddha, cultivated and upheld by the Sangha, and handed down through the generations.

The Sangha represents upholding the Dharma and should be highly honored and valued. Because Sangha members perpetuate and transmit the Buddhadharma, they symbolize the mind of detachment and enlightenment that brings salvation to sentient beings. To truly practice Buddhism, you should acknowledge, accept, and take refuge in the Three Jewels.

The next step is to take the five precepts, which prescribe correct behavior. Some people do not take the precepts for fear they will violate them. They think, "If I do not take them, I can keep my freedom. If I take the precepts, I will not be free." This is like saying that if you take the precepts, you will not create any bad karma, but if you don't, you can go ahead and do evil.

In reality, whether you take the precepts or not, your actions still affect your karma. This is fundamental cause and effect. If you do not accept the precepts, your potential for doing bad things is greater. If you do take the precepts, it may help to prevent you from doing wrong. Violating a precept after taking it is certainly better than not taking it at all. You will at least have the merit of having upheld the precept. Take one precept and you have the merit of one precept; take it for a day and you have one day's merit; take it for a minute and you have one minute's merit. Violating a precept only damages a particular objective for a certain period of time. Upholding the precepts brings merit to sentient beings all through your life. So the precepts are a safety net for cultivating the Way.

What are the precepts? First: no killing of living beings; most important, not to kill human beings, and after that, not to deliberately kill animals. If you maintain a vegetarian diet, this is adhering most closely to this precept; but if for some reason this is unsuitable for you, you should at least not participate in killing animals.

Second: no stealing. Willfully taking property that does not belong to you, whether private or public, is stealing. If you inadvertently profit at the expense of others and you make good and repent, you will be cleansed of this fault.

Third: no sexual misconduct. Sex between married couples is not wrongful lust. Such conduct serves to maintain personal health and family stability, provides the blessings of children, and promotes social harmony. When people who are not married have a long-term relationship that is stable and relatively pure, this is all right too. Although this is not the literal version of the precept, it takes into account present-day social reality.

Fourth: no lying. Most important, this refers to the great lie of claiming enlightenment before you achieve it. People who tell this great lie are aiming to win respect and support from credulous followers, but what they achieve is to bring error and confusion into the minds of others, to mix up ordinary and holy and turn right and wrong upside down. Thus they bear karmic blame for cutting off the life of wisdom of other people. Also, you should not lie in order to spread the Dharma.

Fifth: no drinking alcohol or taking drugs. This is not a precept of fundamental importance; rather, it is a protective precept wrapped around the others, established in order to prevent corruption of the first four precepts. When you are intoxicated, it is easier to violate the first four precepts. Some people think that if you drink without getting drunk, it doesn't matter, but at the very least it is damaging to health, and at the worst, it may cause you to hurt others. To nip this in the bud, the best thing is to abstain.

These five precepts are all easy to obey. If you cannot take all five, choose just those you think you can follow. If you take a precept, then, as I recite it, recite along with me; if you cannot accept a precept, do not recite along with me. However, in such a pure karmic condition as we now enjoy, it would be a pity if each of us did not take all the precepts.

You must not be afraid of taking them. If you violate a precept, repent and purify yourself. If it is truly impossible for you to uphold a precept, you can announce to someone, "I am returning my vow of such and such precept." If you later do something wrong, you still have karmic retribution, but at least you won't violate the precept.

Please resolve to take the precepts. Doing so will make it easier for you to illuminate your mind and see your true inherent nature. What joy this will bring!

FAIR EXCHANGE

To embrace the Buddhadharma with your heart and mind is the greatest wealth you can have. Wisdom and compassion are precious beyond measure. At retreat's end this morning, you took refuge in the Three Jewels of the Buddha, the Dharma, and the Sangha. If you received them with a sincere mind, they are in your possession as true wealth, not the ephemeral, bounded wealth of material things. If you maintain your faith in the Three Jewels, their wealth cannot be taken away from you.

Material wealth is useful for supporting ourselves, the Three Jewels, and others. Physical health is important for the strength and energy it gives us to practice. But these things are limited by nature; they suffer impermanence. As with the body, a healthy mind is one where thoughts, moods, and emotions are stable and balanced. Constant internal conflict is unhealthy. Also disruptive to mental equilibrium are overly positive reactions to praise and overly negative reactions to criticism.

You have all worked hard for seven days. In exchange, you have received the Three Jewels and spiritual wealth. I would say that is a fair exchange.

END OF RETREAT

There is a Chan saying: "One does not expound the Dharma with the mouth, and one does not practice Chan with the legs." While speaking the Dharma and sitting are part of Chan, they are not its whole, true essence. Some people become upset if they are unable to sit in the lotus position. In reality, refining the mind is more important to Chan practice than training the legs. In ordinary life, the mind is master, and if your inner mind is confused, this will incline your surroundings toward chaos. If your inner mind is roiled, you are more apt to be disturbed by external events. Conversely, as the *Vimalakirti Sutra* says, if your mind is pure and clean, then sentient beings are pure and clean and the whole world is pure and clean. People try to alter their surroundings in accord with their wishes, but because not everyone wants the same thing, there is no way to satisfy everyone. Therefore, while it may indeed be a good thing to improve the environment, it is even more important for everyone to improve her or his own mind. First we take afflicted false thinking and transform it into wisdom and compassion that accord with Buddhadharma. After that we can do a better job of changing the world around us.

When the same unpleasant thing happens to two people, one may react in anger, while the other may retain his composure. Chan and Zen people should model themselves after the second person; such people can see clearly what is happening and know how best to deal with it. The mind should not be slave to events or lose perspective; one's qi (chi) should not be thrown off balance. Face the facts, do your best; what you can't do, leave for later. What need is there to feel vexed?

The point of Chan is to be empowered in the midst of daily life. So with these thoughts, I wish you good fortune—may your wishes be fulfilled, may your body and mind be at peace.

Notes

The following abbreviations are used in the notes. For further information regarding the numbers that follow these abbreviations, see item 8 in "Conventions Used in this Book," which is in the front matter.

T.   *Taisho shinshu daizokyo*

X.   *Xuzang Jing (Extended Buddhist Canon)*

Part 1. Exhortations on Investigating Chan by Master Boshan

1.   The "mind of birth and death" refers to a mind that is still entangled in samsara, the cycle of birth and death.

2.   This is another name for buddha-nature, self-nature, or the truth of emptiness.

3.   This is an allusion to a story in Chapter 8 of the *Lotus Sutra* in which the Buddha told of a traveler who became drunk. Wanting to help, a man sewed a precious jewel in the lining of his drunken friend's robe while he slept, and then left. When the drunken man awoke, he continued on his journey, enduring all kinds of hardship, unaware of his hidden wealth. When the two friends met again later, the traveler related his stories of hardship. His friend then told him about the jewel that he could have used to relieve his suffering. The meaning of the Buddha's story is that the Dharma is like a precious jewel that is available to us, even as we may be unaware that it is there.

4.   The six roots are the six sense faculties: eyes, ears, nose, tongue, body, and thoughts.

5.   The "it" in this context seems to refer to the doubt sensation. When the

doubt sensation is present, motion and stillness will no longer be a problem, the mind will naturally be pure, and the sense faculties will naturally be expansive.

6. The "ferret" is an analogy of the self, which is clever and always on the move. Even though tamed, it can still be aggressive and harm its surroundings.

7. The "eight winds" refers to being desirous of and averse to gain and loss, praise and blame, benefit and harm, good reputation and defamation.

8. In the twelve years of the Chinese zodiac, there is no year of the donkey.

9. See *T.* no. 2012b, 48: 387b.

10. "Earnest" is a rendering for *qie*, which has many connotations, such as sincerity, thoroughgoingness, dedication, perseverance.

11. The three natures of good, evil, and indifference form a division of the Hinayana treatise *Abhidharmakosha*. The last type of nature is further divided into the kind of indifference that is an impediment to practice and the kind that is not. All kinds of vexations come from the evil-nature category. See *T.* no. 1558, 29: 7b.

12. "Taut" is a rendering for *jin*, which literally means tight, steady, firm.

13. "Integrated and pervasive" is a translation of *ronghuo*. It is literally a simultaneous state of "fusion and openness" in one's practice.

14. These words were spoken by Chan master Sengcan (d. 606), the third patriarch of Chan. See *T.* no. 2010, 48: 376b.

15. These appear to be the words of Master Xuansha Shibei (835–908), cited by the author of the *Gateless Gate* collection of gong'an cases in his postscript. See *T.* no. 2005, 48: 299a.

16. "Witty or clever mind" is a rendering for *lingli xin*. This mental state has other negative connotations, such as being overly intellectual, being insincere, and desiring shortcuts in practice.

17. Literally the lord of the sixth heaven of the desire realm, Mara also symbolizes the passions and obstructions that arise during practice.

18. "Subconsciousness" is a rendering for *shishen*, which is literally translated as "the spirit in one's consciousness." It can be taken as some kind of maya, or illusion, that manifests in the course of practice.

19. "Occasions of encounter dialogues" in Chinese is *jiyuan*, which refers to those extemporaneous dialogues between a master and a disciple in collections of gong'an cases.

20. This appears in chapter 2 of the *Lotus Sutra*. See *T.* no. 262, 9: 7a.

21. This appears in the chapter on Bodhisattva Vajragarbha in the *Sutra of Complete Enlightenment*. See *T.* no. 842, 17: 915c; for an English translation, see Sheng-yen, *Complete Enlightenment: Zen Comments on the Sutra of Complete Enlightenment* (Shambhala Publications, 1999), 175.

22. There are numerous collections of gong'ans produced in the Song dy-

nasty (960–1279) that cite these words by Master Dongshan. However, I am unable to find the citation in the master's discourse record. The first time these words are cited appears in *Transmission of the Lamp in the Jingde Era,* completed in 1004. See *T.* no. 2076, 51: 329a.

23. I have not been able to find the exact location of this quote. I have, however, come across a similar expression, "Practice should be like a single man facing ten thousand enemies . . . ," in an anthology of Chan teachings called *Precious Admonitions in the Chan Forest.* See *T.* no. 2022, 48: 1029a. The master who said this was Xuetang Daoxing (1089–1151) of the Chan sect of Linji.

24. This case appears in *Five Lamps Meeting at the Source.* See *T.* no. 1565, 80: 115a. The Boat Monk is Huating Decheng, a student of the Caodong master Yangshan Weiyan (745–828). Decheng resided on a boat, ferrying people across the river and teaching them Chan. One day a young monk named Shanhui (805–881) came to seek out this monk for instructions. After some exchange of words, Decheng realized the potential of Shanhui, so he posed a question to him. When Shanhui tried to answer, Decheng knocked him off the boat into the river and retorted, "Speak, speak!" At this point the young monk became enlightened. Decheng pulled him up and said, "Today I have finally caught a big golden fish!" The two stayed all night on the river, sometimes talking, sometimes silent. In the morning Decheng bade farewell to Shanhui and left him on the shore. He said to him, "I studied under Yangshan for thirty years. Today I have repaid his kindness. From now on, you need not think of me again." Then he rowed the boat to the middle of the river and tipped it over and disappeared "without a trace." Shanhui later became a Chan master at Mount Jia.

25. See *Transmission of the Lamp in the Jingde Era, T.* no. 2076, 51: 437a.

26. *Sack,* in Chan, is often used as a reference for the physical body. So in this context, Boshan may have experienced a state where the body suddenly disappeared.

27. Master Baofang is the same person as Wuming Huixing, the teacher of Boshan. Masters often take the name of the monasteries where they reside. At this time Wuming Huixing was residing at Baofang Monastery.

28. This passage is actually recorded in Wuming Huixing's discourse record with a note, "Verse given to Boshan upon his first meeting with the master." See *X.* no. 1432, 72: 210b.

29. See note 3.

30. Chang'an was the capital of the Tang dynasty (618–907) empire. It is located in present day Xi'an Province.

31. *Wu* in Chinese is "no" or "nothing." This refers to the gong'an involving

Master Zhaozhou: "Does the dog have buddha-nature or not?" Zhaozhou replied, "*Wu!*" In Zen the word that is used is *mu*.

32. "The cypress tree" is referred to in case number 37 of the *Gateless Gate* collection of gong'ans. This one involves Master Zhaozhou. A disciple asked him, "What is the meaning of Bodhidharma coming from the West?" Zhaozhou replied, "Oh, because of the cypress tree in the courtyard!" Zenkei Shibayama, *The Gateless Barrier: Zen Comments on the Mumonkan* (Shambhala Publications, 2000), 259.

33. This case appears in the *Pointing at the Moon* collection of gong'ans attributed to Master Puan Yinsu (815–878?). When Puan met Weishan Lingyou (771–853), he asked the latter, "The myriad dharmas return to one, but where does the one return to?" Weishan held up his dust whisk vertically. At this gesture, Puan had an insight. See *X*. no. 1578, 83: 728a.

34. "The ten directions": the eight points of the compass, plus up and down.

35. *Bodhi* is the Sanskrit word for wisdom.

36. The "light of your eyes drops to the floor," in Chan, refers to the threshold of death.

37. *Small Vehicle,* or *Hinayana,* can be seen by some as a derogatory term. However, for Chinese Buddhists, this term does not refer to any historical reality within Indian Buddhism but to a disembodied and ahistorical abstract concept against which Mahayana (Great Vehicle) Buddhism is contrasted. In this context, the term *Hinayana* refers to a focus on the path of individual liberation, as opposed to the Mahayana focus on the bodhisattva path.

Part 2. Discourse on Chan Training from the Records of Master Yuanyun Jiexian (1610–1672)

1. Sun Wu is the author of *The Art of War,* a classic work on military strategy. He is also known as Sun Tzu and Sun Zi.

2. Muzhou, also known as Daoming, was a Dharma heir of Huangbo. Muzhou helped the young Yunmen (ca. 864-949) gain his first awakening. Yunmen later became famous for being the founder of the Chan lineage that bears his name.

3. The Five Houses of Chan were five prominent schools of classical Chan Buddhism: the Caodong (Jap., Soto), Fayan, Guiyang, Linji (Jap., Rinzai), and Yunmen schools. Of these only the Caodong and the Linji schools still exist.

4. Head seat (*banshou*) is a position in the Chan Hall; the person's task is to aid the Chan master in teaching the practitioners.

5. The "Three Mysteries" refers to Master Linji's methods of Chan training, which included the mystery of the essence, which is Dharma teach-

ing on interpenetration of phenomena; the mystery of words to break a practitioner's attachment to doctrine; and the mystery of mystery, all of which are methods of arousing awakening in the practitioner through gestures (shouting and beating) as well as silences.

6. The Five Stations of the Caodong school (also known as the Five Positions) are (1) the relative in the absolute, (2) the absolute amid the relative, (3) emerging from the absolute, (4) approaching the pinnacle of both, and (5) arriving in the middle of both.

7. "Dragons" is a rendering for the Sanskrit word *nagas,* which are considered in Chinese Buddhism as benevolent protectors of the Dharma.

8. These ascetic practices are encouraged in many Buddhist sutras. For example, the *Lotus,* the *Surangama,* the *Avatamsaka,* and the *Bramajala* sutras. They can also be found in *Jataka* tales, or stories of the Buddha's past lives.

9. In Hindu and Buddhist cosmology, Mount Sumeru is a mountain in the center of the universe.

10. See *Record of Linji, T.* no. 1985, 47: 487a. For an English translation, see Irmgard Schloegl, trans., *The Zen Teaching of Rinzai* (Shambhala Publications, 1976), 19.

11. The "root of life," in Chan, usually refers to the discriminating consciousness.

12. According to Buddhist belief, the current epoch of Buddhism is the Dharma Ending Age, when Buddhism will disappear from the world until the coming of the next Buddha, Maitreya.

13. The "imprisonment barrier" is the last of the three barriers in Chan. The first barrier is called the initial barrier, referring to the initial seeing of self-nature; the second barrier is called the layered barrier, referring to the necessity for practitioners to break through all kinds of attachments and habit tendencies by deepening their enlightenment; the imprisonment barrier is the last barrier to thorough, complete enlightenment.

14. Meditation on the skeleton refers to the second of the Five Methods of Stilling the Mind, i.e., contemplating the [impurities of the] body. Contemplating (counting) the breath and contemplating the body are the first and second of the Five Methods of Stilling the Mind. The other three are contemplating loving-kindness, countemplating causes and conditions, and contemplating the four boundless mentalities (dharmas). Sometimes the last one is replaced by recollection of the Buddha. See Sheng-yen, *Hoofprint of the Ox* (New York: Oxford University Press, 2001), 65–91.

15. This passage is a paraphrase of what appears in Dahui Zonggao's (Miaoxi's) collected writing called *The Treasure of the Eye of the Dharma.* See *X.* no. 1309, 67: 629c.

Notes

16. These approaches are part of Linji's Four Hosts and Guests Positions. See *T.* no. 1985, 47: 501a.
17. Chan masters often give a positive twist to emptiness, calling it wondrous existence.
18. *Gates* is often used to refer to sense faculties; "four gates" may refer to the eyes, ears, nose, and mouth. The six passages may refer to the six sense objects of sight, sound, smell, taste, touch, and thought.
19. All of these cases are contained in the *Gateless Gate* collection of gong'ans, except the "myriad things return to one" case, which is from the *Transmission of the Lamp in the Jingde Era*. See *T.* no. 2076, 51: 277a. For an English translation of the *Gateless Gate*, see Zenkei Shibayama, *The Gateless Barrier: Zen Comments on the Mumonkan* (Shambhala Publications, 2000).
20. "Circumstantial device" is a rendering for *jiyuan*. The functioning of *jiyuan* means how masters physically demonstrate their understanding through gestures instead of words.
21. Deshan Xuanjian is known for using a stick to beat practitioners. He would often respond to any question by saying, "You deserve thirty blows."
22. In the *Record of Linji* he states that he uses different types of shouts to receive practitioners. Thus he is known for his shouts.
23. Muzhou slammed the door on Yunmen three times when Yunmen sought instruction from him. The last time, Yunmen stuck his foot in the doorway of Muzhou's hut trying to get inside, but Muzhou still shut the door on him. In pain, Yunmen gained his initial enlightenment. Thomas Cleary and J. C. Cleary, trans. *Blue Cliff Record.* (Shambhala Publications, 1992).
24. Fenyang recognized Zhiming as a vessel of the Dharma, but he refused to admit him to his private room for two years. Instead, he spurred his great enlightenment by constantly berating him and finally attacking him in apparent anger to drive him away. Thomas Cleary and J. C. Cleary, trans., *Blue Cliff Record.*
25. These two gong'ans appear in *Gateless Gate* cases number 14 and 2, respectively.
26. This gong'an appears in *Transmission of the Lamp in the Jingde Era*; see *T.* 2076, 51: 310c.
27. This is case number 42 in the *Gateless Gate.*
28. "Go forth among people" and "appear among people" may refer to when they become teachers themselves.
29. "Kernel can pop within those cold ashes" refers to a state of practice where in stillness there is still something dynamic. A similar Chan

expression is "withered tree still blossoms." "Dead men on the ground level" seems to refer to those whose discriminating minds have ceased but nothing has changed with them; they are still ordinary people.

30. "Fundamental question" is that which drives the practitioner in his or her Chan practice. Masters of old call it the mind that set out to resolve birth and death, or the basic question of wanting to know "Who am I?"

31. *Asura* (Skt.): a demonic spirit inhabiting one of the six realms.

32. The seven devices are pedagogical metaphors invented by Linji in training students. They are: using (1) the sword that kills self-grasping, (2) the sword that gives life to wondrous functioning, (3) the talisman that secures both mountains and rivers to rid oneself of demons of doubt, (4) concealment to point to the difficulty of perceiving reality, (5) the removal of clues to capture the attachments of practitioners, (6) the exchange of ordinary eyes with wisdom eyes, (7) the sword of holiness to remove practitioners' notion of holiness and loftiness.

33. Caoxi (pronounced *ts'ao hsi*) is another name for the sixth patriarch, Huineng, because in the final days of his life he lived at Caoxi.

34. The point in all of these cases is to throw back exactly what the practitioner seeks: fire seeking for fire—ridiculous! Cloudless cloud ascending—there's no such thing! Taking the reflection of the moon on water as the real moon?

35. This is the way devised by Dongshan Liangjie (807–869), one of the founders of the Caodong school. The bird leaves no traces in the sky, and the mysterious way is one that is beyond existence and emptiness. Both describe how a practitioner continues his or her cultivation after enlightenment.

36. In Chan, there is life even in a withered tree. This is a metaphor for the fact that after the Great Death of self-attachment, there is the Great Life of compassion.

37. *Shravaka* (Skt): one who seeks personal liberation in nirvana.

38. *Pratyekabuddha* (Skt.): a self-awakened buddha who has achieved liberation through observing into the nature of conditioned arising.

39. Ritual wine is used for venerating ancestors. Jiexian is using the term here as a metaphor for venerating earlier generations of Chan masters for carrying on the teaching.

Part 3. The Essentials of Chan Practice by Master Xuyun (Empty Cloud; 1839–1959)

1. "See your self-nature," that is, to have an experience of enlightenment, typically referring to the first time one has the experience. "Self-nature" refers to *bodhi*, or buddha-nature.

2. This is an allusion to a passage in the *Diamond Sutra*. A. F. Price and Wong Mou-lam, trans., *The Diamond Sutra and the Sutra of Hui-neng.* (Shambhala Publications, 1990).

3. See the glossary: *gong'an, huatou.*

4. The use of lowercase *dharma* here refers to phenomena, as opposed to *Dharma,* the teachings of the Buddha.

5. See the glossary: *five* skandhas.

6. See *T.* no. 945, 19: 147c7.

7. See *T.* no. 945, 19: 109c7.

8. This is a reference to the Pure Land practice of reciting the name of Amitabha, the Buddha of the Western Paradise. This practice does not require the effort of raising the doubt sensation.

9. In the Chan context, a "clear-eyed person" is one who is already enlightened.

10. See the glossary: *incense stick.*

11. "Oblivion" is a rendering of *wuji,* which also connotes absent-mindedness.

12. See *X.* no. 1400, 70: 686c13. There is a slight discrepancy between what's quoted by Xuyun and what is in the version we have in the canon; Xuyun cites him as saying, "May my tongue be pulled out for cows to plow on forever," which is repeated in the next quote. I have translated according to the version in the canon.

13. See *X.* no. 1400, 70: 696c06.

14. A "single taste" is a Chan expression referring to how an enlightened mind operates in daily life, where everything is experienced as the Dharma. In the *Lotus Sutra* the Dharma is said to be of a single taste, the taste of liberation. See *T.* no. 262, 9: 19b7.

15. This is a verse that appears in case number 12 of the famous Chan book *The Gateless Gate,* a collection of stories of gong'an. The master who said this was Yanhuan (n.d.). See *T.* no. 2005, 48: 294b26.

16. This passage appears in Hanshan's *Journal of Dream Roaming.* See *X.* no. 1456, 73: 469b08.

17. This Chinese expression, "dragons and elephants," is often used for outstanding monastics within Buddhist circles. The Chinese conceive of these two animals as the most powerful creatures in water and on land. The Chinese also tend to use the word *dragon,* for its mystical powers and strength, as an adjective to describe the amazing speed of an animal, such as a "dragon horse." According to this definition, then, the translation should be "dragon elephants."

18. See note 8 in part 1.

19. This is an allusion to a story in chapter 7 of the *Lotus Sutra,* where the Buddha shows that the arhats' attainment of nirvana is like an illusory

city, a temporary rest stop, and that they must go on to the bodhisattva path.

20. This is in reference to a gong'an case in the *Transmission of the Lamp in the Jingde Era* in which an old woman burned down the hut of the monk whom she had supported for twenty years. The story goes that one day, in order to test the monk, the old woman asked her daughter to hug the monk when she brought his meal. She did that, and the next day the old woman asked the monk how he felt when her daughter hugged him. He replied that it was like "a withered log leaning on a cold cliff." Upon hearing this, the old woman regretted that she had been supporting this monk and chased him out of the hut, after which she burned it down.

21. This is an expression for experiencing the moment of enlightenment.

22. Hanshan, the Tang dynasty poet, not Hanshan Deqing, the Ming dynasty master.

Glossary

Abbreviations: C. = Chinese, J. = Japanese, S. = Sanskrit

Amitabha Buddha: (S., lit., "boundless light") Amitabha Buddha is the central object of devotion in the Pure Land school of Buddhism, in which recitation of Amitabha's name is the path toward rebirth in the Western Paradise (the Pure Land). The Pure Land is a blissful state of mind in which continued cultivation of full enlightenment (buddhahood) is possible without being subject to human rebirth.

anuttara-samyak-sambodhi: (S.) Unexcelled perfect enlightenment of the Buddha.

arhat: (S., lit., "worthy one") One who has gained personal liberation through practice and thus attained nirvana. The arhat has accomplished the Path and in that sense "has no more to learn," has extinguished all passions, and will not again enter the cycle of birth and death. See also **nirvana.**

bodhi: (S., lit., "awakened") *Bodhi* is the wisdom that comes with experiencing the true nature of self as illusory and realizing that phenomena are empty of abiding self-nature. The Mahayana tradition recognizes three levels of *bodhi:* the *bodhi* of individual liberation, the *bodhi* of liberation for the sake of others, and the *bodhi* of complete enlightenment of buddhahood.

bodhicitta: (S., lit., "awakened mind") A mind that has been aroused to aspire to Buddhist enlightenment.

Bodhidharma: Indian (some say Central Asian) monk, ca. 470–543, considered to be the twenty-eighth patriarch of Indian Buddhism, who went to China in the sixth century to spread Buddhism. Bodhidharma was notable for his emphasis on the practice of *dhyana* (meditation) as a means for directly cultivating enlightenment. He is considered to be the first patriarch of Chinese Chan Buddhism.

bodhimandala: (S., lit., "seat of *bodhi*") The *bodhi* seat, or site of enlightenment. Metaphorically, this refers to one's meditation cushion, but in fact the *bodhimandala* is anywhere that emptiness (in the Buddhist sense) can be recognized, which is, of course, in everything and everywhere.

bodhisattva: (S., lit., "awakened being") The bodhisattva is the role model in the Mahayana tradition, a sentient being who vows to remain in the world of samsara, postponing his or her own full liberation until all other sentient beings are delivered.

Buddha: Historically, the Indian prince Siddhartha Gautama, born ca. 624–564 B.C.E., who renounced princely life and strove for enlightenment, thus attaining the designation of Buddha, which means "awake," or enlightened. See also **Three Jewels.**

Buddhadharma: (S., lit., "Dharma of the Buddha") The teachings of Buddhism taken as a whole. See also **Dharma.**

Caodong: One of the two major surviving sects (Soto in Japan) of Chan Buddhism, the other being the Linji (J., Rinzai) sect. Like the Linji sect, Caodong espouses sudden enlightenment but with greater emphasis on the practice of silent illumination (*shikantaza*), as opposed to the methods of gong'an and huatou. See also **gong'an, huatou, silent illumination.**

dana: See *paramitas.*

Dharma: (S., lit., "holding") Central "truth" or beliefs of Buddhism, as taught by the Buddha. As a convention often used in English, *Dharma* (with an upper case *D*) refers to the teachings of the Buddha, while *dharma* (with a lower case *d*) refers to an object, an event, or any physical or mental phenomenon. See also **Three Jewels.**

dharmakaya: See *trikaya.*

dhyana: (S., "meditative absorption") A term designating certain states of meditative absorption cultivated by Buddhist practitioners as a technique for attaining enlightenment. Chan Buddhism derives its name from the Chinese transliteration of *dhyana*, while Zen Buddhism derives its name from the Japanese transliteration of *chan*. See also *paramitas.*

Eightfold Noble Path: After becoming enlightened under the Bodhi Tree, the Buddha gave his first sermon, which was on the Four Noble Truths. The fourth noble truth, which is the truth of the way out of suffering, consists of the Eightfold Noble Path: right view, right intention, right speech, right action, right livelihood, right effort, right mindfulness, and right meditation.

five precepts: The five basic precepts of Buddhism are not to kill, not to steal, not to engage in sexual misconduct, not to lie, and not to take intoxicants.

five *skandhas:* The five *skandhas,* or aggregates, are the constituents of the sentient being's experience of the world. They are form, sensation, perception, volition, and consciousness. The first *skandha,* form, is the material component; the other four are mental in nature. Operating together, the five *skandhas* create the illusion of separate existence and the notion of self, or ego.

four great vows: The four great vows are taken and repeated by those on the bodhisattva path: *I vow to deliver all sentient beings, I vow to cut off endless vexations, I vow to master limitless approaches to the Dharma, I vow to attain supreme buddhahood.*

gong'an: (C., lit., "public case," or "law case") A Chan method of meditation in which the practitioner energetically and single-mindedly pursues the answer to an enigmatic story (the gong'an) about an encounter between a master and a disciple. The gong'an can be answered only by abandoning logic and reasoning, through directly generating and breaking through the "doubt sensation" under natural causes and conditions. Famous gong'an encounters were recorded and used by masters to test their disciples' understanding, or they served as a catalyst for enlightenment. The term *gong'an* is often used interchangeably with *huatou,* a question that is usually derived from a gong'an. Thus, gong'an refers to the story itself as well as to the method of practice. See also **huatou, koan.**

Great Vehicle: The Mahayana (Great Vehicle) path of Buddhism, followed by those who have taken the bodhisattva vows. See also **bodhisattva, four great vows, Mahayana.**

Guanyin: The Chinese name for Avalokiteshvara Bodhisattva, the bodhisattva of compassion.

Hinayana: (Lit., "small vehicle") a designation for the Buddhist path of individual liberation. A Hinayana practitioner would be anyone in any tradition who practices for self-enlightenment or personal liberation. See also **Mahayana.**

huatou: (S., lit., "the source of words before they are uttered") A method used in Chan to arouse the doubt sensation. The practitioner meditates on such baffling questions as "What is nothingness?" "Where am I?" or "Who is reciting the Buddha's name?" Thus, the term *huatou* can refer to both the method itself, as well as to the question. One does not rely on experience, logic, or reasoning to resolve the question. Often these phrases are taken from gong'ans, or in Zen, koans. At other times they are spontaneously generated by the practitioner. In Zen the term for *huatou* is *wato,* and it is often used interchangeably with *koan.* See also **gong'an.**

Huineng (638–713): Dajian Huineng (J., Diakan Eno) The sixth patriarch of the Chan school, considered to be a founder of the "sudden enlightenment" tradition of Chan. As a young monk he became enlightened when he heard someone recite some lines from the *Diamond Sutra.*

incense stick: An incense stick, or incense board, is a thin wooden slate that is used to strike meditating practitioners on the shoulders to wake them from drowsiness or to spur them on to greater effort. Nowadays, the use of the incense stick is mostly at the request of the sitter. In Zen the incense stick is called *kyosaku.*

kalpa: (S.) Referring to an immensely long period of time between the arising of a universe and its descent into chaos.

koan: Japanese transliteration of *gong'an,* the meditation practice developed in Chan Buddhism. See also **gong'an, huatou.**

Linji (d. ca. 866–867): (J., Rinzai) Master Linji was the founder of the sect of Chan Buddhism that bears his name. The Linji sect was characterized by its emphasis on meditation and the use of the gong'an and huatou methods to create a "doubt mass" in the mind of the practitioner. In this practice the resolution of the doubt mass is an essential step toward realizing enlightenment. The Linji sect is one of two remaining Chan sects, the other being the Caodong (J., Soto). See also **Caodong.**

Mahayana: (S., lit., "great vehicle") Followers of the Mahayana path vow to attain supreme enlightenment for the sake of delivering all other sentient beings from suffering. See also **Great Vehicle, Hinayana.**

Mara: (S., lit., "murder, destruction") In Buddhism, Mara epitomizes death and symbolizes the passions that overwhelm human beings. It also refers to unwholesome influences that obstruct the path to enlightenment.

Middle Way: The path that was espoused by the Buddha, to neither follow extreme asceticism nor pursue desires without restraint.

nirvana: (S., lit., "extinction") Total extinction of desire and suffering and achieving transcendent bliss; the state of liberation through full enlightenment.

no-self: The Buddha's central teaching that there is no isolated, self-existing entity that can be grasped as the self, which is merely a construct of the mind.

paramitas: (S., lit., "that which has reached the other shore") *Paramitas* are the "perfections," that is, actions cultivated by practitioners on the path of liberation to "the other shore" (nirvana). The six basic *paramitas* are giving (*dana*), morality (*sila*), patience (*ksanti*), diligence (*virya*), meditation (*dhyana*), and wisdom (*prajna*). The ten *paramitas* are practiced by those who have taken the bodhisattva vows. They consist of the six basic *paramitas* plus four others: expedient means (*upayakausalya*), vows (*pranidhana*), power (*bala*), and all-knowing wisdom (*jnana*).

prajna: See *paramitas.*

Pure Land: The Land of Supreme Bliss, or the Western Paradise, of Amitabha Buddha. It is a pure realm that came into existence due to the vows of Amitabha Buddha. Anyone who sincerely invokes Amitabha's name and expresses the wish to be born there will ultimately be reborn in the Pure Land. See also **Amitabha Buddha.**

samadhi: (S., lit., "make firm") In early Buddhism *samadhi* referred to a deep state of meditative concentration where desires have been left behind. It is characterized by a state of mind-body unification, of unity of self and environment, where the mind dwells single-pointedly on the one thought of self-awareness. In the later Mahayana, a deeper *samadhi* was asserted in which there is not even the notion of self. In this context *samadhi* is not separate from wisdom, and the fully enlightened mind is therefore always in *samadhi,* not just during formal meditation. See also *dhyana.*

samsara: (S., lit., "journeying") The relentless cycle of birth and death and suffering in which ordinary, unenlightened sentient beings are deeply entangled until they achieve liberation in nirvana. There are three realms within samsara: the desire realm, the form realm, and the formless realm. Human beings exist in the desire realm.

Sangha: (S., lit., "crowd," or "host") One of the Three Jewels of Buddhism, the other two being the Buddha and the Dharma. The Sangha Jewel consists of the community of monks and nuns, beginning with the Buddha and continuing till today. The Sangha also includes the lay community of Buddhist practitioners. Taking refuge in the Three Jewels is a formal act of entering the practice of Buddhism. See also **Three Jewels.**

shikantaza: (J., transliteration from the Chinese *zhiguanda zuo*) The meditation practice of *shikantaza* is associated with the Soto school of Japanese Zen and espoused by Zen Master Dogen as the most effective and direct way to cultivate enlightenment. The practice is also referred to as "just sitting." In Chan Buddhism the method is known as *mozhao,* or silent illumination. See also **silent illumination.**

sila: See *paramitas.*

silent illumination: Chan meditation method that simultaneously effects calming of the mind (*samadhi*) and insight (*prajna*) through dropping all attachments and wandering thoughts and focusing one's awareness on the act of sitting. The method is most closely associated with the Caodong school of Chan (Soto school of Zen). See also *shikantaza.*

six realms: In Buddhism, samsaric existence is composed of six realms, which are divided into two groups. The lower realms consist of the animal realm, the hell realm, and the realm of hungry ghosts. The higher realms consist of the human realm, the realm of the jealous gods, and the realm of the gods (*devas*). The inhabitants of these realms have unresolved karma and are therefore subject to reincarnation. See also **nirvana, samsara.**

skandhas: (S., lit., "heaps," or "aggregates") See **five** *skandhas.*

Small Vehicle: See **Hinayana.**

tathagata-garbha: (S., lit., "seed of the *tathagata,* the perfected one") The term refers to the buddha-body in the form of ultimate reality, which is also the reality that is indwelling in all sentient beings, that is, "buddha-nature."

Three Jewels: The Three Jewels of Buddhism are the Buddha, the Dharma, and the Sangha. The Buddha is the primordial teacher of Buddhism, the Dharma is what he taught, and the Sangha is the community of believers and followers. See also **Buddha, Dharma, Sangha.**

trikaya: (S., lit., "three bodies") The *trikaya* is the Mahayana belief in the threefold nature of the fully realized Buddha, consisting of the *dharmakaya, sambhogakaya,* and *nirmanakaya.* The *dharmakaya* is the transcendent body of all buddhas, perfect and devoid of characteristics. One interpretation of *sambhogakaya* is that it is an object of devotion, the "body of delight," being the accumulated result of the Buddha's merit. The *nirmanakaya* is seen as the incarnated form of a buddha who has chosen to return to help sentient beings. In the current epoch, the *nirmanakaya* manifested as the Indian prince Shakyamuni, who became the Buddha.

wato: Japanese transliteration of the Chinese *huatou,* the method used in Chan to arouse the doubt sensation. See also **huatou.**